Political Women in Japan

Political Women in Japan

The Search for a Place in Political Life

Susan J. Pharr

UNIVERSITY OF CALIFORNIA PRESS

Berkeley / Los Angeles / London

University of California Press
Berkeley and Los Angeles, California
University of California Press, Ltd.
London, England

© 1981 by The Regents of the University of California

Printed in the United States of America

1 2 3 4 5 6 7 8 9

Library of Congress Cataloging in Publication Data

Pharr, Susan J
   Political women in Japan.

   Bibliography: p.
   Includes index.
   1. Women in politics—Japan.   2.   Political social-
ization.   I.   Title.
HQ1236.P46   305.4'2'0952   80-12984
ISBN 0-520-04071-6

To Gladys Chappelear Pharr

Contents

Tables and Figures

FIGURES

Preface

The success of a book such as this one depends almost entirely on the goodwill and cooperation of those sought as informants. It is they who command rich data, and it is they who have the choice of whether or not they will make it available to a foreign researcher. In a way, this book is the direct yield of one hundred political women making a decision to talk to me candidly about their lives. They met me in coffee shops, political party headquarters, the meeting room of their political group, or in their own homes, sometimes with babies in their laps. They took me in tow to meetings, rallies, and demonstrations. They introduced me to their parents, their husbands or other male friends, their children, and to fellow members of their political groups. They revealed to me, in addition to the specific data I sought, endless insights into the nature of contemporary Japanese society and into the problems and struggles of women throughout the world who are attempting to make a place for themselves in political life.

The one hundred political women who were informants for this study have made it possible. Their anonymity is preserved throughout, and the debt to them is beyond measure.

In addition to the informants themselves, a great many Japanese both in and outside the political world added greatly to my understanding of political women and woman's role in general in the total social environment. I should like to express my appreciation to Takahashi Akira and Doi Takeo,[1] both of Tokyo University, to Takenaka Kazurō, then of Doshisha University and now of Tsukuba University, and to Inoue Teruko of Wako University, for their help in shedding light on the data and for assisting me with introductions. I owe thanks to many officials in all of Japan's major political parties for introducing me to political women, but special thanks must go to Murakawa Ichirō and Watanabe Kazuko of the Liberal Democratic Party and Takenaka Ichirō of the Japan Socialist Party for their time and assistance. I am grateful to

? Akamatsu Ryōko, then of the Ministry of Labor and now one of Japan's delegates to the United Nations, for her contribution to my understanding of women's changing roles and status, and to her husband, Hanami Tadashi, Professor of Law at Sophia University, for his help as an authority on laws affecting women workers. To both I owe a debt of friendship as well as of gratitude for aid rendered. Many political women older than the age range set for this study shared with me their experiences and reminiscences about the prewar world and prewar suffrage movement, as well as their views of women's place in the political world today. Of these I owe particular thanks to Ichikawa Fusae, a member of the upper house of the parliament and a long-time advocate of women's rights, Mizusawa Yōko of the Women's Democratic Club, and Inoue Fumiko, a participant in the prewar Christian movement for women's rights. I must also express thanks to Matsuoka Yōko, Higuchi Keiko, Kobayashi Tomiko, Terada Meisei, and numerous other well-known political women and men in contemporary Japan who gave me their time and help.

I owe a deep debt of gratitude to four women who at vari-

---

1. Throughout this book, personal names are given in Japanese fashion, that is, with the family name appearing first.

ous stages of my research assisted in the interviewing and who became personal friends as well. Masuzawa Fumiko aided me throughout the interviewing stage. Her friendly, exuberant manner, her tact and diplomacy in the face of many a tight situation, greatly aided my attempts to secure the cooperation of numerous informants who were at first unsure about me and about being interviewed. Sakagishi Setsuko, political woman, mother, and feminist, not only helped me with the interviewing, but greatly enriched my understanding of the lives of Japanese women. Ōno Yasuko and Satō Ikuko provided invaluable help and companionship as well as gracious introductions to their families.

I must express thanks, not only to individuals, but to institutions for their assistance. I should like to thank Kenneth Butler, Arahari Kazuko, and the staff at the Inter-University Center for Japanese Language Study in Toyko for their practical help while I was in Japan, as well as for their inspired and able language training, and the staff of the Institute of International Relations at Sophia University, where I was a Visiting Foreign Research Scholar during my two-year stay in Japan in 1971 and 1972. The East Asian Institute at Columbia, with Gerald Curtis as Director and Deborah Bell as Administrative Assistant, provided a comfortable and stimulating environment for the initial write-up of my research. Finally, two years as a staff member at the Social Science Research Council in New York made an incalculable contribution to my development and growth as a social scientist and provided me with the tools, the will, and the fresh perspective needed to rethink and revise the book. The Council also made possible a return trip to Japan in 1975, which allowed me to gather further data. The research would not have been possible without funding from the Ford Foundation, the Yoshida Foundation of Toyko, and the East Asian Institute of Columbia University. A grant from the Graduate School of the University of Wisconsin made it possible for me to complete the book.

To many colleagues in this country I owe much appreciation. My work has greatly benefited from discussions with Walter Slote, a clinical psychologist in New York with extensive field experience in Asia. I am indebted to Gerald Curtis for his help in the original design and conception of this project. His advice—that researchers owe it to themselves to study those topics that they find personally interesting as well as intellectually engaging—led me to the topic of this book. To Herbert Passin I owe much of my initial interest in Japan. Discussions with him over the years have given me access to an endless flow of perceptions about an extraordinarily complex social system. Stanley Heginbotham deserves many thanks for his help with methodology and organization at many stages of the research and write-up. To James Morley I express appreciation, not only for the understanding he has given me of the Japanese political system, but for his personal help and encouragement over the years. In addition to the above, Ezra Vogel, David Plath, Patricia Steinhoff, Ellis Krauss, Scott Flanagan, and Lewis Austin read all or parts of the manuscript and offered invaluable comments and criticism. I should like to thank Carol Lohry Cartwright and Shari Graney for typing various drafts of the book, Gladys Castor for her skilled editorial work, and Philip Lilienthal and Phyllis Killen of University of California Press for their help and guidance. To Stephen Butts, who read the manuscript at many stages and who was there through both the darkest and the finest moments, I express my deepest gratitude and thanks.

These acknowledgments would be incomplete without special tribute to Tsurumi Kazuko, Professor of Sociology at Sophia University, who was my mentor while I was in Japan. Dr. Tsurumi's help came to me in so many ways that it is difficult to find words to express my appreciation. Her numerous introductions to Japanese women in and outside of the political world, her thoughtful critique of my initial interview schedule, her insightful comments on my data where my findings confused or perplexed me, as well as her own example as an extraordinary Japanese woman, gave me the initial opportunity to pursue my research and the confidence to interpret its results.

None of the above, of course, bear responsibility for my findings, but to all I owe my sincerest appreciation.

Madison, Wisconsin
January 1980

1

Women's Search for a Place in Political Life

The twentieth century has seen a worldwide revolution in the extension of political rights to women. Less than ninety years ago there was no major country in the world where women were guaranteed the right to participate in politics on an equal basis with men. Today only a handful of states, most of them little-populated Arab nations, legally bar women's participation in political life. In several major waves of change in this century, the ideal of political equality for women has spread from those states where it originated to the rest of the world and has been translated into legal guarantees.

The degree to which women's right to participate in politics at all levels is accepted in custom as well as in the laws varies widely. In no nation are women fully represented at the elite level proportional to their numbers in the population. Meanwhile, in many countries, women's right to participate in the

most basic of political activities, such as voting, attending political meetings, or discussing politics, is still denied full social
approbation, as is evidenced by wide discrepancies between
the voter turnout for men and women and by survey data
showing a substantial proportion of the population in most
countries still uncertain about whether women belong in political life.

Why women remain marginal in politics, despite legal
guarantees, has been the subject of much recent study. The
most comprehensive explanation—one that is emerging in
bare outline form from the work done to date—draws on social learning theory and holds that political participation involves roles that, like any others, can be learned.[1] For women
confronted with the option of becoming politically active, the
task is not an easy one, however. There is inherent conflict
between the norms and expectations associated with the
female-gender role, as defined in all modern societies, and
the norms and expectations linked to political roles. Less than
a century ago politics was the exclusive domain of men in all
major societies, and thus political roles by definition were
male roles until quite recently. It follows that, even when
legal constraints are removed, women enter the new terrain
of politics only by incurring certain risks to their basic identity
as women. Adjusting their concept of self and role to include
new forms of expression and behavior once barred to them
involves a complex process of change that is at once personal
and social. For the process, here called *role redefinition*, goes
on not only at the level of individual women, but at the
societal level as well, as society, in response to individual
women's struggles, adjusts prevailing definitions of woman's
role to accommodate the new behavior.

The process of role redefinition is going on very gradually,
at different rates, in all countries today. In the United States

1. For key studies that treat women's adoption of political roles as involving a role learning process, see John J. Stucker, "Women as Voters: Their
Maturation as Political Persons in American Society," in *A Portrait of Marginality*, ed. Marianne Githens and Jewel L. Prestage (New York, 1977), pp.
264–283; Marjorie Lansing, "The American Woman: Voter and Activist," in
Women in Politics, ed. Jane S. Jaquette (New York, 1974), pp. 5–24; Commission of the European Communities, *European Men and Women* (Brussels,
1975); and Virginia Sapiro, "Is the Child the Mother of the Woman? Socialization to Political Gender Roles among Women," *Journal of Politics*, in press.

and many other countries where women's suffrage was first granted, the process has advanced to the point that most forms of political participation below the elite level, including voluntary political and civic activism, are now seen as acceptable for women.[2] In such countries, the major question is no longer why more women do not give their time and energies to political groups and causes, but why their activism brings so few payoffs in terms of women's greater representation and power at the elite level. In Japan, as in most societies of the world today, the major battle for acceptance of women's right to participate in politics is going on at a much lower level. The threshold beyond which women's involvement in politics will be judged inappropriate or only marginally appropriate is still quite low, and citizen modes of participation, including political voluntarism, are the central focus of the process. In no country is the process completed.

If definitions of woman's role have served to constrain women's political participation in the past and to varying degrees today in all societies, we must seek to understand how these constraints operate at the level of the individual woman, and how they are overcome as women, individually and collectively, move toward a view of themselves as political beings. At the same time, recognizing that women's participation in politics, even in the face of numerous barriers, is a reality in the twentieth century, it is important for us to look at the appeals and satisfactions of political activism for women. Exploring the multifaceted process of role redefinition involved in women's passage into politics is the central concern of this book.

The study focuses on Japan as a setting for an examination of the experiences of women in coming to terms with political roles. There are a number of reasons why Japan is an ideal setting for analyzing a worldwide process. Japan today is uniquely positioned between the advanced industrial societies of the West and the less-developed countries. Economic indicators now place Japan squarely among the Western postindustrial societies. At the same time, many social indicators reflect the recentness of Japan's emergence as a

2. See chapter seven for a review of major findings supporting this conclusion.

modern state. Japanese popular culture carries dramatic re-
minders as well. Japan's emergence from a feudal past is so
close in time that the term "feudalistic" is still used today by
leaders and the public alike to refer pejoratively to outmoded
attitudes and customs.

As a non-Western nation and as a country that developed
late, drawing heavily on the models provided by the advanced Western societies, Japan has much in common with
the underdeveloped world today. This is especially true
when it comes to the way in which Japanese women gained
political rights. As will be explored more fully in the last chapter, the women's rights and suffrage movements that took
shape in the nineteenth and early twentieth centuries in a
number of Western countries were the logical outgrowth of
two centuries of ferment over the issues of human rights and
equality. For all the struggles that accompanied those movements in the original suffrage states, the basic principles upon
which the movements rested had gained acceptance by the
time they emerged. The force of right, in other words, was on
the side of the pro-suffragists, and the task was to get old
principles extended to cover the needs and demands of a new
group. Outside the original suffrage states, however, the process of gaining acceptance for women's rights has faced even
more formidable odds. Women in much of the non-Western
world gained political rights, not as the gradual outcome of
internal changes, but as the result of external contact and
influence, whether in the context of a colonial situation, as in
India or Malaysia, a revolution guided by Western ideology,
as in the People's Republic of China, or in other situations of
foreign influence, such as the one represented by occupied
Japan. Where suffrage movements arose outside the original
suffrage states, typically they were led by a Western-
educated elite whose views were far out of step with those of
most of the population. Thus, in much of the world, women's
political rights, once gained, have lacked roots, and the process of role redefinition necessary to incorporate political activities into most people's definition of appropriate behavior
for women has been a particularly onerous one.

Nowhere has this been more true than in Japan. As the
book shows, full political rights were granted to Japanese
women in 1945 as an accident of military defeat. Although a

women's rights movement and, later, a suffrage movement, had taken shape in the first decades of the twentieth century in Japan, the leaders were educated, urban women whose views were ahead of their times. The impact of these movements, despite their symbolic importance today to Japanese women, was extremely limited in their own day. Political rights were thus "given" rights, handed to Japanese women over the heads of their nation's defeated leadership by the American military occupation. The key problem for women in Japan, like that for women in so much of the world today, has been to translate legal rights into power and to bring customs in line with what the laws say.

Japan is an ideal laboratory for studying the process of political role redefinition for another reason. Socioeconomic variables concomitant with industrial change and development have a major influence on women's position in society, including their degree of participation in the public sphere.[3] The poverty, illiteracy, and lack of educational opportunity that are generally found alongside low levels of economic growth have a major constraining effect on the political participation of both women and men. In many less-developed countries where women recently have acquired the legal right to participate in politics, patterns of mass political participation for both sexes are so affected by these exogenous variables that it is almost impossible to talk meaningfully about gender differences and role conflict as constraints on women's political behavior.[4] Outside a revolutionary context, politics—especially most citizen modes of participation—represents leisure-time activity that is engaged in only when basic needs are met.[5] The precondition that makes possible the entry of men and women into political life is the elimina-

3. Janet Z. Giele, "Introduction: Comparative Perspectives on Women," In *Women: Role and Status in Eight Countries*, ed. Janet Z. Giele and Audrey C. Smock (New York, 1977), pp. 1–32.

4. The effects of poverty on political participation in Bangladesh can be cited as an extreme example. See Audrey C. Smock, "Bangladesh: A Struggle with Tradition and Poverty," in *Women: Role and Status in Eight Countries*, ed. Janet Z. Giele and Audrey C. Smock (New York, 1977), pp. 81–126.

5. Jeanne N. Knutson, *The Human Basis of the Polity* (Chicago, 1972), pp. 22–26, 187–190. Knutson's study presents compelling evidence that persons with high physiological needs are unlikely "to join with others in more personally involving types of political activities" (p. 190).

tion of constraints born of a survival situation. Conversely, rising levels of prosperity and education, the spread of literacy, and other factors all make way for increased citizen awareness of politics and the growth of participant societies in which the average citizen, male or female, theoretically has the option of becoming politically involved.

In Japan, with the third highest gross national product in the world, these preconditions are fully in place. Prosperity has reached such levels that 90 percent of the Japanese people today regard themselves as middle class.[6] Universal literacy was achieved long ago, and today the Japanese are among the best-read people in the world. The country is more than 70 percent urban and linked by a communications and transportation network second to none. Political information is widely available.[7] In short, the economic and social constraints that limit citizen political participation in the less-developed countries are largely absent. Japan thus provides an ideal setting for isolating and studying those constraints growing out of definitions of woman's roles and place that continue to limit women's political participation at some level in even the most advanced and prosperous societies.

The Study

To find out why certain women become involved in politics and what constraints they face, the logical persons to ask are politically active women themselves. Intensive interviews were conducted with one hundred Japanese women between the ages of eighteen and thirty-three who were active in voluntary political groups.

The study focused on political volunteers because it is they, it will be argued later on, who are at the forefront of the role-

6. Taketsugu Tsurutani, *Political Change in Japan* (New York, 1977), p. 20.

7. Literacy is nearly 100 percent. Although Japan's population (115 million in a land area about the size of California) is only about half that of the United States and is only sixth in the world, its three top dailies (*Asahi*, *Yomiuri*, and *Mainichi*) rank first, second, and third throughout the world in number of copies printed. Eighty-two percent of all Japanese homes have television sets. See Robert E. Ward, *Japan's Political System* (Englewood Cliffs, N.J., 1978), pp. 51–52 and 226–228.

redefinition process today in Japan. As a result of the timing and circumstances surrounding the granting of political rights to women there, voting and other forms of participation in the "less active" category have gained acceptance. The strug- gle over role redefinition has shifted upward, and today it centers on middle-range activity of the type represented by political volunteerism. The last chapter will place this change in the context of world trends.

The level of involvement among the women varied widely. Within their respective groups, some one-fourth held leader- ship positions, one-half were regular participants, and the remaining women participated more sporadically. All the women, whatever their level of activism, are referred to throughout as "political women," meaning simply that they gave a significant portion of their time to politics. The term is used by a number of political scientists today as a corrective to a concept of "political man" that claimed to encompass all political behavior but that failed to take adequately into ac- count the behavior and experiences of women.[8]

The women were drawn from more than fifty voluntary po- litical groups that are part of the political scene in contempo- rary Japan. Represented among the groups are all of Japan's major political parties, a substantial number of major or- ganized interest groups, and a large array of protest groups and movements, including environmental protection groups, student protest groups, and women's rights groups. Ideolog- ically, they span the entire spectrum. At one extreme is the Liberal Democratic Party, the conservative party in power. At the other is the Red Army, a radical militant sect whose members have been involved in a number of terrorist ac- tivities nationally and internationally. Within the limits set for the study, the aim was to include women from the broadest possible range of political parties, organizations, and move- ments in contemporary Japan. A list of political groups from

8. The term *political woman* has gained currency as a result of Jeane Kirkpatrick's important book by that name: Jeane J. Kirkpatrick, *Political Woman* (New York, 1974). For an example of the many works in which *politi- cal man* has been used to refer to all human behavior in the universalistic sense, see Seymour M. Lipset, *Political Man* (New York, 1960). Kirkpatrick confines her use of the term *political woman* to elites (*Political Woman*, p. 23n.); here, however, it is used more broadly to refer to women who are politically active, whatever their level of involvement.

which the women were selected and an account of how the sample was chosen are included in the appendixes.

The study focuses on women between the ages of eighteen and thirty-three for several reasons. First and foremost is the importance, personal and political, of the stages of the life cycle represented by those years. Late adolescence and early adulthood are the periods in a woman's life when key decisions are made regarding education, work, and marriage, and how these and other pursuits are to be combined. How women decide these issues has major consequences for the pattern of their political participation in adult life, then and later on. The actual age range in which the decisions are concentrated, of course, varies according to the society. In societies where women marry in their early to mid teens, all these challenges may have been met before age twenty. In Japan, however, the average age of marriage for women is twenty-four.[9] The average woman completes her family by age thirty.[10] Thus major choices are concentrated in the age range set for the study.

A second reason for focusing on younger women arises out of the study's concern with issues relating to political development and role change. Among women in Japan today, it is young women who have the greatest potential for change in the area of political participation. Japanese women above the age range for the study spent a major part of their lives in a highly repressive society in which political rights for women were largely denied. Although some of these women—including the most prominent and highly visible political women in Japan today—underwent major reversals of values later on in life and are politically active now, the learning process itself is obviously quite different from the one undergone by women who have never experienced such restrictions. An activist who was thirty-three at the time she took part in the

9. Ministry of Labor, Women's and Minors' Bureau, *The Status of Women in Japan* (Tokyo, 1977), p. 26. In 1974 the average age of marriage was 24.5 years for women and 26.8 years for men.

10. Japan Institute of Labor, *Japan Labor Bulletin* (July 1, 1973). In 1972, the average Japanese woman gave birth to her first child at age 25.3 years and the second child at age 27.9 years, according to a Survey of Fertility conducted in that year by the Ministry of Welfare. The average number of children per couple was 2.1.

study was a "postwar woman."[11] She was educated entirely in the new order instituted after 1945 and grew up taking women's political rights for granted.[12] It is this woman, and those born after her, who will determine future patterns of women's political participation in Japan.

Each of the women chosen for the study was interviewed for an average of three hours, although in many cases the sessions ran much longer and extended over several meetings. A number of standard questions were used, but otherwise the interviews were open ended. An interview topic list is included in the appendixes. To supplement the interviews, background data were collected in meetings with some two hundred women and men whose views could be thought to shed light on what it means to be a political woman in Japan.

To analyze how and why certain women, unlike most women, become involved in politics in Japan is to venture into uncharted waters. Few systematic studies have explored the experiences of political women in any country until quite recently. Most of the work that has been done is in preliminary stages and has centered almost exclusively on women in the United States.[13] Furthermore, in the vast literature con-

11. It may be noted that Japanese themselves constantly use "prewar" and "postwar" to point up meaningful generational differences in personal experience. For one example that deals with postwar women, see Tsurumi Kazuko, *Social Change and the Individual: Japan Before and After Defeat in World War II* (Princeton, 1970).

12. A woman who was thirty-three when the interviewing began in 1971 was born in 1938; by the time she entered elementary school, the prewar system had been discredited and the postwar reforms introduced during the occupation were under way.

13. Works on political women in the United States that were especially useful in this research were Jeane J. Kirkpatrick, *Political Woman* (New York, 1974), and *The New Presidential Elite* (New York, 1976); Edmond Constantini and Kenneth H. Craik, "Women as Politicians," *Journal of Social Issues* 28 (1972): 217–236; Marcia M. Lee, "Towards Understanding Why Few Women Hold Public Office," in *A Portrait of Marginality*, ed. Marianne Githens and Jewel Prestage (New York, 1977), pp. 118–138; Naomi Lynn and Cornelia Butler Flora, "Societal Punishment and Aspects of Female Political Participation," in ibid., pp. 139–149; Marianne Githens, "Spectators, Agitators, or Lawmakers," in ibid., pp. 196–220; M. Kent Jennings, "Men and Women in Party Elites," *Midwest Journal of Political Science* 4 (November, 1968): 469–492; Barbara G. Farah and Virginia Sapiro, "New Pride and Old Prejudice" (Paper presented at the Annual Meeting of the Southern Political Science Association, Nashville, 1975); Charles Bullock and Patricia Hays, "Recruitment of

cerned with why people become politically active, few writers have taken gender differences into account. Indeed, few studies have even acknowledged that gender is relevant to the process by which some people become activists and some do not. And yet we know, from simple observation of the world around us, that women in all societies are underrepresented in political life. If gender-related variables constrain the active political participation of the great majority of women, then it is relevant to ask how political women deal with or overcome those same constraints in the course of becoming active in politics.

important

To ask this question is quite different from asking how and why certain women early in life become *psychologically* predisposed to becoming active. It is assumed throughout this study that all political activists, male or female, have basic needs and drives that to some extent operate behind, or guide, their decision later on in life to become involved in politics.[14] Political psychologists have done much important work in linking certain types of needs with different forms of political expression, but in all cases the presence of such needs is no more than a precondition for political activism. There is nothing to guarantee that people with particular types of needs will choose politics as an outlet for their re-

Women for Congress," *Western Political Quarterly* 25 (September, 1972): 416–423; Mary Porter and Ann B. Matasar, "The Role and Status of Women in the Daley Organization," in *Women in Politics*, ed. Jane S. Jaquette (New York: 1974), pp. 85–108; Emmy E. Werner and Louise M. Bachtold, "Personality Characteristics of Women in American Politics," in ibid., pp. 75–84; Emmy E. Werner, "Women in Congress: 1917–1964," *Western Political Quarterly* 19 (1966): 16–30; Maureen Fiedler, "The Participation of Women in American Politics" (Paper presented at the Annual Meeting of the American Political Science Association, San Francisco, 1975).

Several works on political women outside the United States proved helpful. See Maurice Duverger, *The Political Role of Women* (Paris, 1955); Barbara Jancar, "Women and Elite Recruitment into the Central Committees of Bulgaria, Czechoslovakia, Hungary, and Poland" (Paper presented at the Annual Meeting of the Midwest Political Science Association, Chicago, 1977); and Ingunn Norderval Means, "Women in Local Politics: The Norwegian Experience," *Canadian Journal of Political Science* (September 1972): 365–388.

14. See James Chowning Davies, "Where From and Where To?" in *Handbook of Political Psychology*, ed. Jeanne Knutson (San Francisco, 1973). This basic view of how individuals become "predisposed" to participating in politics goes back to Harold D. Lasswell, *Psychopathology and Politics* (New York, 1960), originally published in 1930.

lease. Alternative outlets are obviously available in any society, from making work the focus of one's physical, emotional, and psychological energies, to directing these energies into the domain of interpersonal relations, as so many women do in concentrating on the family. Most of the work done by political psychologists, then, leaves unanswered the question of why women who have basic needs that hypothetically "predispose" them to act politically are less likely than men to choose politics as an outlet.

If we look beyond the psychological roots of activism, the answer appears to lie in exploring how political women, unlike most women, come to see politics as a possible forum for self-expression. In making such an inquiry, the importance of two interrelated processes looms larger. The first is gender-role socialization, the process by which women learn gender-appropriate behavior as it is defined by their society. The second is political socialization, by which individuals learn politically relevant attitudes and behavior patterns. The outcome of the first process, in the great majority of women in Japan and in most societies today, is a woman whose view of self and role precludes becoming politically active under all but the most unusual of circumstances. The dominant ideology of woman's role in contemporary Japan rules out active political involvement unless, as will be shown, political duties can be seen as an extension of primary role commitments to a husband, father, or other significant male, which thereby "legitimates" the political activism. The outcome of the second process is ordinarily a woman who is less interested than men in politics, has a lower sense of political efficacy than men, discusses politics less often and is much less likely to be involved in politics than men. In Japan, voting is an exception to this overall pattern of lesser political participation for women. Because of the unique circumstances surrounding the introduction of women's suffrage there, voting is the one major form of political activity that has gained full acceptance as appropriate female activity under the dominant definition of woman's role.

If this is the pattern for the majority of Japanese women, what can be said about the processes of political socialization and gender-role socialization as they affected women who later became politically active? An examination of the political socialization experiences of the respondents revealed that there was little in their early and adolescent experiences in the family that would have predicted their later entry into politics. The families from which they emerged were neither more nor less politically interested and involved than most Japanese families. Nor was there anything unusual about the allocation of economic and political roles within the family. The fathers of politically active women, like those of most women today, were breadwinners who were much more likely than their wives to be interested in politics. The mothers were housewives who, according to their daughters' reports, professed little interest in politics.

What the study found, however, was that, despite the absence of obvious factors in the home that might have sparked their initial interest in politics per se, certain aspects of their experiences were highly relevant to their decision later on to become politically active. These were features of women's gender-role socialization that had functioned to make them receptive to the possibility of challenging the dominant definition of woman's role. Some degree of gender-role change, then, was an essential precondition for their later activism.

Based on this essential finding, the study argues that women find their way into politics by way of a complex, two-stage process. According to this view, a woman's actual entry into political life—in this case, her decision to join a political group—is determined by the same factors that lead men into politics: she is the right person (in terms of psychological predispositions) in the right place at the right time (in terms of situational variables). As the book indicates, contemporary Japanese society puts both men and women in many situations—the university, with its many student political groups; the company or factory, with its union; the neighborhood, with its opportunities for participating in civic or protest groups or political parties—in which they have the option of becoming politically active. But what the theory suggests, however, is that psychological and situational variables, in isolation, cannot account for the political involvement of women. For most women there is an additional stage on the way toward activism during which they become open to the possibility of challenging the dominant definition of woman's role. Unless women have passed through this prior stage, they will not cross over the threshold into politics.

The study then explores the nature of the changes that occur during this "extra" stage. Three aspects of the gender-role socialization process stood out in the experiences of the women. First, a "permissive" family atmosphere had func- tioned to create an environment in which role experimentation became possible. The second factor was a complex dynamic operating in the mother-daughter relationship. Typically, the mother, while meeting traditional role expectations herself, had de-selected herself as a role model, conveying indirectly what one mother said openly to her activist daughter: "Don't imitate me." The mothers' ambivalence about woman's role, it is argued, may grow out of a retrospective dissatisfaction with the restricted lives they led in prewar Japan and out of their desire to experience vicariously the greater freedom available to young women today in a variety of areas: work, education, sexual mores, dress, and so on. Although mothers often verbally counseled caution in relation to role experimentation and, in many cases, expressed negative attitudes toward their daughters' political involvement, typically they had indirectly conveyed strong support for role change and, in some cases, for political participation at key periods of the daughters' maturation. A third factor was the special place of alternative role models in the process just described. Typically, a father, brother, or other person, generally a male, had served as a model to daughters for learning the behavior associated with the political role. Seldom were these men active or conscious sponsors of role change. The fathers' views of appropriate behavior for women were more restrictive than those of the mothers. But indirectly, through their example, they provided an important basis for their daughters' political involvement later on.

Beyond tracing women's steps into political life, the study looks closely at the costs and benefits, the satisfactions and dissatisfactions, of political involvement for women over the years from age eighteen to thirty-three. The costs and dissatisfactions of activism are greatest at those points in the life cycle when female role demands are highest. At such points the dropout rate from politics is high. The study shows, however, that politically active women adopt a variety of strategies that make it possible for them to reduce the role strain that typically accompanies their political involvement. They may "gender-type" their own political activities, limiting them to types of behavior that are more consonant with the dominant definition of woman's role; they may compartmentalize roles, screening their political activity from potential critics; or they may defy their critics and demand that those around them accept their own emerging definition of the female gender role that sees political behavior as fully appropriate for women.

These latter women are at the cutting edge of social change. By confronting those who would limit or curtail their political activity, they offer a direct challenge to the dominant definition of woman's role and force change in it. In a larger sense, however, all political women, no matter how modest their degree of involvement or how carefully they may disguise their activism from any detractors, are agents of change. As a result of their collective efforts, prevailing notions of woman's role are gradually expanded to include new forms of activity that once were wholly proscribed for women. Through their struggles, political women show others the way.

2

The Background to Contemporary Struggle: Gaining Political Rights in Japan

Japanese women's views of their place in political life have undergone profound changes over the past three and a half decades. Women gained full political rights, in a legal sense, in 1945 as the accidental by-product of Japan's defeat in World War II and subsequent occupation by American forces. Prior to that time, their participation in politics had been extremely limited. For much of the prewar period, not only was voting proscribed, but women were legally barred from most citizen modes of political participation during an era when women in many Western societies were gaining full political rights. A women's suffrage movement took shape in Japan in the early decades of the twentieth century, but its base of support was far too limited for it to have the kind of broad, consciousness-raising effects that such movements had in a number of Western countries. The particular legacy of Japan's past, combined with the unique circumstances surrounding the introduction of full political rights for women in 1945, have had major consequences for the Japanese women's views of their political roles and options in the postwar period up through the present. That is the subject of this chapter.

When Japan began its rush to modernize in 1868, the country was emerging from almost seven centuries of feudalism presided over by a class of male warrior elite, the samurai. Whereas Western countries over the same period had produced a smattering of powerful queens, such as Elizabeth I, Mary Queen of Scots, Isabella of Spain, Catherine the Great, and Queen Jadwiga of Poland, the Japanese pantheon of political leaders included few women of even token note. Nor were women even in a position to exert much informal influence on the conduct of politics. By the Tokugawa period (1603–1867), central government policy had required that male elites with national political roles to play leave their families behind in the provinces when they came to the capital to deal with political affairs. Many women of the elite class were thus even physically peripheral to Japanese political life.[1]

In the early decades of the modern period (1868–), what status women were to occupy in the new order was not clear. Plagued by economic problems and pressured by the West, Japan's crumbling feudal structure had given way by the mid-nineteenth century to a new leadership pledging its determination to modernize the country. It took several decades to put together a new system of guided democracy based on

1. According to standard accounts, Japanese women occupied a status more nearly equal to men's in prehistorical and early historical times up through the eleventh and twelfth centuries, but suffered a decline in status in later centuries with the spread of feudal institutions. See Morosawa Yōko, *Onna no rekishi* (The history of women), vol. 1 (Tokyo, 1970), and Takemure Itsue, *Josei no rekishi* (The history of women), vol. 4 of *Zenshū* (The Collected Works) (Tokyo, 1966). For a summary of major developments in women's history prior to 1868 and a bibliography of relevant English and Japanese language sources, see Susan J. Pharr, "Japan: Historical and Contemporary Perspectives," in *Women: Role and Status in Eight Countries*, ed. Janet Z. Giele and Audrey C. Smock (New York, 1977), pp. 219–227.

Western models, and for a time the situation was quite fluid. News of feminist movements under way in other countries found its way to Japan, and Western ideas and ideologies gained popularity. As a result, some voices were raised on behalf of women's rights. Women's suffrage became an issue as early as 1876 in one of Japan's newly founded prefectural assemblies.[2] A small number of women joined in a broadly based movement for people's rights (*jiyū minken undō*). Japan's first suffragist, Kishida Toshiko (1863–1901), campaigned throughout Japan on behalf of this movement and combined her appeals for democratic rights with appeals on behalf of women.[3] As the people's rights movement developed into a party movement in the 1880s, some of the most liberal factions supported women's suffrage and included suffragists in their ranks. Various male leaders took up causes relating to women's rights. One of these, Mori Arinori (1847–1889), in his position as one of Japan's representatives abroad, advocated contractual marriage based on egalitarian principles. It was largely through his influence that the Japanese government in 1871 sent five young girls to America for an education, an action stirring such wonder in Japan that one contemporary Japanese writer compares it to man's arrival on the moon.[4] Fukuzawa Yukichi (1835–1901), another liberal leader whose views grew from his travels in the West, became an important advocate of raising women's status, if for no other reason than that it would improve Japan's image in the eyes of the West.[5]

As the new government took shape, however, and reaction to the earlier period of borrowing from the West set in by the 1880s, the ambiguity surrounding woman's status in the

2. Harada Tomohiko, *Nihon josei shi* (History of Japanese women) (Tokyo, 1965), p. 194. The issue arose in Hamamatsu, but disappeared when Hamamatsu merged with Shizuoka prefecture.

3. Murakami Nobuhiko, *Meiji josei shi* (The history of Meiji women), vol. 2 (Tokyo, 1970), pp. 74–101.

4. See Tsunatake Furuya, "Meiji Women: Landmarks They Have Left," *Japan Quarterly* 14 (July–September 1967): 319–320.

5. This criticism of Fukuzawa's motives is elaborated in Yoshimi Kaneko, *Fujin sansei ken* (Women's political rights), vol. 1 of *Gendai nihon josei shi* (Contemporary history of Japanese women) (Tokyo, 1971), p. 15. For his writings relating to women, see Carmen Blacker, *The Japanese Enlightenment: A Study of the Writings of Fukuzawa Yukichi* (Cambridge, 1964), pp. 67–89.

new society disappeared. The new Meiji Constitution of 1890, which provided for a parliament and introduced limited manhood suffrage, dealt with women's political rights by omitting mention of them. Meanwhile, a Peace Preservation Law introduced several years earlier to control a variety of liberal causes explicitly barred women from organizing or even joining political groups and from attending meetings where political matters were discussed.[6]

Over the decades following the passage of the Peace Preservation Law, various women, most of them from the urban, educated, upper classes, organized themselves in support of feminist causes. Their activities strikingly paralleled developments taking place in many non-Western countries during the same period. Using arguments and organizational strategies borrowed from Western feminists, Western-educated urban women in Republican China and in colonial India similarly were pressing for women's rights in the first decades of the twentieth century and in settings where the ideas they advanced were equally out of step with prevailing norms and values in their societies.[7]

The most prominent of the early groups in Japan was the Bluestockings Society (Seitōsha), named after the eighteenth-century salon of avant-gard British intellectuals. Formed in 1911, this group had the ostensible goal—and indeed almost any other would have been in violation of governmental restrictions then in force—of providing a literary outlet for talented women writers through its publication *Seitō* (Bluestockings). Soon, however, the magazine became a vehicle for feminist criticism, and its members debated issues ranging from the meaning of motherhood to women's suffrage. The group's founder, Hiratsuka Raichō (1886–1971), became one of Japan's foremost suffragists and perhaps the country's best-known prewar feminist leader. *Seitō* itself was frequently censored by the government and suspended publication in 1916.[8] But soon after, Hiratsuka, joined by

6. See Wakamori Tarō and Yamamoto Fujie, *Nihon no josei shi* (A history of women in Japan), vol. 4 (Tokyo, 1965), pp. 67–150.

7. See Kay Ann Johnson, "The Politics of Women's Rights and Family Reform in China," Ph.D. dissertation, University of Wisconsin, Madison, 1976.

8. See Nancy Andrew, "The *Seitōsha*: An Early Japanese Women's Organization, 1911–1916," *Papers on Japan*, East Asian Research Center, Har-

Ichikawa Fusae (1893–), another prominent suffragist who was still active in women's causes in the 1970s, formed a New Women's Association (Shin Fujin Kyōkai) in 1919 to press for women's political rights.

The targets of the new group's efforts were those restrictions of the Peace Preservation Law that made it difficult for women's rights groups to meet, let alone make a bid for suffrage. The successful, if modest, outcome of their feminist struggle at this stage is reflected in the words of a Japanese activist writing in English for foreign readers: "After a few years, as a result of their earnest work, notwithstanding prejudice all around, a law was passed and the regulation preventing women from listening to political lectures was taken away."[9] With the revision of the Peace Preservation Law in 1922, women gained the right to organize and attend political meetings (although the same law continued to bar them from joining or forming political parties).

Various women's groups, led by the Women's Suffrage Alliance (Fusen Kakutoku Dōmei) pressed for suffrage in the years that followed. Ichikawa Fusae, who had spent the period from 1920 to 1924 in the United States in contact with such American suffragists as Carrie Chapman Catt, founder of the League of Women Voters, and Alice Paul, organizer of the National Woman's Party, became the key figure of this period.[10] A tall woman who smoked and wore her hair short,

vard University, vol. 6 (Cambridge, Mass., 1972); Pauline Reich, "Japan's Literary Feminists: The Seitō Group," trans. Pauline C. Reich and Fukuda Atsuko, Signs 2 (Autumn 1976), 280–291; Ken Miyamoto, "Itō Noe and the Bluestockings," Japan Interpreter 10 (Autumn 1975), 190–204; and Ide Fumiko, Seitō (Tokyo, 1962). Hiratsuka Raichō wrote an autobiography that is available in Japanese: Genshi, josei wa taiyō de atta (In the beginning, woman was the sun), 3 vols. (Tokyo, 1971). The title of the work refers to the much-quoted "manifesto" of the Bluestockings that appeared in the first issue of its magazine in 1911: "In the beginning, woman was truly the sun. She was a genuine person. Now, woman is the moon, the sickly pale moon that can shine only with the light of another. . . . We must now restore our vanished sun" (translated in Andrew, "The Seitōsha," p. 57). The reference to woman as the sun goes back to Japanese mythology in which the Sun Goddess, Amaterasu Ōmikami (from whom Japan's present imperial line traces its descent), played a central role.

9. Michi Kawai and Kubushiro Ochimi, Japanese Women Speak (Boston, 1934), p. 125.

10. See Dee Ann Vavich, "The Japanese Woman's Movement: Ichikawa

she was an object of ridicule in the Japanese press for her manner as well as her convictions. But her single-minded commitment to suffrage over other issues helped to hold together a movement that was by that time heavily factionalized. For a time after 1928, there was some hope that the movement might achieve its aim. The Seiyūkai, one of the two leading political parties of prewar Japan, took up the issue of women's suffrage. Almost overnight, the tone of reporting from a press long critical of the suffragists became more favorable. The high point in what Ichikawa has called the "period of hope" was the passage, in 1931, of a modified women's civil rights bill by the lower house of the Imperial Diet. But the far more powerful upper house was never to give its approval to the measure. The bill had only limited support in the first place, but to seal its fate the movement received a wave of bad publicity shortly before the vote was taken. A women's rally held in support of the measure in February 1931 erupted into bitter ideological debate and then violence when a man from the audience attempted to drag Ichikawa from the stage. The defeat of the suffrage bill the following month in the upper house, by a vote of 184 to 62, was a foregone conclusion.[11]

Although there were immediate plans to reintroduce the measure in the next session of the Diet, history then inter-

---

Fusae, A Pioneer in Woman's Suffrage," *Monumenta Nipponica* 22 (1967): 401–436, and Patricia Murray, "Ichikawa Fusae and the Lonely Red Carpet," *Japan Interpreter* 10 (Autumn, 1975): 171–189. Ichikawa has written an autobiography covering the prewar years (*Ichikawa Fusae jiden: senzenhen* [Autobiography of Ichikawa Fusae: the prewar years], Tokyo, 1974) and plans to write another volume covering her postwar career. She has served in the upper house of the Japanese parliament almost continuously since 1953, and is probably Japan's most famous political woman today.

11. Vavich, "Ichikawa Fusae," pp. 418–420. At least some of the problems of the Japanese suffrage movement during this turbulent period were due to factionalism within Japan's left-wing political movement. Many of the suffrage movement's supporters had loyalties to proletarian parties as well, and wanted to co-opt the movement on behalf of their particular party. Ichikawa stood firm against her left-wing critics: "I honestly believe that what I am doing is right. . . . Whatever they say, there will be a day when everything is resolved. . . . I will dedicate all I have—time, power, money—for this movement." (Translated from an autobiographical statement by Ichikawa in Vavich, p. 416.)

vened. The Manchurian Incident in 1931 led to the increased ascendancy of a highly antifeminist military in civilian affairs and a reordering of national priorities that left women's suffrage a dead issue. In an increasingly repressive society, those advocating women's rights causes were harassed and their publications rigorously censored. Women's suffrage activists gradually turned their energies to the problems, mounting in the Depression years, of working women and widows. They were instrumental in getting several important measures passed by the Diet to benefit these groups. But as far as a movement for women's political rights was concerned, the "period of hope"—and mild hope at that—had ended.

From the late 1930s, when Japan's expansionist activities in Asia accelerated, until 1945, when the war ended, women, including those who had been active in the feminist causes of earlier decades, were buffeted by larger forces: the national mobilization policy of the government, the economic hardships imposed on the nation before and during the war, and the patriarchal attitudes of Japan's wartime leadership.[12] The suffrage movement itself literally disappeared when women's groups of all kinds were subsumed in 1942 under a state-directed Greater Japanese Women's Association (Dai Nihon Fujinkai) organized in support of the war effort.

In 1945 Japan's defeat brought an era to a close. In that same year enfranchisement came, handed to Japanese women over the heads of a discredited leadership by the American occupation in a series of developments to be discussed shortly. Looking back at the prewar period, one may speculate on the great imponderable of what would have happened to women had the war and the occupation not intervened in Japanese history. Would the Japanese women's movement finally have gained sufficient support to win a sympathetic hearing from the government? Or, as the work

12. See Thomas R. H. Havens, "Women and War in Japan, 1937–45," *American Historical Review* 80 (October 1975): 913–934. Not only was it impossible to advance the cause of suffrage during this period, but there were few of the kind of economic opportunities that opened up to American women during the war. As Havens shows, while the percentage of women in the work force shot up in the United States, Germany, the USSR, and England, Japanese women were greatly underutilized (p. 918). Despite a desperate labor shortage, Japan's wartime leadership exhorted women to reproduce, not produce (p. 933).

of many structural determinists seems to suggest, would suffrage, along with other political, social, and economic gains,
have come to women anyway as a result of larger social and
economic forces at work in the prewar period that were push-
ing Japan toward its status today as an advanced industrial
society?[13] Of the two positions, the second is undoubtedly
more persuasive than the first. For although feminist activities in prewar Japan had great symbolic importance, their
scale and influence were clearly limited. The monthly circula-
tion of *Seitō* at its peak never reached more than three
thousand.[14] The First National Meeting for Women's Suffrage held in 1930 at the height of the "period of hope" drew
less than five hundred women.[15] Much of the support for the
movement came from women, along with some men, who
were in movements (the people's rights movement and later
the labor movement and the proletarian parties) that themselves lacked a broad base of support in prewar society. By
any estimate, then, the prewar suffrage movement had a long
way to go at the point of its gradual demise after 1931. And
indeed, even those who see major consequences for women's
social and political status in larger economic structural
changes taking place in a given society are quick to acknowledge the lag effect produced by such political variables as elite
attitudes. In Japan today, most who argue that women's gain
of political rights was inevitable, for whatever reason, readily
admit that the occupation sped up the process immeasurably.[16]

On April 10, 1946, Japanese women voted and ran for political office for the first time. Over the more than thirty years

13. See Janet Z. Giele, "Introduction: Comparative Perspectives on
Women," in *Women: Role and Status in Eight Countries*, ed. Janet Z. Giele and
Audrey C. Smock (New York, 1977), pp. 1–32, which links economic change
to changes in women's status.

14. Andrew, "*Seitōsha*," p. 49.

15. Vavich, "Ichikawa Fusae," p. 419.

16. Ichikawa's position is typical: "Without the Occupation or the defeat
of Japan, the realization of women's constitutional rights would not have
been achieved so quickly." (Quote from a 1964 interview cited in Vavich, p.
426.) Many writers, however, argue that technological and other changes
paved the way for postwar gains in status for women, independent of the
role played by the occupation. See, for example, Kazuo Kawai, *Japan's American Interlude* (Chicago, 1960), p. 244.

since the end of the war, the political climate in Japan has changed in fundamental ways. In stark contrast to the prewar situation, women in postwar Japan confront a wide range of options when it comes to playing a political role. Not only may they vote, but they may compete for top political offices, and between these two extremes there are no legal barriers to playing any number of political roles in the "more active" category.

Actually exercising newly acquired legal rights is, of course, a different matter. In no country of the world today has full and equal political participation of women been realized, despite the removal of legal restrictions. It is important, then, to look at the degree to which women in Japan have been able to translate political rights into political influence and power. Only against this backdrop can the activities and aspirations of young women entering political life today be understood.

The place to begin is with the single political act most basic to the functioning of a democratic society, voting. The Allied occupation got under way almost immediately after the defeat in 1945 and lasted until 1952. As part of the effort to democratize Japan, the occupation, under General Douglas MacArthur as Supreme Commander for the Allied Powers (SCAP), undertook a far-reaching series of reforms ranging from a land reform to a series of women's rights measures, of which the cornerstone was women's suffrage. The rationale for granting suffrage to women was spelled out clearly in documents of the period. It was hoped that in a nation seen by the Americans as aggressive and militaristic, women would use the ballot on behalf of peace, and that as educated citizens they would teach future generations of Japanese the ways of democracy.[17]

Gaining the vote and other political rights, however, represented a fundamental break with the past, and many occupation officials and Japanese wondered if women were capable of responding to the changes so quickly. The first postwar election was set to be held only a few months after the granting of suffrage. Ichikawa Fusae, who had worked continuously since the defeat to secure women's political rights in the new order and to educate women in the use of the ballot,

17. Ibid.

direly predicted that no more than 10 percent of Japanese women would turn out for the election.[18]

When the results were in, however, women's voter turn-out had far exceeded the most optimistic expectations. The voting rate was 67.0 percent for women and 78.5 percent for men, an exceedingly small gap, particularly when compared with the performance of women in other countries in early postsuffrage elections. In most European countries, such as Germany, Sweden, Finland, and Norway, gaps of 10–15 percentage points between the voting rates for men and women appeared for decades after the granting of suffrage.[19] In the United States available data indicate that men may have out-voted women by a two-to-one margin in the first postsuffrage election.[20] Ironically, the male/female gap in the 1946 Japanese election was less than the gap in the most contemporaneous United States presidential election, held in 1948.[21] This irony undoubtedly went unnoticed by most Americans involved in the occupation, for whom it was an article of faith that the United States was the home of the world's most liberated women.

After this impressive beginning in 1946 the gap between the voting rates for men and women in Japan closed gradually over the postwar period, paralleling a trend found in virtually all of the advanced industrial societies. If we look at the process historically, however, what is surprising is the degree of change that occurred in Japan in such a short period of time. Not only do Japanese women vote, but they have become super-voters. Since 1968, the voting rate of Japanese women relative to that for men has been higher than that for any society for which voting data by sex are available. In other advanced industrial societies women's voting rate, even today, generally lags behind that for men by from one to ten

18. Supreme Commander for the Allied Powers (SCAP), General Headquarters, Government Section, *Political Reorientation of Japan* (Washington, D.C., 1949), p. 321.

19. Herbert Tingsten, *Political Behavior* (London, 1937).

20. John J. Stucker, "Women as Voters: Their Maturation as Political Persons in American Society," in *A Portrait of Marginality*, ed. Marianne Githens and Jewel L. Prestage (New York, 1977), pp. 270–271.

21. Marjorie Lansing, "The American Woman: Voter and Activist," in *Women in Politics*, ed. Jane S. Jaquette (New York, 1974), p. 8. The female voting rate lagged behind that for men by 13 percent in the 1948 U.S. presidential election; the gap was under 12 percent in Japan in 1946.

percentage points, whereas in Japan, not only has the gap closed, but women's voter turnout in national elections has consistently exceeded that for men in every national election since 1968 (see table 1). Women's voting turnout tends to be even higher relative to men's in local elections, especially in

TABLE 1   *Comparison of Male and Female Voting Rates in Japanese National Elections, 1946–1976* (in percentage)

A. LOWER HOUSE

General Election	Voting Rates		Difference
	Female	Male	
22nd (April 10, 1946)	67.0	78.5	−11.5
23rd (April 25, 1947)	61.6	74.9	−13.3
24th (January 23, 1949)	67.9	80.7	−12.8
25th (October 1, 1952)	72.8	80.5	−7.7
26th (April 19, 1953)	70.4	78.4	−8.0
27th (February 27, 1955)	72.1	78.0	−5.9
28th (May 22, 1958)	74.4	79.8	−5.4
29th (November 20, 1960)	71.2	76.0	−4.8
30th (November 21, 1963)	70.0	72.4	−2.4
31st (November 29, 1967)	73.3	74.8	−1.5
32nd (December 27, 1969)	69.1	67.9	+1.2
33rd (December 10, 1972)	72.5	71.0	+1.5
34th (December 5, 1976)	74.1	72.8	+1.3

B. UPPER HOUSE

General Election	Female	Male	Difference
1st (April 20, 1947)	54.0	68.4	−14.4
2nd (January 4, 1950)	66.7	78.2	−11.5
3rd (April 24, 1953)	58.9	67.8	−8.9
4th (July 8, 1956)	57.7	66.9	−9.2
5th (January 2, 1959)	55.2	62.6	−7.4
6th (July 1, 1962)	66.5	70.1	−3.6
7th (June 4, 1965)	66.1	68.0	−1.9
8th (July 7, 1968)	69.0	68.9	+0.1
9th (June 12, 1971)	59.3	59.1	+0.2
10th (July 7, 1974)	73.6	72.7	+0.9

SOURCE: Ministry of Labor, Women's and Minors' Bureau, *The Status of Women in Japan,* 1977, p. 3.

large cities. As an example, their turnout in an important 1967 election for the governorship of Tokyo prefecture was 4 percent higher than that for men.[22] How are we to account for the extraordinary changes that have taken place in Japan over the postwar years in the area of women's voting behavior, and what do they tell us about women's views today of their place in political life?

The process by which women, once barred from a sphere of male activity, come to participate in it once legal barriers are removed is thought to involve role learning, or what may be termed *role redefinition*.[23] In other words, as time passes, an adjustment takes place in dominant definitions of woman's role, and the behaviors associated with the activity gradually come to be viewed as appropriate for females. In the chapters ahead, a major aim is to explore the dynamics of role redefinition by examining the experiences of individual women today who are at the cutting edge of role change in the area of political participation in Japan. In a larger sense, however, the process of role redefinition has been under way for all Japanese women in the postwar period as beneficiaries of new political rights once reserved for men. The process of change experienced by individual women is best understood in the context of this larger process of role redefinition. For this reason it is especially useful to explore how and why voting gained general acceptance among women in such a short period of time. For it appears that in Japan, at least where voting is concerned, the process of role redefinition is now complete, as evidenced by the disappearance of the male/female gap.

The general outlines of the process by which voting gained acceptance among Japanese women can be partially reconstructed from available data. Based on what is known about the factors linked to participation in political life, we would expect to find increased voter turnout associated with a rising sense of political efficacy among women as they came to see themselves as political actors with a legitimate role to play in political life.[24] And indeed, this is the case. The starting point of this long process may be seen in data from the early post-

22. Taki Fujita, "Women and Politics in Japan," *Annals of the American Academy* 375 (January 1968), p. 93.

23. See chapter one.

24. Jeanne Knutson, *The Human Basis of the Polity* (New York, 1972), p. 187.

war period. Raper and his associates, interviewing Japanese villagers only a few years after the granting of suffrage, found that men viewed women's political role with "some amusement, if not contempt."[25] They found that village women talked mainly to one another about politics, thereby avoiding criticism or belittlement from their husbands and other men who saw them as overstepping the boundaries of appropriate female behavior.[26]

The researchers concluded that women may have voted in the first postwar elections more out of fear of criticism from their female neighbors and their own children than from any positive feelings associated with voting.[27] That negative rather than positive affect attached to the act of voting in the early postwar years is further suggested by the results of election studies conducted in the early 1950s. In a survey of women's attitudes toward voting conducted in 1951, 73 percent of those questioned said that they voted because "not voting is a bad thing," a reply that rings more of a fear of negative sanctions than of positive, efficacious feelings about voting.[28] In the same survey, only a small minority of women (26%) said that they had voted "because politics will be influenced if I express my opinion," a response indicative of more efficacious feelings about their new citizen role.[29] From this starting point early in the postsuffrage years, there is every evidence that women's acceptance of and adjustment to the role of voter progressed steadily over the years. Not only was the male/female gap in turnout closing, but women's attitudes toward voting were changing. Surveys through the 1950s and 1960s show a declining percentage of women who voted only because "not voting is a bad thing."[30]

25. Arthur F. Raper, Tamie Tsuchiyama, Herbert Passin, and David L. Sills, *The Japanese Village in Transition*, General Headquarters, Supreme Commander for the Allied Powers, Report No. 136 (Tokyo, 1950), p. 207.

26. Ibid., pp. 206–208.

27. See Sumie Mishima, *The Broader Way* (New York, 1953), pp. 238–239, for a first-hand account of the pressure on women from other women to vote.

28. Results of a "Survey on Women's Civic Consciousness" conducted by the Women's and Minors' Bureau of the Ministry of Labor, cited in Matsushita Kei-ichi, *Gendai fujin mondai nyūmon* (An approach to problems of women today) (Tokyo, 1970), p. 283.

29. Ibid.

30. Ibid. Matsushita presents data from six surveys conducted from 1951 to 1967 to document this change in voter attitudes.

By 1976, only 3.8 percent of those questioned chose that reply. Most women, instead, said they voted "because it [vot-
ing] is a natural right" (44%) or because their vote could "do
good for politics" (47.7%).[31] These responses are important
evidence that positive, more efficacious feelings about the act
of voting have been on the increase as part of the process of
role redefinition in Japan in the area of political behavior. By
the late 1960s, voting had become a routine activity fully in
keeping with the norms and expectations associated with
woman's role.

So far, the discussion has traced some of the steps over
time in the process of role redefinition. It has not, however,
explained why the process proceeded as quickly as it did, and
from such an auspicious beginning. While noting that attitudes toward voting have changed as part of the process of
role definition, it is perhaps even more important to explain
why so many women voted—for whatever the reason—at
the outset of the postwar period when voting was a
thoroughly new activity for them. The explanation is certainly
not obvious, given women's low turnout in most countries in
early postsuffrage elections, and given the absence of a variable that has been thought critical to women's acceptance of
suffrage in many countries: the "consciousness-raising effects" of a long and widely supported women's suffrage
movement.[32] As was indicated earlier, the prewar women's
suffrage movement in Japan lacked the popular support that
would have allowed it to function in that way.

What Japan had that other suffrage states did not have,
however, was a unique setting for change created by the in-
tervention in its history of an occupying force committed to
improving the status of women. When one studies the aftermath of the granting of women's suffrage in Western countries, one is struck by how little most governments did to encourage women to exercise their newly acquired right. In
most of the original suffrage states, the vote was granted to
women grudgingly over much opposition from those in
power. If leaders hard pressed by suffragist movements

31. Ibid.
32. See Stucker, "Women as Voters," p. 272; also see William H. Chafe,
The American Woman (New York, 1972), for a discussion of the aftermath of
the suffrage movement in the United States.

finally conceded women's legal right to vote, they were
hardly prepared to go further and to campaign on behalf of
the cause or to attempt to resocialize women to accept voting
as appropriate female activity. If any campaign was launched,
it was generally to discourage women from voting rather than
to encourage them. In the American South, for example,
women's suffrage met so much resistance from the traditional
leadership that a "magnolia curtain" effectively kept the vast
majority of Southern women from the polls in the early postsuffrage years.[33] Outside the United States, support from
above for women's use of the ballot has often been even less.
In Egypt, for example, a few months before women's suffrage
was declared in 1956, Islamic legal scholars issued an official
religious ruling that women were unfit to vote.[34] With little
support from key authority figures for role change, it is little
wonder that the vast majority of Egyptian women even today
stay away from the polls.[35] Exercising a newly acquired right
in a setting where the leadership is hostile—or at a minimum,
neutral or divided—over the issue puts the individual in the
position of going it alone, of violating role expectations with
little support from those leaders and institutions in a position
to influence values and attitudes in society.

Occupied Japan, then, appears to have provided a unique
setting for change. For a brief period of seven years, the
Americans, with the full powers of the American military and
the Allies behind them and with a clear goal (democratization) to justify their commitment to women's rights, were in a
position to carry out what may be the world's greatest experiment with feminism outside a revolutionary context. In a
period when Japan's own leadership was discredited and in
disarray and when overt resistance to occupation policy was
impossible, the occupation in Japan functioned much like a
revolutionary council following a highly successful military
coup in support of a far-reaching program of social change.
Since universal suffrage was considered a cornerstone of that

33. Stucker, "Women as Voters," p. 273.

34. Audrey Chapman Smock and Nadia Haggag Youssef, "Egypt: From
Seclusion to Limited Participation," in *Women: Role and Status in Eight Countries*, ed. Janet Z. Giele and Audrey C. Smock (New York, 1977), p. 67.

35. In 1971 there were 900,000 registered female voters and 7 million registered male voters in Egypt (ibid.).

program, the occupation launched a multi-media campaign to promote women's use of the ballot in the months prior to the April 1946 election. Japanese women leaders who had been prominent in the prewar suffrage movement, as well as other noted Japanese women, were brought in to promote voting. They appeared on radio talk shows and, in some cases, campaigned in the countryside alongside occupation officials urging women to vote. Movies on the prewar Japanese suffrage movement and on the value of women's political participation were soon in production. Materials shipped over by the League of Women Voters of the United States were quickly translated and widely disseminated.

It is little wonder that Japanese women by the late 1940s were telling social scientists that "not voting is a bad thing." The message from above was that voting was a major responsibility that women should shoulder if Japan was to become a democratic and peace-loving society. Although most members of the occupation would have been the last to see themselves as radical feminists, the program they set in motion to alter sex-role stereotypes and to redefine voting as highly appropriate and essential activity for women may have been more extensive than anything attempted elsewhere in the area of political role change for women.[36] We may speculate that had the leadership in the original suffrage states been willing to promote—as well as permit—women's suffrage earlier in the century, the gap between the voting rates for men and women would have closed long ago, and Western women's fears of "tarnishing their femininity" through voting would long since have been laid to rest.[37]

In our examination of why women in Japan gave so much support to women's suffrage in the postwar years, one other factor, also linked to the special role played by the occupation, deserves mention. This is the particular symbolic value that appears to have attached to voting from the time of the introduction of women's suffrage. Gaining the vote in Japan came at the vanguard of a whole range of occupation reforms designed to upgrade women's status in society and the fam-

36. See Susan J. Pharr, "A Radical U.S. Experiment: Women's Rights Laws and the Occupation of Japan," in *The Occupation of Japan: Impact of Legal Reform.* ed. L. H. Redford (Norfolk, Va., 1978).

37. Robert E. Lane, *Political Life* (New York, 1959), p. 213.

ily. But among the reforms, suffrage had a unique place. The average woman in 1947 was not in a position to test new constitutional and legal guarantees by obtaining a divorce, by running for elective office, by trying to obtain a job with pay equal to that for a male worker. As Raper and his associates reported in their study of thirteen villages in 1947–1948, voting was the only new right that women did not regard as "theoretical."[38] As far as other guarantees in the Constitution and Civil Code were concerned, most women felt that these had little relation to their everyday lives. Voting, however, was different, for it involved a single, easily performed act for which constitutional guarantees were clear and unequivocal. By voting, a woman could show her support for the new rights given to all women by the occupation. Practically speaking, too, voting took on special significance, since women's showing at the polls was regarded by the media, Japanese politicians, and the occupation itself as a key index to women's acceptance of their new status. That voting is still linked in the popular mind with other status gains for women is reflected in the results of a recent survey in which women were asked about the meaning of women's political participation. Fifty-three percent, by far the greatest percentage for any reply, said that it meant that "women's status is rising."[39]

As a final commentary on the process of role redefinition in relation to voting that has occurred in Japan, it should be pointed out that the overall pattern of change is similar to that found in other advanced industrial societies. As in the United States, higher voter turnout for women relative to the male rate is found among younger women (see table 2). Although a traditional "collectivity orientation" found among older voters and those in rural areas assures a high voter turnout for

38. Raper et al., *Japanese Village*, p. 208.
39. Sankei Shimbun, *Iken to ishiki no hyakka jiten* (Encyclopedia of opinion and thought) (Tokyo, 1972, p. 225). Other replies by women in the same survey, the results of which were released in December 1970, were as follows: women's political participation, even if it's a kind of duty, doesn't accomplish anything (1.0%); has become a deterrent to war (7.1%); [means that] the ideal of equal rights for men and women now prevails (27.5%); [means that] political injustice is disappearing (6.4%); other (2.8%); don't know (1.9%).

TABLE 2   *Japanese Women's Voting Rate by Age Group, Compared with That for Men* (in percentage)

	Age Group				
	20–29	30–39	40–49	50–59	60+
Women	74.7	86.2	89.3	87.4	77.2
Men	66.5	84.2	87.1	91.9	84.7

SOURCE: Ministry of Labor, Women's and Minors' Bureau, *Me de miru fujin no ayumi* (A look at women's progress), Tokyo, 1971. Figures based on 1969 study of voting in Lower House election.

both men and women in the older age groups,[40] it is among these older and more traditional segments of the population that women's voting rate lags behind that for men. Younger women, who have grown up taking voting for granted as appropriate female activity, are the ones responsible for closing the male/female gap in Japan, as in the United States.[41]

To trace the process by which Japanese women have come to terms with their political rights in postwar society, the focus so far has been on voting. Among Western political scientists, changes in women's voting behavior are thought to be closely associated with changes in other measures of mass political behavior, an assumption for which there is much empirical evidence.[42] In Japan, however, the pattern of women's political behavior has numerous inconsistencies that are best traced to the special circumstances surrounding

40. See Bradley M. Richardson, "Urbanization and Political Participation: The Case of Japan," *American Political Science Review* 67 (June 1973): 433–452, and Jōji Watanuki, "Patterns of Politics in Present-Day Japan," in *Party Systems and Voter Alignments, Cross-National Perspectives*, ed. Seymour M. Lipset and Stein Rokkan (New York, 1967).

41. See Lansing, "American Woman," p. 10. In the 1972 presidential election, the voting rate for women exceeded or equaled that for men among people below age forty-five. Among the older age groups, however, the rate for women lagged well behind that for men.

42. See Jane Jaquette, "Review Essay: Political Science," *Signs* 2 (Autumn 1976), p. 148. This does not mean, of course, that changes in mass political behavior automatically lead to changes in patterns of participation and representation at the elite level; obviously, as many writers note, this has not happened, as is evidenced by the few women in elite positions throughout the world despite changes in women's political behavior at the mass level.

TABLE 3 *Political Participation, Interest, and Information among Upper-Middle-Class Men and Women in Large Cities in Japan* (in percentage)

	M	F	Difference
Always votes in national elections	69.7	70.4	+0.7
Attends rallies (four or more)	25.4	14.3	−11.1
Works for political parties (more than once)	21.1	12.5	−8.6
Discusses national politics (more than once a week)	71.4	68.0	−3.4
High political interest	28.5	14.3	−14.2
High level of political information	51.2	42.3	−8.9

SOURCE: Jōji Watanuki, "Social Structure and Political Participation in Japan," Laboratory for Political Research, Report No. 32 (Iowa City, Iowa, 1970), p. 14, derived from Table 4. Data were collected during 1966 and 1967.

the introduction of women's political rights in Japan. While voting is fully accepted as appropriate female activity, all other measures of political cognition, affect, and behavior reveal major male/female differences. Even among those subsets of the population where the voting rate for women is well ahead of the male rate, such as among upper-middle-class, urban residents, substantial male/female gaps appear for all other measures (see table 3). In the United States, in contrast, available data suggest that sex differences in all types of citizen political participation have virtually disappeared among comparable segments of the population.[43] Among Japanese women of lower socioeconomic standing, the disparity between their voting behavior and other types of political behavior is even more pronounced, with the greatest disparity found among poor, rural women.[44]

The best explanation for Japanese women's greater acceptance of voting over other types of political activity is probab

43. Ibid.; also, see Maureen Fiedler, "The Participation of Women in American Politics." Paper presented at the Annual Meeting of the American Political Science Association, San Francisco, 1975, p. 6.

44. Jōji Watanuki, "Social Structure and Political Participation in Japan," Laboratory for Political Research, Report no. 32 (Iowa City, Iowa, 1970).

bly the one just mentioned: the special place occupied by women's suffrage among the occupation's battery of reforms. Although the occupation supported many changes affecting women and pressed women toward more active citizen roles on all fronts, there can be no question that women's suffrage was the centerpiece of the measures in the political area and, as such, was the primary target of the consciousness-raising campaigns referred to earlier. It seems likely, then, that role learning proceeded at a much faster pace where voting was concerned than in other types of political participation.

Earlier we set out to examine the degree to which Japanese women have been able to convert the new political rights they acquired during the occupation into political influence and power. Here the ultimate test, of course, is office-holding. It is important to look at the representation of women at the elite level as background for the chapters ahead because women's success rate at the elite level is the ultimate measure of women's acceptance in political life, and a barometer for gauging external barriers that may limit women's more active political participation.

Women's gains in Japan at the elite level have been extremely modest in an absolute sense, but roughly comparable to those of women in other advanced industrial democracies. The first postwar election in 1946 brought thirty-nine women to the more powerful lower house of Japan's bicameral Diet, to make up 8.4 percent of that body's total membership. Many factors account for this relatively impressive showing, which has never been matched in subsequent elections for either house (see table 4). One factor almost certainly was the depleted state of male leadership at that time, which was due not only to the occupation's purge of many political leaders accused of war responsibility, but also to the fact that many experienced male leaders were discredited in public eyes by the defeat. Another factor was that the electoral laws in effect in the first postwar election were more favorable to less established candidates than laws enacted the following year.[45] Following their impressive showing in the first lower-house election, women's success rate suffered a gradual decline over the

45. Joseph A. Massey, "The Occupation and the Sheriff of Nottingham: The Legacy of Election Reform," in *The Occupation of Japan: Impact of Legal Reform*, ed. L. H. Redford (Norfolk, Va., 1978).

TABLE 4   *Number and Percentage of Women Elected to the Diet,*
1946–1976

A. LOWER HOUSE ELECTIONS

Election	No. of Women Elected	Percentage of Total Membership
22nd (April 10, 1946)	39	8.4
23rd (April 25, 1947)	15	3.2
24th (January 23, 1949)	12	2.6
25th (October 1, 1952)	12	2.6
26th (April 19, 1953)	9	1.9
27th (February 27, 1955)	8	1.7
28th (May 22, 1958)	11	2.4
29th (November 20, 1960)	7	1.5
30th (November 21, 1963)	7	1.5
31st (November 29, 1967)	7	1.4
32nd (December 27, 1969)	8	1.6
33rd (December 10, 1972)	7	1.6
34th (December 5, 1976)	7	1.4

B. UPPER HOUSE ELECTIONS

Election	No. of Women Elected	Percentage of Total Membership
1st (April 20, 1947)	11	4.4
2nd (January 4, 1950)	12	4.8
3rd (April 24, 1953)	19	7.6
4th (July 8, 1956)	15	6.0
5th (January 2, 1959)	13	5.2
6th (July 1, 1962)	17	6.8
7th (June 4, 1965)	17	6.8
8th (July 7, 1968)	13	5.4
9th (June 12, 1971)	13	5.4
10th (July 7, 1974)	18	7.1

SOURCE: Ministry of Labor, Women's and Minors' Bureau, *The Status of Women in Japan,* 1977.

NOTE: In the lower house there were 466 seats until the 26th election; from the 26th to the 30th elections, 467; in the 31st and 32nd, 486; in the 33rd, 491; and in the 34th, 511. In the upper house there were 250 seats until the 10th election, when the number of seats rose to 252.

TABLE 5   *Percentage of Women in National Legislative Bodies and
Total Labor Force in Advanced Industrial Societies*

Country	National Legislatures (% Women)	Total Labor Force (% Women)
Canada	1.6 (1968)	33.9 (1973)
France	1.6 (1969)	34.5 (1968)
United States	2.3 (1974)	39.4 (1974)
Japan	3.4 (1974)	37.8 (1974)
United Kingdom	4.1 (1970)	35.7 (1966)
Austria	8.2 (1970)	38.9 (1972)
West Germany	8.8 (1963)	36.0 (1971)
Norway	9.3 (1968)	37.1 (1972)
Sweden	10.4 (1968)	37.1 (1972)
Denmark	11.2 (1970)	40.1 (1972)
Poland	12.4 (1968)	46.0 (1970)
Czechoslovakia	17.6 (1967)	44.7 (1970)
Finland	21.5 (1970)	42.1 (1970)
USSR	28.0 (1968)	50.4 (1970)

SOURCE: Data for countries other than U.S. and Japan from Janet Z. Giele
and Audrey C. Smock (eds.), *Women: Roles and Status in Eight Countries,* New
York: Wiley, 1977, table 2, p. 17. Labor force data for U.S. and Japan from
U.S. Dept. of Labor and Japanese Ministry of Labor, *The Role and Status of
Women Workers in the United States and Japan,* U.S. Government Printing
Office, 1976, pp. 74 and 205. Political data on Japan for 1974 derived from
table 4 above.

postwar period. In the upper house, the House of Council-
lors, the pattern is less consistent, but the percentage of seats
has remained in the range of 4 to 7 percent over the last three
decades. Overall, the proportion of women's representation
in the national legislature puts Japan slightly ahead of the
United States, Canada, and France, slightly behind other advanced industrial societies, and well behind those with
socialist and communist systems (see table 5). When patterns
of office-holding for Japan and other countries are compared,
perhaps the most striking difference is in the area of women's
representation at the local level (see table 6). In most other
advanced industrial societies, including all those in table 7,
representation at the local level exceeds that at the national
level. In Japan the opposite is true. The low level of women's
representation at the local level is initially hard to understand

BACKGROUND TO CONTEMPORARY STRUGGLE 37

TABLE 6   *Number of Men and Women and Percentage of Women Elected to Office at the Local Level in Japan for Selected Years, 1955–1975*

Year	Prefectural Assemblies M	F	F(%)	Municipal Assemblies M	F	F(%)	Town or Village Assemblies M	F	F(%)
1955	2,430	32	1.3	21,240	158	1.0	114,015	445	0.4
1960	2,607	36	1.4	17,724	190	1.1	63,699	275	0.4
1965	2,565	41	1.6	17,732	198	1.1	56,712	311	0.5
1966	2,536	40	1.6	17,867	201	1.1	55,634	326	0.6
1967	2,688	38	1.4	18,259	221	1.2	53,850	303	0.6
1968	2,659	37	1.4	17,786	225	1.2	52,894	272	0.5
1971	2,705	26	1.0	20,133	350	1.7	49,453	198	0.4
1975	2,796	32	1.1	19,807	360	1.8	48,008	217	0.4

SOURCE: Ministry of Labor, Women's and Minors' Bureau, *The Status of Women in Japan*, 1977, p. 5.

TABLE 7   *Percentage of Women in Elective Assemblies Below National Level in Selected Countries*

Country	Percentage of Women	Year
Japan	0.9	1975
France	2.4	1971
United States	6.0	1971
Norway	9.5	1972
United Kingdom	12.0	1971
Czechoslovakia	19.9	1967
USSR	42.8	1968

SOURCE: Giele and Smock (see table 5). Figure for Japan is derived from table 6 above.

given Japanese women's greater interest in local over national affairs, as is documented by many studies, and their high turnout in local elections, frequently ahead of that for men.[46] These characteristics in other countries are almost always ac-

46. See Bradley M. Richardson, *The Political Culture of Japan* (Berkeley and Los Angeles, 1974).

companied by greater representation of women in local elective assemblies. Two explanations for the inconsistency in Japan may be offered. First, in line with what was stated earlier, the widespread acceptance today accorded voting as appropriate female activity has not carried over fully to other forms of political behavior, with the greatest lag found in the rural and more traditional areas. Second, special external constraints operate in local politics in Japan, particularly at the town and village level, that greatly limit women's chances for representation there. Local politics typically involves traditional patterns of relations between leader and follower and other characteristics that represent "old boyism" in an extreme form.[47] The difficulties faced by women seeking support and endorsement from the political "ins" in a system based on cronyism are well known.[48] Today, however, Japanese politics below the national level is undergoing profound change, particularly in cities. Increasingly, conservative politicians identified with machine politics have been voted out in favor of reform-minded progressive politicians. This trend is likely to reduce some of the external barriers that have made women's entry into local politics so difficult until now.

In examining women's degree of success in gaining entry to the elite, it is important to look at one final area, their success rate in gaining nonelective elite positions. Gains in this area are especially significant in Japan, for they tell us how much support women have received from Japan's leadership in the search for full equality of participation in politics. Has the Japanese government been willing to carry forward the occupation's "revolution from above" by appointing women to public office and by promoting them to positions of power within the bureaucracy? This answer is clearly no. Only two women have been appointed to cabinet positions in the postwar period, both for short-term, token appointments.[49]

47. See Scott C. Flanagan, "The Japanese Party System in Transition," Comparative Politics 3 (January 1971): 231–254.

48. Mary Cornelia Porter and Ann B. Matasar, "The Role and Status of Women in the Daley Organization," in Women in Politics, ed. Jane S. Jaquette (New York, 1974), pp. 85–108.

49. One served as Health and Welfare Minister from July to December 1960, the other, as Director General of the Science and Technology Agency from July 1962 to July 1963. Fujita, "Women and Politics in Japan," p. 95.

TABLE 8   *Percentage of Women in National Administrations for Selected Countries from a 53-Nation Study, 1971*

Rank	Country	Percentage of Women
1	France	22.5
2	Hungary	16.0
3	United States	15.2
11	Sweden	9.4
22	United Kingdom	7.5
35	Thailand	5.5
52	Japan	1.2
53	Pakistan	0.7

SOURCE: Alexander Szalai, *The Situation of Women in the United Nations,* United Nations Institute for Training and Research (UNITAR), Report No. 18, 1973, p. 4. The ILO study included only those countries where a breakdown figure by sex was available for women working at the professional (as opposed to clerical) level in their respective national administrations. For this reason a number of countries were not included, such as India, the USSR and the People's Republic of China.

A recent United Nations study revealed that Japan had fewer women in positions of responsibility within the bureaucracy than all but one of the fifty-three countries for which data were included (see table 8). In 1973 there was only one woman in the Japanese government serving at the level of bureau chief (*buchō*).[50] Few would argue that lack of availability explains the extremely low percentage of women in key administrative positions. Attitudes held by male leaders appear responsible. As one of Japan's most successful women bureaucrats has stated, "In spite of the fact that more and more young women pass the public service examinations, and with brilliant records, the posts open to woman are as yet very limited and their promotion is much slower compared to that of men."[51] All evidence suggests that Japan's conservative postwar leadership has played a weak rather

50. Ministry of Labor, Women's and Minors' Bureau, *Seminar in (sic) Public Administration Officers on Women's Problems 1973 Fiscal Year* (Tokyo, 1973).
51. Fujita, "Women and Politics in Japan," p. 95.

than a strong role, then, in carrying forward the occupation's program of support for women's political participation, and that women today who wish to follow conventional routes to political power are likely to confront many external barriers along the way.

As was noted at the outset, women gained full political rights in Japan as an accident of war and military defeat, with little in the way of a historical or cultural legacy to support the radical change that came after 1945. The nearest thing Japan had to such a legacy was the prewar suffrage movement. Although the impact of the movement was limited in its own day, it is important to note, in looking to the chapters ahead, that the suffrage movement did give young women today a pantheon of women leaders to study and admire in a society whose history otherwise has provided relatively few role models for women who are challenging conventional role definitions. It is significant that political women today often refer to Japan's suffrage leaders when they are discussing their own struggles, disappointments, and aspirations.

With so few preconditions laid down for the changes that occurred after 1945, women's full acceptance and implementation of new political rights granted by an alien, occupying military force was hardly a foregone conclusion. And, indeed, the pattern of women's political participation in postwar Japan has been uneven. Despite the acceptance women have accorded voting, their degree of participation in other modes of citizen political expression and behavior lags far behind that for men. Central to the concern of the chapters ahead, this finding indicates that many constraints, internal and external, continue to limit women's more active participation in political life.

These developments in Japan form a backdrop against which the experiences of politically active women today may be viewed. Young women entering voluntary political groups and other political activities in the "more active" category are participating in a larger process by which all Japanese women have undergone fundamental adjustments in their notion of self and role in accepting certain forms of political behavior as appropriate for women. In their experimentation with more active political roles, the young women who are the focus of this study are unusual only in that they are taking the process many steps forward into a gray area of behavior where role redefinition is far from complete. Their experiment places them squarely in the front ranks in Japanese women's struggle for full political participation.

3

The Outcome of Gender-Role Socialization: Women's Evolving Views of Life and Role

If the potential conflict between the demands of woman's role and the demands of political roles discourages or limits the political participation of the great majority of women, then the key question is why and how certain women overcome similar constraints to become politically active. The answer to this question is the concern of this chapter and the two that follow it. This chapter lays the groundwork by exploring the outcome of the gender-role socialization process for women activists as it is reflected in several distinct views of woman's role found among the respondents, and by

Portions of this chapter appeared in Susan J. Pharr, "The Japanese Woman: Evolving Views of Life and Role," in *Japan: The Paradox of Progress,* ed. Lewis Austin (New Haven, 1976), pp. 301–327.

exploring how a political role for women is seen under the terms of each view. Chapter four focuses on the political socialization process as it was experienced by political women, and asks how their experiences were different from those of most women. Chapter five draws on chapters three and four to offer some first steps toward a theory of individual change to explain why certain women become involved in politics.

The woman activist, whatever her political ideology, has often been regarded as a spokesperson for women's full economic and social equality, who supports a political cause while simultaneously proclaiming liberation from the restrictive homemaker role. This view was set out with particular clarity by Duverger a number of years ago in his important work on patterns of women's political participation in Europe. Women's entry into political life, he wrote, was "a clear challenge" to the "antifeminist tradition" and a deliberate attempt to substitute "a new system which concedes the complete equality of the sexes in every field."[1] The public and even highly trained observers of human behavior such as political psychologists have often appeared to share the view. It was fully in keeping with popular stereotypes that Lasswell described a female activist he studied as a woman with "an enormous masculine complex" who had chosen "masculine goals" and who had "ruled out the female role as far as she could."[2]

If the public and the political scientist have assumed that political activism and feminism went hand in hand, what they have meant by "feminism" has frequently been unclear.[3] Almost by definition, politically active women could

1. Maurice Duverger, *The Political Role of Women* (Paris, 1955), p. 151.

2. Harold D. Lasswell, *Psychopathology and Politics* (New York, 1960), pp. 121–124.

3. Until recently, writers have drawn dichotomous distinctions in talking about ideologies of woman's role. There was a "traditional" or "feminine" ideology, on the one hand, and on the other, a "modern" or "egalitarian" role view. See, for example, Mirra Komarovsky, "Functional Analysis of Sex Roles," *American Sociological Review* 15 (August 1950): 508–516, in which gender roles are designated as either "feminine" or "modern." Kammeyer used the same dichotomy, substituting "traditional" for "feminine" to describe older views of woman's role. See Kenneth Kammeyer, "Birth Order and the

not subscribe to any view of woman's role that wholly precluded activities outside the home. But this hardly means that all political activists are militant feminists. Indeed, as a number of recent studies have shown, such a conclusion masks a complex reality. In all modern societies today, there are major differences of opinion on how women should conduct their lives. The role ideologies of activists, like those of nonactivists, reflect these differences, but the question is how and to what degree.[4]

Before proceeding, it is important to clarify what is meant by "ideologies" of woman's role. There are at least three dimensions that must be considered when roles are discussed.[5] First, there are "role demands" placed upon the individual by society. Second, there are "ideologies" of a given role, which constitute the individual's response, at the ideational level, to the demands society is trying to impose on her. Finally, there is the individual's actual behavior in the role ("role performance"). Most writers discussing role deal with role demands.[6] This study does, too, in identifying a definition of woman's role, to be discussed shortly, that is the dominant definition today. But since the study focuses on individual women, it is important to look at their response to society's perceived demands, as expressed in role ideologies, as well as examine the role demands themselves.

One further point must be clarified: the meaning of "woman's role" itself as a category of analysis. In the sociological

Feminine Sex Role Among College Women," *American Sociological Review* 31 (August, 1966): 508–515.

4. The writer who perhaps has best captured the complexity of differences of opinion on the subject of women's proper roles and place is Dahlstrom, who identifies the six distinct role ideologies, each of which has advocates, in the debate over gender roles in Sweden. Edmund Dahlstrom, *The Changing Roles of Men and Women* (Boston, 1962), pp. 170–182.

5. The distinctions made here follow those presented by Daniel J. Levinson: "Role, Personality and Social Structure in the Organizational Setting," in *A Source Book for the Study of Personality and Politics*, ed. Fred I. Greenstein and Michael Lerner (Chicago, 1971), pp. 63–64.

6. For a statement of this position, see Ralf Dahrendorf, "Homo Sociologicus" in *Essays in the Theory of Society* (Stanford, 1968), pp. 35–38. Dahrendorf argues that in discussing social role, we should "invariably" confine ourselves to expected behavior: "Our concern is invariably with the individual as confronted with demands generated outside himself, or with society as it confronts the individual with such demands" (p. 37).

literature on women, "woman's role" refers to woman's combined role as wife and mother, or, as some designate it, "homemaker."[7] Here and throughout, the term is used in that sense. However, when the discussion turns to "competing ideologies of woman's role," what is meant is something broader. If woman's role in most societies centers in the home, the ideological issue is whether things should remain that way. What is at issue is whether—and if so, how—woman's role as wife and mother should be combined with various other social roles, such as those of worker, student, or, as in this study, political activist.

The political women introduced in the first chapter were from a wide variety of socioeconomic, geographic, and educational backgrounds. Although they were far better educated and far more likely to be from middle-class and upper-middle-class backgrounds than the average Japanese woman, 30 percent had not had an education beyond the high school level, and 20 percent were of working-class background. Furthermore, there were sharp differences in their life experiences. One third were married, the rest single. More than half were working; the other half were students or full-time housewives, in many cases with limited or no work experience. As was indicated earlier, their political affiliations spanned the political spectrum, from the conservative political party in power to radical student sects or feminist groups. Naturally, among such a diverse group there were broad differences of opinion on such a controversial subject as what woman's proper role and place should be. First there was a Neotraditional perspective. Proponents of this view held that the wife-mother role is primary in a woman's life and that, in general, all other life activities should be subordinated to it. Aspects of this view, as expressed by political women today, distinguish it from a still more traditional ideology of woman's role current before the war, but its links to the past are strong. Those who are called New Women had a second point of view, which represents a subtle change from the

7. Most major writers use the term in this way, although it is recognized that they are speaking about several roles, or more technically, a role set. For the difficulties of analyzing woman's role or roles with the fine distinctions employed by Parsonian sociologists in discussing role, role set, position, and so on, see Elizabeth Janeway, *Man's World, Woman's Place* (New York, 1971), pp. 84–85.

Neotraditional perspective. New Women accepted the traditional assumption that the domestic role should be central to their lives as women, but in what is a major change in attitude, they held at the same time that women should be able to engage in numerous other activities not relating to the homemaker role. Finally, there was the *Radical Egalitarian* view. Radical Egalitarians not only believed that adult women should feel free to play many roles simultaneously, but they also challenged the very basis of contemporary social arrangements by rejecting traditional patterns of gender-role allocation that have made it woman's duty to maintain the home.

The above ideologies came to light in interviews with political women. Among the sample, the New Women's view predominated. Sixty percent of the sample were New Women, with the remaining 40 percent divided almost equally between Neotraditionalists and Radical Egalitarians. It is apparent, however, that the same three views are in competition in a number of countries today.[8] In a society at any moment in history, one view generally prevails over the others in the degree of acceptance accorded it.[9] Drawing upon survey results, on background interviews with many nonactivists, and on the findings of many studies conducted in Japan, we find that Neotraditionalists hold the view that is the dominant ideology of woman's role in today's Japan.[10]

8. For a discussion of gender-role ideologies operating in other societies today, see Dahlstrom, *Changing Roles of Men and Women,* and Jessie Bernard, *Women and the Public Interest* (Chicago, 1971).

9. See Florence Kluckhohn's discussion of cultural ranking among value orientations, in Florence R. Kluckhohn, "Some Reflections on the Nature of Cultural Integration and Change," in *Sociological Theory, Values, and Sociocultural Change,* ed. Edward A. Tiryakian (New York, 1963).

10. Most major studies of the Japanese family portray woman's roles and attitudes in a way that is consistent with the Neotraditional ideology, supporting the conclusion that it is the dominant view. See, for example, Ezra Vogel, *Japan's New Middle Class* (Berkeley and Los Angeles, 1963); Robert O. Blood, *Love Match and Arranged Marriage* (New York, 1967); George DeVos and Hiroshi Wagatsuma, "Status and Role Behavior in Changing Japan," in *Sex Roles in Changing Society,* ed. Georgene H. Seward and Robert C. Williamson (New York, 1970), pp. 334–370; and Linda Perry, "Mothers, Wives, and Daughters in Osaka" (Ph.D. dissertation, University of Pittsburgh, 1976). Works by Japanese scholars also support this conclusion. See Koyama Takashi, *Gendai kazoku no oyako kankei* (The parent-child relation in the contemporary family) (Tokyo, 1973); Isomura Ei-ichi, Kawashima Takeyoshi, and Koyama Takashi, eds., *Gendai kazoku kōza* (Lectures on the

The New Women's view is a variant pattern among women at large, tolerated, but denied full social approbation by a great many people, including many older-generation Japanese.[11] Finally, the Radical Egalitarian view is highly marginal, going far beyond what most Japanese men and women can understand, much less accept. It might be pointed out that even the Neotraditional view reflects the high degree of social change characteristic of the postwar period. Certain beliefs held by Neotraditionalists were seen as either variant or deviant for much of Japanese history prior to 1945.

The three role ideologies that come to light in interviews with political women reflect major currents of thought and feeling among the Japanese population at large and, in fact, among people in many societies today. But to understand how political women feel about woman's role, it is important to explore at more depth what each of these views means in the context of Japanese society, and to study the implications of each for a political role for women.

The Traditional View of Woman's Role

All three of the views discovered in interviews with the informants respond to definitions of woman's role in force in earlier periods of Japanese history. As background, then, the traditional view of woman's role deserves a brief

---

contemporary family), 6 vols. (Tokyo, 1955–1956). Some recent survey results confirm the preference of women in the age range twenty to thirty-four for an ideal family arrangement in which "the husband works and the wife looks after the home," and in which housekeeping and childcare are the adult woman's primary life activities. See Sumiko Iwao, "A Full Life for Modern Japanese Women," in *Text of Seminar on Changing Values in Modern Japan*, ed., Nihonjin Kenkyūkai (Tokyo, 1977), pp. 98–99.

11. The degree of support for the New Woman's view is suggested by the results of a major 1973 survey in which slightly less than 30 percent of women in the age range twenty to thirty-four said that if at all possible, they would prefer to continue working after having children. In contrast, more than 70 percent of women in the same range preferred to stop working either when they married or when they had children, and thereafter to devote themselves to the home. Sumiko Iwao, "Modern Japanese Women," pp. 100–101. These findings further substantiate the thesis that although the Neotraditional view is supported by a comfortable majority of young women today, the New Women's view has a substantial following.

treatment. In prewar society and before, certainly for all of recorded history, the great majority of people in Japan believed that women were intended for one major role in life, that of wife and mother. Behind this view were certain interrelated assumptions. Men and women were seen as essentially different beings. Though each was acknowledged to have special talents and abilities, it was men who were superior in most areas of endeavor. They were therefore entitled to many rights not shared by women, and by the same token, they had certain duties and responsibilities women were thought incapable of assuming.

Men led, made decisions, and provided for the basic unit of society, the family. Women often contributed their labors on behalf of the family, but it was widely understood that a married woman's work plans were subject to her husband's approval and were secondary to his own plans as the main provider. Man answered to society for a household that bore his name. It was an orderly chain of authority. Woman answered to man, and man, to society.

These assumptions, taken together, constituted the traditional view of woman's role. They defined woman's goals and rewards and set her priorities. Largely cutting across the lines set by class and regional differences, they provided a comprehensive framework within which most women ordered their lives. In a woman's youth, ideally she prepared for the day when she would become a wife and mother. In adult life, the homemaker role came first, and activities not relating to home and children were by definition secondary.

Society did offer a range of alternative role options to women. To become part of the demimonde (*mizu shōbai*) of geisha, entertainers, and prostitutes who provided leisure activities for virtually an all-male clientele, to eschew normal family arrangements for a solitary life as a nun, a scholar, a writer, or the like—these were also possibilities, open throughout history to certain of the very beautiful, the very talented, and the unconventional among women, or, for many who made their way into the demimonde, to the poor and the fallen. But to elect or even consider these routes was hardly the normal course for the great majority of Japanese women, who sought the security of a permanent marriage arrangement.

The traditional view was in virtually no respect unique to Japan. The assumptions just described have operated in most societies evolving from patriarchal traditions. What was unusual to Japan, in comparison with most major nations, was the persistence of the view, with only minor challenges, almost halfway into the twentieth century. After Japan emerged in the 1860s from centuries of feudalism and national isolation, most of these assumptions passed intact into the modern period and were reaffirmed by legal code and custom until the end of World War II.

Three features of the traditional view as it operated in Japan had particular impact on the lives of women before the war and influence attitudes today. The first was the degree to which differences in the status of men and women were thought natural and legitimate. Whereas in Europe, romantic and chivalrous traditions had developed in the feudal era to soften the very real lines of status difference between men and women, in Japan, with different feudal traditions, the lines were very stark. In the prewar period women showed deference to men of their own as well as of higher classes through the use of polite language and honorific forms of address, through bowing more deeply than they, walking behind their husbands in public, and in numerous other ways deferring to men. Ideally, in the extended family arrangement common before the war, a new bride coming into the house was expected to acknowledge her inferior status in a number of ritualized ways: getting up first in the morning, going to bed last at night, taking her bath only after all other family members had bathed, eating after other family members, and taking the least choice servings of food.[12]

Another feature of the traditional view, supported not only in custom but in legal codes until the end of World War II, was the husband's authority over the wife. In the prewar family system, the head of the household assumed full legal responsibility for all family members. When she married, a woman could act in legal matters only with the approval of

12. See Susan J. Pharr, "Japan: Historical and Contemporary Perspectives," in *Women: Role and Status in Eight Countries,* ed. Janet Z. Giele and Audrey C. Smock (New York, 1977), pp. 227–231, for further discussion and citations relating to prewar conceptions of woman's proper roles in society and the family.

her husband's family. The Civil Code consistently favored the husband in provisions relating to divorce, marriage, property rights, and other questions coming under family law. Adultery constituted legal grounds for divorce only if committed by the wife. When there was a dispute over the custody of a child, the wishes of the husband prevailed. It was regarded as proper, if painful for the wife, for a husband to divorce her and to keep the children in his own family to bear his family name. Similarly, if a man fathered children by women other than his wife, he was legally entitled to adopt them into the family. If her husband died, a wife came under the authority of her eldest son as soon as he came of age. Most women in prewar Japan spent their entire lifetime before and after marriage as legal dependents of male family heads.[13]

A final feature of the traditional view that affects beliefs today is the notion that husband and wife belong in separate spheres of activity. As many writers note, industrialization supported gender-role specialization by taking husbands out of the family productive unit (the farm or shop) and into the office or factory.[14] But the prevalence of attitudes supporting gender-role segregation today is also traced to the strength of this aspect of the traditional view in prewar society, especially among the upper classes. Upper-class married women in prewar Japan played few roles in affairs outside the home circle and neighborhood. In contrast to Europe and the United States, where upper-class leisure patterns brought husbands and wives together in many social contexts, Japan provided few such opportunities. Wives hardly ever ventured into the demimonde, where many well-to-do men spent their leisure hours. Gender-role divisions were less rigid among the working classes, where work roles were often shared and where families had limited means for leisure

13. For a useful summary of the major provisions of family law under the old system, see B. James George, "Law in Modern Japan," in *Twelve Doors to Japan*, by John W. Hall and Richard K. Beardsley (New York, 1965), pp. 509–514.

14. See Ester Boserup, *Woman's Role in Economic Development* (New York, 1970); William J. Goode, *World Revolution and Family Patterns* (New York, 1970); and Gail Lapidus, "Modernization Theory and Sex Roles in Critical Perspective," in *Women in Politics*, ed. Jane S. Jaquette, pp. 243–246. For the effect of industrialization on women in Japan, see Ronald P. Dore, *City Life in Japan* (Berkeley and Los Angeles, 1958), p. 116.

activities. But the more restrictive view of woman's role that was the norm among upper-class people found support among the other classes during the period prior to World War II. As prosperity spread in prewar Japan, it was natural for those ascending the social ladder to aspire to the style of life of those above them.[15] Gender-role divisions stressed in the upper-class version of the traditional view of woman's role thus survived the twentieth century and spread to other levels of society, accelerated by industrialization.

All three aspects of the traditional view had implications for the way that woman's place in politics was seen under its terms. The denial of political rights to women was the logical outgrowth of the position of male family heads vis-a-vis female family members. In the status hierarchy of the family, it was thought natural that the male head, in keeping with his superior status, should represent his status inferiors in any contact the family had with higher authorities. Furthermore, given the clear division between the roles allocated to husbands and wives respectively, it was seen as reasonable for one family member, the male head, to have complete monopoly over a given role, in this case the political role. The denial of women's legal right to participate in politics was but a reflection of widely shared attitudes about the proper roles of men and women in the family and society.

The traditional view of woman's role has been challenged from many sides in the postwar period. Japan's surrender in 1945 set off a series of changes that have affected women at almost every level of Japanese life. In addition to the political guarantees discussed in chapter two, numerous legal measures were introduced to benefit women. The Constitution of 1947 explicitly forbade discrimination on the basis of sex. Through reform of the Civil Code, the American occupying forces attacked the basis of women's inferior status in the family by guaranteeing women free choice of a spouse, equal recourse to divorce, equal property rights, and so on. Meanwhile, democratization and legal reform have been supported by other postwar forces. Urbanization has sped the demise of the extended family system. Even where status differences are acknowledged within the urban nuclear family, they are

15. See Takashi Koyama, *The Changing Social Position of Women in Japan* (Paris, 1961), pp. 33–38.

far less ritualized than before. Prosperity, another force for change in postwar Japan, has made higher education and other opportunities available to daughters as well as sons. Improvements in home facilities resulting from a higher standard of living have lightened the burden of housework, freeing women for other pursuits. These recent forces for change impinge on the traditional view of woman's role described earlier, leading to the three role ideologies that emerged in interviews with young political women.

Neotraditionalists

Honda Akiko was typical of political women in the sample who held a Neotraditionalist's view of woman's role. At nineteen she was an office worker with but one main thought for the future: marriage. In her off hours she was engaged in volunteer work for the Clean Government Party (Kōmeitō), a middle-of-the-road political party with links to one of Japan's "new religions." At the time of the interview she was eagerly awaiting the day when she would become twenty and could be an official member of the party. Meanwhile, she participated in party activities by helping an older sister, already a party member, count out campaign pamphlets at home.

Akiko was the youngest of four girls, the daughter of an iron-parts maker who had worked hard all his life and a mother who had spent most of her married life doing double duty as a housewife and part-time factory worker. Together they had struggled to make a living for the six of them, and if they had a single ambition for a family of four daughters, it was to see them marry into a life of greater ease than they had known.

After high school graduation Akiko immediately had taken a job in a large company. There she performed the duties that thousands of young Japanese women today undertake for a few years before marriage. She was what is called an "O.L." in Japan, an "office lady" hired to do routine office work, to pour tea for company members several times a day, and to create a pleasant working environment for the men who did the serious work of the office. To have suggested to Akiko that she apply for the kind of job done by the men would have been like suggesting that she try for the position of prime minister. In the Japanese business world, men and women are almost always hired for different kinds of work, and there is little way in present-day society that she could have crossed those lines.[16] More important, in her own mind she really did not see herself as able to do the work that men do. As she explained in words reflecting the strong status distinctions referred to a moment ago, "Men are superior to women in every field. Women have a narrower mind, a more limited view." Not only would that kind of work have been beyond her abilities, as she saw it, but it would have interfered with her main life plan of becoming a full-time housewife and mother to the exclusion of most other pursuits. At nineteen, Akiko's role ideology was well formulated, and the steps necessary for translating it into reality were spelled out clearly in her mind:

> As for me, I have no special person in mind, but I have a dream of marriage. It is stronger now than when I was graduating from high school. My dream is to create a warm atmosphere in a home even if it turns out to be a humble home. To find someone, first I must polish myself. That is what I am doing now. I am improving myself so that I can find an ideal husband.

For Akiko's plans, her job was perfectly suited to her needs. Her salary was low, necessitating that she live with her family, but she had funds to pay them for her upkeep so that she did not feel herself a burden on them. Beyond that, she had pocket money for clothes, makeup, magazines, and an occasional trip to a coffee house with former high school friends and girlfriends from the office. At work, she had a chance to gain the kind of practical experience with life that most young women today feel is an important credential for marriage. She was "polishing herself," and in the back of her mind was

16. A national survey of business executives and labor union officials conducted in 1974 found that women were completely absent from even the lowest management ranks in 50 percent of Japanese firms. Japan External Trade Organization, "Female Employment in Japan," *Now in Japan* 19 (December, 1975): 3–4.

the hope that through her job she might be able to meet and marry one of the middle-class salaried workers who are symbols of postwar prosperity in Japan.

Once she found someone suitable, Akiko planned to quit her job. It was her earnest hope, shared by a great many young women today whose mothers in their early married years struggled to combine housework and child rearing with a tiring industrial job or hard work in a home productive unit in prewar Japan, that she would be able to give full time to what she saw as the central life task of making a home.[17] But Akiko was realistic. If she did not meet a white-collar worker, and ended up marrying someone of her own class, she was prepared to work, for it is not yet possible for most young working-class couples in Japan to live on the husband's salary alone. When asked if she would work after marriage, her answer showed that the question touched on a subject that occupied many of her thoughts.

> If there is no way around it, of course I will. I'm hoping, though, that I won't have to. I would rather stay at home and keep a perfect house. I'd prefer that life—waiting for my husband to come home.

17. Among the 20 percent of the sample who were from blue-collar backgrounds, their mothers (and grandmothers) typically felt that the ideal for a woman was to be a full-time housewife. By their daughters' accounts, a number of these mothers hoped that their daughters would be spared the experience of having to start out their married life while holding an industrial job. In a number of cases, the mothers' own experiences as young women workers in prewar Japan appeared to have influenced this view. Although working conditions improved gradually over the prewar years, women workers for most of the period were grossly underpaid relative to men and frequently were exploited. Many young women in the period of Japan's rapid industrialization were contracted out by their fathers (generally, impoverished farmers) who could borrow in advance against their salaries. Since women could be hired at salaries much lower than those for male workers, factories competed for their services and sometimes practically kidnapped them for jobs in the spinning mills. Dormitories housing young women workers were in some cases walled in to keep them from running away. Hosoi Wakizō, *Jokō aishi* (A tragic history of girl operatives) (Tokyo, 1954, originally published in 1925); Uno Riemon, ed., *Shokkō mondai shiryō* (Data on the problems of factory operatives) (Osaka, 1912); and Murakami Nobuhiko, *Meiji josei shi: onna no shokugyō* (The history of Meiji women: women's employment), volume 2 of series (Tokyo, 1971), pp. 127–184. Valuable sources in English are Keizo Shibusawa, *Japanese Life and Culture in the*

So far, Akiko's views, as described here, appear to put her in the category with prewar traditional women. It is important to indicate several of the key ways in which her view is neotraditional rather than traditional. A major area of change was in her attitude toward education. In the prewar period, girls were educated in a separate girls' track with a program explicitly designed to prepare them to become "good wives and wise mothers."[18] Today most people regard the serious study of basic subjects as necessary for youth of both sexes. Ministry of Education figures show that when choosing among several curriculum options in senior high school, only 11 percent of the girl students elected the home economics concentration that almost surely would have been the natural preference of a great many prewar girls, had they been confronted with study options.[19] The level of women's educational aspirations has also been rising. Whereas relatively few girls went on beyond their six years of compulsory schooling in prewar Japan, it is now within the ordinary hopes and expectations of most young Japanese women like Akiko to go to senior high school. Just as in the United States, the rate of advancement to senior high school is higher now for girls than for boys and stands at 93 percent.[20]

Attitudes toward higher education are also changing. Akiko herself had not sought education beyond the high school level. But her older sister, another Neotraditional woman, had managed to finish junior college by working part time. In the prewar years, the percentage of women advanc-

Meiji Era, trans. Charles Terry (Tokyo, 1958), and Koji Taira, *Economic Development and the Labor Market in Japan* (New York, 1970).

18. For an analysis of the goals and content of women's education in the prewar period, see Fukaya Masashi, *Ryōsai kenbo shugi no kyōiku* (Education to be a virtuous wife and wise mother) (Tokyo, 1966). English sources are somewhat limited, but Ronald S. Anderson, *Japan: Three Epochs of Modern Education* (Washington, D.C., 1959), p. 38, gives a description of the girls' track curriculum.

19. Results of a study cited in Yasumasa Tomoda, "Educational and Occupational Aspirations of Female Senior High School Students," *Bulletin of the Hiroshima Agricultural College* 4 (December 1972): 248.

20. The figure is for 1975; for males it is 91 percent. Ministry of Labor, Women's and Minors' Bureau, *Fujin rōdō no jitsujō* (The status quo of women workers), Report no. 133 (Tokyo, 1976), p. 84.

ing to higher education generally was around 1 percent.[21] By 1975, it stood at 35 percent.[22] Many of these women, like Akiko's sister, attend junior colleges, where they make up 86 percent of the enrollment, rather than four-year colleges and universities, where they represent only 21 percent of the total; but compared with the prewar situation, these developments are remarkable.[23] Following from their attitudes toward woman's role, many Neotraditionalists want a college degree as a new kind of marriage credential, which many people now see as necessary for a young woman of the middle or upper class who wants to attract a suitable husband. Because Neotraditional women want to marry a man who is somewhat superior to them intellectually, they are careful not to become more educated than the kind of men they hope to marry. Junior college is a particularly safe choice because it makes them eligible to marry almost any college-educated male. On the other hand, Neotraditionalists of upper-middle-class backgrounds, feeling fairly assured that they can marry a graduate of one of the top universities of Japan, may attend a middle-ranking university or a four-year women's college. Of the Neotraditional political women in the study, 75 percent of those with higher education had attended junior colleges or women's colleges.

Views of marriage itself have also changed, as evidenced by present-day attitudes toward mate selection. Japan still has an arranged-marriage system, which most Neotraditionalists see as an acceptable way to meet a mate.[24] Overall, however, the percentage of "love" marriages (renai kekkon) has outpaced that of arranged marriages (miai kekkon). A report issued several years ago by the Economic Planning

21. In 1920 the enrollment rate for women was 0.4 percent (for males, 3 percent); in 1930 it was 1.1 percent (for males, 6.4 percent); in 1940 it was 1.2 percent (for males, 8.1 percent). See Tomoda, "Educational and Occupational Aspirations," p. 247.

22. Ministry of Labor, Women's and Minors' Bureau, The Status of Women in Japan (Tokyo, 1977), p. 7. The figure for males is slightly less, at 34 percent. The figures include those attending night classes while employed.

23. Ibid., p. 8.

24. The arranged-marriage system itself has undergone profound change. Parents or go-betweens formally introduce young people whom they judge to be suitable to each other; the couple then date, but either side is free to break things off. Defenders of the system point out that it is not unlike "computer dating" in the United States, except that the persons matching up two young people know them better than any computer can.

Agency showed that in large- and medium-sized cities, about 60 percent of all marriages were "love" matches.[25] Akiko's preference for finding her own mate, then, is usual in postwar Japan. In a recent study, 83 percent of those under twenty years of age who were questioned said they would prefer to have a "love" marriage.[26] The actual figures as cited above lag behind these expressed desires, but nevertheless the change in attitudes is a major one.

Neotraditionalists' feelings toward work also reflect major signs of change. In the prewar period, many young girls took jobs for wages because of severe family hardship. Many, enamored with the traditional view described earlier, would have preferred to stay home to prepare for marriage by studying cooking, flower arranging, and other feminine arts. Today, however, Neotraditionalists like Akiko as a matter of course take a job for a few years before they marry. Of women in the age group twenty to twenty-four, 67 percent are in the labor force.[27] As was indicated by figures cited earlier, most of the others are in higher education. Obviously, few young women today stay home preparing for marriage, and for most—whether for pocket money, for personal enrichment, to find a husband, or, recently, to save money for a trip abroad—taking a job has come to be seen as a necessary stage of growing up.

A final area of change, central to this study, is in attitudes toward political participation. In contrast to traditionalists, who see women as having no place at all in political life, Neotraditional women, activist or nonactivist, have accepted certain political roles as fully appropriate for women. The process of role redefinition, as discussed in chapter two, has been completed where voting is concerned, and other forms of political participation in the "less active" category, such as discussing politics, expressing opinions on political issues, and professing to have an interest in politics, are gaining acceptance.

25. Economic Planning Agency, *Kokumin seikatsu hakusho* (Report on national life) (Tokyo, 1971), p. 30. Data are from a 1966 study.

26. Sankei Shimbun, *Iken to ishiki no hyakkajiten: Sankei Shimbun 1000-nin chōsa kara* (Encyclopedia of opinion and thought: from Sankei Shimbun's survey of 1000 persons) (Tokyo, 1972), p. 85.

27. Ministry of Labor, Women's and Minors' Bureau, *Fujin rōdō*, 1976, p. 31.

At the same time, however, the Neotraditionalist view of the place of politics in a woman's life typically puts definite restrictions on the political roles permitted her. Under ordinary circumstances, active political participation of the kind represented by joining a political group is unacceptable under the terms of the Neotraditional ideology. It is unacceptable before marriage because political activism is considered unfeminine and therefore is potentially damaging to a woman's marriage chances. After marriage it is unacceptable because—unlike the short-term act called for in voting—it involves time and energy that, according to the Neotraditional view, should not be diverted from the performance of the wife-mother role. For a married woman to engage in political activities out of her own personal interest in a political group or issue is seen as selfish behavior and in violation of her primary responsibility to serve her family's needs and to subordinate her own interests to those of her husband. When the demands of the wife-mother role ease once the children are well on their way in school, more active political involvement becomes somewhat more acceptable, although it remains subject to a husband's approval. With her husband's permission, a Neotraditional woman above the age range for this study may attend political functions or join a political group as a delegate of the family, representing its interests. But if her husband shares the Neotraditional view of woman's role, it is unlikely that such permission would be granted, even if it were requested, unless her childcare duties were completed. For the women in the age range eighteen to thirty-three set for this study, active political participation was normally off limits under the terms of the Neotraditional role ideology.

This leaves open, of course, the question of how Akiko, along with the other nineteen Neotraditionalist political women in the sample, became politically active under the terms of the same definition. All of them fully supported the view just described of women's proper place in the political world. In each case, however, special circumstances obtained that made it possible for them to be involved in politics without violating the terms of the Neotraditional ideology. The nature of these "special circumstances" is central to the book, and will be analyzed in detail in chapter five.

New Women

Only 20 percent of the sample held the Neotraditional view of woman's role just described. The remaining 80 percent had role ideologies that challenged assumptions basic to the Neotraditionalist ideology. The large majority of them, 60 percent of the entire sample, were New Women.

A woman who typified many of the New Women was Takai Setsuko, a quietly dressed young woman of twenty-three who at the time of the interview was the Japanese equivalent of a Nader's Raider. As a specialist on the chemical composition of fabrics, she was a persuasive and committed advocate of consumer protection, working full time at the headquarters of the Housewives' Association (Shufuren) in Tokyo.[28]

In Setsuko's early experience one sees little that sets her apart from the Neotraditional woman. She grew up far from a major urban center in a village in southern Shikoku, the smallest of the four main islands that make up Japan, and she told me forthrightly that when she graduated from high school she had no particular thoughts except about someday getting married like her girlfriends. But over the summer after graduation, she talked to former high school classmates back from their freshman year in various colleges in Tokyo. She had said to herself, "I've been thinking in my own limited world. I ought to go to college." Her father, a local official, was not enthusiastic, expressing fears that in their rural locale a college education would hurt her marriage chances. But he agreed finally to pay for her schooling. Five years before the interview, Setsuko had come to Tokyo to attend a women's college, where she majored in home economics. So far she was on the Neotraditional course.

But at some point in her senior year in college, something appears to have changed in Setsuko. She was then doing her graduation essay, a requirement of all seniors, and she be-

28. Founded in 1948, the Housewives' Association is one of the largest women's organizations in Japan, with branches throughout the country. The organization works to improve and rationalize housework, a concern that has led it to focus much of its energy on protesting against inflation and promoting protection of consumers. Interviews with Housewives' Assocation officials, May 1972.

came increasingly interested in the topic, which dealt with the safety of commercial fabrics used for clothes. She began interviewing manufacturers and members of consumer groups, including persons working at the Housewives' Association, and she was shocked to find that many widely used fabrics are flammable and dangerous. Late in her senior year, she decided that she would have to do something with the knowledge she had acquired from her research, and she began to formulate plans. Her family back home, worried about a daughter alone in distant Tokyo, wanted her home after graduation. In letters, they were beginning to mention likely candidates for an arranged marriage. But Setsuko pressed to be allowed to follow her own course, and in the end her parents reconciled themselves. She accepted a job that she had been offered at the Housewives' Association and set out to find an apartment in Tokyo. Because she had heard that many Tokyo landlords might be reluctant to rent to a young single woman, she began looking for a place long before her job began. Most young women from other parts of Japan who work in Tokyo live with relatives or women-friends. Their reasons are partly financial, but many would also be afraid that if they lived alone they would endanger their reputation and thereby hurt their marriage chances. Setsuko, however, went ahead with her plan because, she said, she wanted a taste of the independent life. At the time of the interview she was living by herself in a tiny apartment, and spent most of her time in activities related to her job at the Housewives' Association.

When Setsuko was asked about the future, she immediately began talking about her plans to improve her competence at the job she was doing. When asked about her marriage plans, she obviously felt great discomfort. She wanted to marry, but only if she could continue her job afterward. She was wondering if she could find a husband in Japan who would understand how she felt.

Whereas Neotraditionalists, even when they became deeply absorbed in a job or other activity, were apt to see it as only a passing phase of youth before they took on their main life role, many New Women like Setsuko did not want to give up their outside interests. They wanted to marry, and they accepted the gender-role division in marriage that allocates to women the role of homemaker and child tender. But they wanted to play other roles as well.

What New Women wanted in terms of the actual content of the marriage relationship varied with the individual. Some, while handling their job or other activities, wanted to assume all the traditional obligations that go along with the homemaker role. They talked of taking on full childcare responsibility, paying for it themselves, and said that they would expect no help from their husbands with housework. Others (though they, too, did not question the assumption that housework was women's responsibility) expressed the view that the husband should lend an occasional helping hand.[29] In their criteria for a husband, some New Women still openly held certain traditional views and said forthrightly that they wanted someone more intelligent than they. Others said that they preferred someone closer to their own age (but generally, slightly older) and of similar educational attainment. All expressed the hope that in the marriage they ultimately entered there would be somewhat greater companionability and more opportunity for sharing thoughts and feelings than tend to go along with the Neotraditionalist's model of marriage. Most New Women, however, were engaged in an experiment with woman's role in which neither their ideology nor the behavioral requirements for implementing it were clearly formulated in their own minds. Those who were not married had no clear model of what they actually wanted in the marriage relationship, and those who were, knew mainly what they did not like. If Freud were to talk to the New Women of Japan today, he might well be led to repeat his famous query, "What do women want?" New Women do not yet know in precise terms. They are searching for answers themselves.

29. For Japanese husbands to help with housework is still uncommon. A 1973 national survey found that the average housewife spent six hours and forty-three minutes a day on housework; the average husband spent six minutes. Ministry of Labor, Women's and Minors' Bureau, *Status of Women in Japan*, 1977, p. 29. In contrast, one study shows that American husbands typically spend from one to two hours per day, even if their wives are full-time housewives. U.S. Department of Labor and Japanese Ministry of Labor, *The Role and Status of Women Workers in the United States and Japan* (Washington, D.C., 1976), p. 141.

Many New Women who were not yet married had difficulty finding men who shared their view of woman's role
and place. The problem of finding a husband was compli-
cated by the fact that the arranged-marriage system, which
even the most independent-minded Neotraditionalists considered a reasonably acceptable fallback, was largely unsuited
to their needs. Even with all the recent changes in the system,
it still functions to bring two people together in a traditional
marriage relationship in which the wife is expected to follow a
course set by the husband. As one New Woman, a freshman
economics major at Tokyo University, commented, in words
that echo the views of a great many New Women:

> There are two kinds of arranged marriages in Japan. One is the
> old feudalistic kind in which parents and relatives put a lot of
> pressure on the parties concerned. The other is the modern
> kind, which is basically an introduction method. I don't like
> either kind. I don't want to have to agree with a man's opin-
> ions about everything.

Even when New Women found a marriage prospect on their
own, they often ran into problems. Many men who want to
assert their independence by having a "love" match still have
traditional expectations concerning woman's role. Although
they may feel strongly attracted to New Women at school or
in the office, when it comes to marriage they often feel a
strong pull toward Neotraditional women, and uncertainty
about whether a marriage to a New Woman would work.[30]

For married women who had come to the New Woman's
view within a traditional marriage relationship, there were
other kinds of problems. The experience of Tanaka Keiko
provides an example. At thirty-two, she was a member of a
Tokyo women's group made up of upper-middle-class Tokyo
suburban housewives, all of whom wanted part-time or full-
time jobs. At age twenty-five, Keiko, a graduate of a women's
college, had had an arranged marriage to a young engineer
whom she had dated only eight times before the wedding
ceremony. Following the accepted pattern—which she herself thought quite natural at the time—she quit her job at an
electric company near her home in Kyoto when she married,

---

30. See the discussion in chapter six of the "marriage crisis" as it affects
young political women.

and moved to Tokyo to make a new life with her husband. At the time of the interview seven years and two children later, she wanted a part-time job as soon as the children were both in school. Her reasons were those heard with increasing frequency in Japanese upper-middle-class suburbia: housework was monotonous, she had too much free time, and she was lonely in a community where she still knew very few people after seven years.[31] Her husband was frankly astonished at her attitude. From his standpoint, he had gone above and beyond the traditional responsibilities to a wife by providing her with a more-than-adequate home, a car which she was able to use during the day, and ample spending money. Since he provided so well, it made no sense to him that his wife would want to work. He also had the view, held by most people who hold a Neotraditional view of woman's role, that children require a mother's full-time physical presence and fairly constant attention, not only in the early years, but well into the school years and even late adolescence as well, and that giving herself over to these tasks should be a woman's highest satisfaction and main life purpose. Thus he could only see his wife's plan, which called for placing the children in a day-care center or in the care of outside help for a few hours several afternoons a week, as serious neglect of her responsibilities and a failure of moral purpose as well. To heighten the tension, his own mother vehemently agreed with him and sided with him in disputes. This was a traditional marriage undergoing considerable strain as the discussion continued. Some New Women who came to their view after marriage had achieved more success in gaining their husband's cooperation, particularly where the activity they wanted to take on was a job that would supply needed extra income to the family. But where family income was adequate, husbands generally were much harder to convince. The work

31. These types of grievances had been the basis for the formation of this informant's women's group, which had been organized by the city government of Kunitachi, a Tokyo suburb. The group of twenty-five members published a book in 1973 of the proceedings of its meetings. The purpose of publication, and of the group itself, was to "reach . . . ordinary housewives and women who may be alone and suffering, causing themselves pain, and those who have become concerned [about their problems as women] without knowing it." Kunitachi-shi Kōminkan Shimin Daigaku Seminā, *Shufu to onna* (Housewives and women) (Tokyo, 1973), p. 8.

available even to highly educated women without special skills generally pays very little—in many cases barely enough to pay for day care or a housekeeper to mind the children.[32]

A wide variety of environmental influences have lent support to changes in women's views of their role. The experience of higher education is a major factor. It is true that more than half of all Japanese women in higher education attend junior colleges and women's colleges, many of them following the typical Neotraditionalist path. But the number attending four-year coeducational universities is increasing rapidly. In 1950, women made up only 2 percent of the university enrollment, but by 1975 the figure had risen to 21 percent, a spectacular rate of increase far outpacing that for male students.[33] Even at prestigious Tokyo University the percentage of women students almost tripled between 1960 and 1970, to 10 percent.[34] The importance of four-year educational institutions in supporting change in women's views of their role is well documented. In the sample for this study, 57 percent of the New Women, in contrast to only 35 percent of the Neotraditional political women, had attended four-year institutions.

The experience of working also supports role change. A number of New Women described work experiences that had clearly contributed to major changes in their attitudes about woman's role. Takai Setsuko, who had found an interesting job and wanted to continue it after marriage, was a case in point. Overall, however, this factor may be somewhat less significant in Japan than in the United States. Japan's dual

32. Both public and private day-care facilities are available in Japan, but demand for placement far exceeds available space. As of 1975 there were approximately 17,000 centers accommodating 1.6 million children. Government of Japan, *Seminar in (sic) Public Administration Officers on Women's Problems 1975 Fiscal Year*, 1975, p. 57. But for the working wife of all but low-income families, it is still difficult to make inexpensive day-care arrangements. Fees at public day-care centers are set on a scale based on ability to pay, with the fee determined by the income of the head of the household. Thus for married women whose husbands provide an adequate income, the fee is likely to take a major portion of any income they can earn.

33. Ministry of Labor, Women's and Minors' Bureau, *The Status of Women in Japan*, 1977, p. 8.

34. Figures based on data provided in Ministry of Education, *Zenkoku gakkō sōran* (National school report) (Tokyo, 1961), p. 2, and (Tokyo, 1971), p. 2.

economy provides relatively limited options for educated and well-qualified women. For example, women held only about 4 percent of the jobs in the category of managers and officials in 1970, compared with 16 percent for women in the United States in the same year.[35] Most New Women in the sample who were working were over-qualified for the jobs they held. As one New Woman, a Tokyo University graduate, remarked bitterly after she was turned down for low-paying editorial jobs at two big publishing houses, "Japan is an escalator society, and women just never get on the escalator."[36]

When it comes to political participation, the New Woman's ideology represents a major change away from the role definition held by the majority today. Although New Women are not always sure about how much activism is appropriate for a woman to engage in, their view holds that activities other than homemaking should be fully permissible for an adult woman so long as they do not interfere with her primary responsibilities to her family. In many ways, voluntary political activities are ideally suited to the needs of women with a New Woman's view. Before marriage women can engage in such activities without making the type of long-term commitment that is necessary in many jobs—a commitment that might have to be terminated after marriage if a husband's job responsibilities required relocation or if childcare duties weighed too heavily. Furthermore, in a society with limited job options for educated women, joining a political group may be easier and less frustrating than experiencing discrimination and rejection from employers.[37] After marriage, vol-

35. Figure for Japan is from Ministry of Labor, Women's and Minors' Bureau, *Fujin rōdō*, 1972, p. 38. Figure for the United States is from U.S. Dept. of Labor and Japanese Ministry of Labor, *Women Workers*, p. 96.

36. In a national survey conducted in 1972–1974, women were asked if they thought that the conditions that would permit women to have an occupation were available in Japan. Only 11 percent of the women thought so. The barriers cited included inadequate nursery facilities (27 percent), household and childcare responsibilities (13 percent), discrimination in salaries and jobs (12 percent), difficulty presented by working hours and holidays (11 percent), and lack of opportunities for women to get suitable jobs (9 percent). Ministry of Foreign Affairs, *Status of Women in Modern Japan: Report on Nationwide Survey* (Tokyo, 1975), p. 26.

37. Among New Women, consciousness of job discrimination was high. This consciousness alone is a deterrent to any attempt to find a satisfying job, apart from the concrete barriers that the women might face if they actually

untary political activities have the appeal that they can be combined more easily than a job with the responsibilities of the wife-mother role, and terminated more easily if a conflict develops.

Many New Women included in the study gave precisely these types of reasons when talking about why they had been drawn to political volunteer groups. In discussing their prior experiences a number of them stated that they had first sought interesting work, before or after marriage. Failing to find it, they had turned to political activities. Alternately, in keeping with their New Woman's view they had been looking for interests that could be combined easily with their other responsibilities and did not require a large commitment of time and energy. Participation in a political group had been ideally suited to their needs.[38] For New Women who become politically active, one critical step in the process is the moment of entry into the political arena itself, and the immediate factors operating behind it. But an equally important stage in the overall process is one in which they move toward a role ideology that sees active political participation as a viable option for women.

Radical Egalitarians

Twenty percent of the political women interviewed for the study were Radical Egalitarians. Typical of them was Suzuki Fumiko, a member of the Red Army (Sekigun), who at age eighteen was one of the youngest political women in the sample.[39]

sought such a job. For a discussion of women's avoidance of situations that are likely to lead to discrimination against them, see Marcia M. Lee "Towards Understanding Why Few Women Hold Public Office," pp. 132–133.

38. See chapter seven for a full discussion of the attractions of political involvement for women.

39. Formed out of several radical factions in 1969, the Red Army is Trotskyist in its view and is thus committed to world revolution. Together with another militant group, the Red Army in the early 1970s formed an organization known as the United Red Army (Rengō Sekigun), which has engaged in a variety of terrorist activities inside and outside Japan. The informant described in the text was active in the Red Army before the merger.

Fumiko's feelings about woman's role came out early in the interview when she was asked how she felt about men and marriage. After thinking for a moment, she made a strong statement of the Radical Egalitarian view and then described the course she had chosen:

> The war destroyed the [traditional] family system in Japan, but the basic problems remain. Marriage in this society involves a relationship between possessor and possessed, not between two individuals who think of each other as equals. My own relationship with a man is not that kind of relationship. It is a face-to-face relationship in which we look directly into each other's eyes. We live together in the course of developing our ideas and thoughts.

Fumiko lived with a man, also a Red Army member, in a tiny apartment they had found together. Both were agreed, she said, that the duties of daily life in the apartment should be shared and that each should have large areas of personal freedom to do what he or she wished.

Fumiko's questioning of the dominant ideology of woman's role appeared to have long roots. She said that even as a child she had had a strong sense of independence and had rejected many types of behavior that were considered "feminine." At an early age she had declared that she would never marry.

Fumiko had grown up in considerable poverty. Her mother, left a widow early in her forties by the sudden death of her husband, a white-collar worker, had suffered severe financial hardship in trying to make her way alone as a woman in Japan. It was this experience, in part, that appeared to have made her supportive of a daughter's search for autonomy. Piecing together a marginal income from her deceased husband's pension and from making kimonos, Fumiko's mother had given her tacit consent, while outwardly voicing disapproval, when her daughter became involved in radical political activities during junior high school days. While her mother sewed upstairs in their large, rambling house in Kamakura outside Tokyo, Fumiko had turned the downstairs into a commune for the Red Army. The year before the interview, Fumiko had dropped out of senior high school and had begun to live with the fellow activist referred to above, with her mother's full knowledge.

Though Radical Egalitarian activists had come to their view by somewhat distinctive routes, and though they differed widely in personal qualities and in such factors as class and educational background, there were certain characteristics they shared. One was a distinct personal style. Whereas virtually all Neotraditionalists and most New Women tended to express themselves somewhat indirectly, uniformly using the polite forms of speech and expression considered appropriate for women, Radical Egalitarians spoke with great frankness and directness. In many cases they used plain forms of speech and slang expressions that are commonly regarded as "men's language" in Japan. For example, in a political demonstration, they might shout "*baka yarō*" at their opponents or at the police, an expression that has the force of "asshole" or "oaf" in English and that most Japanese women (including most of the Neotraditional and New Women interviewed for this study) would eschew as shockingly unfeminine. Asked why they might use such expressions, they reported that doing so made them "feel strong" and assertive, and made it possible for them to express their anger directly and forcefully.

Another characteristic was that most had given considerable thought to where they stood on many issues, both political and personal. Whereas Neotraditionalists and especially New Women often discovered inconsistencies in their behavior and feeling over the course of the interview, Radical Egalitarians, even the younger ones like Fumiko, had gone through fairly extensive self-examination. They were willing, in most cases, to admit shortcomings and failures. But in a way that was quite striking, they had thought things through.

Unlike New Women, who differed from one another about what they wanted in a relationship with a man, Radical Egalitarians were fairly agreed. They uniformly expressed a strong dislike for the widely accepted criteria for choosing a mate in Japan, such as family background, socioeconomic status, and educational attainment. Many were ideologically opposed to the institution of marriage for the kinds of reasons cited by Fumiko.

How women come to an ideology of woman's role so marginal to the dominant view is a complex question that will be discussed more fully later on. Here it should be noted that the types of background—education and work experience—that operate behind role change in the case of New Women also had affected the experiences of many Radical Egalitarians. Fifty-five percent of the Radical Egalitarians, approximately the same percentage as New Women, had attended four-year institutions of higher education, in contrast to only 35 percent of the Neotraditionalists. In the aggregate, the percentage of Radical Egalitarians who had been employed was about the same as for the other two groups, but a number of Radical Egalitarians described job experiences that were clearly contributory toward changes in their views of life and role. Neither factor, of course, adequately explains changes of such magnitude in their view of woman's role.

For the discussion that will follow later on, it is important to note the special role of the political group itself as a setting for role change. Almost all the Radical Egalitarians interviewed for this study were engaged in political activities in which they were pressing for equality as women. This typically involved spending a major portion of time in a subculture in which they were surrounded by persons who gave them strong personal validation. Although a number of them maintained close ties with their families, most lived apart from relatives, generally with members of their political group or with a man who shared their views. Most Radical Egalitarian activists were in one of two main types of groups. Half, like Fumiko, were in radical political sects that are part of the New Left in Japan. These women were opposed not only to current notions of woman's role, but to the general pattern of social and family relations in Japan and other capitalist societies, to the work ethic, to the present government, to all the existing political parties in Japan, including the parties of the Left, and to an educational system in their country which they saw as overcompetitive and dehumanizing. Within their group, many were pressing for their right to participate on an equal basis in all group activities, ranging from assuming leadership roles to engaging in physical combat in pursuit of the group's objectives. Most said that there were major barriers to achieving equality within their sect.

Disputes between male and female activists had broken out in numerous groups over the question of what role women should play in the sect.[40]

The other half were members of radical feminist groups.[41] Many of these women had deserted the New Left because they felt that men in the movement failed to understand the seriousness of their struggle for equality and recognition. Joined by many young women not from the New Left, they had formed numerous women's groups and collectives. Those associated with Tatakau Onna ("Fighting Women") generally held that before women could have equal relations with men they first had to learn to express themselves among women and develop their self-confidence. This group operated several collectives where women lived and studied together. Most supported themselves by taking part-time jobs in coffee shops or wherever they could find work. While living in the collective, many had sexual relations with men out-

40. The conflicts between men and women in New Left groups in Japan parallel the disputes that broke out in Students for a Democratic Society and other American radical groups in the late 1960s. In the United States, these conflicts functioned as catalysts for the emergence of the younger branch of the American feminist movement. See Jo Freeman, *The Politics of Women's Liberation* (New York, 1975), pp. 56–62. Similarly, in Japan, a number of feminist groups in the early 1970s were formed by women who left their radical sects in anger over sex discrimination. The best-known dispute took place in the Middle Core Faction (Chūkaku-ha) in the summer of 1971, when a core of women members staged a protest at a large national rally of the group; subsequently, a number of the women left and formed radical feminist groups and collectives. Interviews with former Chūkaku-ha women activists, May 1972.

41. Japan has a number of organizations and groups committed to improving the status of women in society and in the family, which thus could be considered a part of a "women's liberation movement" in the broad sense in which that term is used in the United States. However, "women's lib" (*ūman ribu*) as used in Japan has a much narrower meaning. Specifically, it refers to a small number of groups that appeared in the early 1970s and that take sexual liberation as a primary objective. A major political goal of these groups is to end the ban on birth-control pills in Japan and to counter government efforts to tighten restrictions on abortions. See Yoshiko Nagano, "Women Fight for Control: Abortion Struggle in Japan," *Anpo* 17 (Summer 1973): 14–20. The actual membership figures for these groups are fairly low, probably numbering in the several hundreds. But interest in their aims and activities is considerably higher than this estimate would indicate. In May 1972, for example, a conference in Tokyo on "women's lib" drew about 3,000 participants.

side it. Here they argued that Japanese women, long sexually repressed in a country with a strong tradition of a double standard, should overcome their timidity and sexual dependence on men by learning to have sexual relations as many men do: with a variety of partners and on their own terms.[42] Radical Egalitarians in several feminist groups not associated with Tatakau Onna had different objectives. Individual members were living with a man, and met occasionally in groups that functioned much like consciousness-raising groups in the United States. These young women felt that women must struggle for equality and recognition, not in a separatist movement, but in a joint struggle waged with a man who shared their view of woman's role and who was willing to try to create a new style of relationship between man and woman in present-day Japanese society.

In the context of the Radical Egalitarian view of woman's role, all forms of political expression become available to women. Because Radical Egalitarians reject the gender-role allocation that makes it women's duty to maintain the home unit in a relationship with a man, the kind of boundaries on political participation arising from the New Women's perspective do not exist, at least in theory. According to the Radical Egalitarians, women should be able to play any political role of their choosing. There can be no gender-based conflict between any "primary" home responsibilities, on the one hand, and political roles, on the other, because Radical Egalitarians reject the notion that gender should determine *any* roles women are to play, other than the biological role of childbearer.

In Japanese society today, the Radical Egalitarian view, which is consonant with a radical feminist perspective found among minorities of women in many countries, is very much at odds with dominant thinking. As was just noted, even within many groups of the New Left, there was often conflict with male activists over women's attempt to translate ideology into behavior. It was highly significant in the study, however, that women with a Radical Egalitarian view of

42. Interview with Tanaka Mitsu, age twenty-eight, leader of Tatakau Onna, Tokyo, May, 1972. Her views on women's liberation are set out in her autobiography: Tanaka Mitsu, *Inochi no onna tachi e* (That women might live) (Tokyo, 1972).

woman's role were found almost exclusively in radical political subcultures, where they found more support for experimentation with political roles and with woman's role itself than is available in any other setting in the Japan of today.[43]

Concluding Remarks

To uncover the process by which certain
women, unlike most women, become politically active, the
first step has been to examine the outcome of the gender-role
socialization process for women activists, as expressed in
their particular views of woman's role. In this investigation it
was shown that each ideology carried with it a definite view
of the place of politics in a woman's life. In the Neotraditional
view, which predominates in Japan today, active political
roles are precluded for women in the age range of this study
under all but the most unusual of circumstances. In the New
Women's view, active political roles are permitted, but only
within certain gender-dictated boundaries. Only in the context of the Radical Egalitarian perspective, a marginal view
very much at odds with prevailing thought in Japan, is equal
political participation, without gender-determined boundaries and limits, fully accepted. In addition to shedding light
on the experiences of women who are politically active, this
analysis leads to a better understanding of why the political
participation of *most* Japanese women is limited when it
comes to more active forms of participation of the type represented by political volunteerism. The view that women
should commit themselves to political groups or causes without accepting certain gender-related restrictions on their participation is very much a marginal view in Japanese society.

43. The relationship between change in role ideology and engaging in
protest activity was recently investigated in a study by James Orcutt of American college students. Using a Guttman scale of attitudes toward female role
behavior, Orcutt found that 90 percent of women who had been highly active
in protest activities had a "modern" role ideology, whereas only 45 percent of
nonactivist women had such a view. James D. Orcutt, "The Impact of Student Activism on Attitudes towards the Female Sex Role," *Social Forces* 54
(December 1975), p. 388.

Espousing it and making it operational appears to be possible only within radical political subcultures where relatively few women are likely to tread.

To explain why certain women *do* become politically active, this chapter has provided the first steps in an analysis that will continue in the next two chapters. Several key points have emerged from this examination of the role ideologies of political women. It is of major significance that 80 percent of the political women in the study had adopted alternative views of woman's role. This finding did not mean—contrary to what Duverger and other writers have suggested—that all political women are by definition militant feminists. Far from it. As was shown, the New Women's view, which reflects far more moderate change in the dominant definition of woman's role, predominated in the sample. On the other hand, the finding indicated that political women, relative to the current balance of opinion and feeling in Japan, were not ordinary women. The large majority of the sample held views of woman's role that challenged the role definition held by the majority of Japanese people. This finding strongly suggests that an important relationship exists between active political participation and role change for women. One possibility, of course, is that women's views of their role undergo change as a *result* of becoming politically active.[44] The congruence between the Radical Egalitarian view and radical political activity lends certain support to that view. What was striking, however, in case history after case history, was the degree of role change and role experimentation that had *preceded* the activism of the 80 percent of the sample who held alternative views of woman's role. The questioning of the dominant role ideology had taken many forms, ranging from Takai Setsuko's decision to seek a more independent life in Tokyo, turning aside numerous opportunities to have an arranged marriage, to Suzuki Fumiko's childhood objections to

44. Although Orcutt adopts this position (in ibid.), he offers no evidence to support it, and his reasoning is not persuasive. He argues that since many *male* protest activists were guilty of sexism in the 1960s, but today have a more liberated view of woman's role, then changes in attitudes toward the female-gender role probably could not precede entry into protest activities in the case of either men *or* women. But there is no reason to assume that the process by which a new ideology of woman's role is adopted will be the same for both men and women.

"feminine" behavior. Even if we allow for the human tendency to remember selectively and to confirm a present identity by seeking roots for it, the pattern was consistent and therefore of major importance. What emerged from the analysis was a picture of a highly complex relationship between changes in women's notions of self and role, on the one hand, and their adoption of an active political role, on the other. Political activism (as in the case of Radical Egalitarians in their political subculture) appeared to support role change and to encourage still further change in many political women, but at the same time, change of varying magnitudes in women's views of their proper role appeared to be a key precondition to most women's entry into the male world of politics.

4

The Effect of Political Socialization
on Political Women

A new view of woman's role that challenges
the prevailing definition is a precondition for the entry of
most women activists into politics. But this is hardly the full
explanation for why some women, but not others, are drawn
to political groups and causes. The kinds of values and attitudes that characterize alternative ideologies of woman's
role, especially the New Woman's view, have many supporters in Japan among nonactivist as well as activist women.
The next question is why *certain* women with a new view of
woman's role become attracted to a *political* outlet for self-
expression. As chapter one indicated, this question assumes
that all political people have a psychological "predisposi-
tion" to participate in politics, but that this is not a sufficient
explanation for why political women choose politics, and
not some alternate outlet, for their basic needs and drives.

Venturing into politics is a big step for a woman to take in Japan, even if she has begun to challenge the dominant view of woman's role that denies her the right to do so. The political sphere is probably the single largest male bastion in contemporary industrial societies, as is evidenced not only by the extraordinarily low levels of women's representation in positions of power, but by the fanfare that accompanies any woman's entry. In Japan, as a legacy of women's exclusion from participation in political groups for so much of the prewar period, many types of political activities in even the middle-range are largely a male preserve. Compared with the consequences of role experimentation in other social arenas, experimentation in the political realm thus involves especially strong sanctions in the form of social disapproval from many people inside and outside a woman's broad circle of significant others. It is therefore reasonable to ask whether special factors operated in the experiences of political women to make active participation a viable option for them. Were their parents unusually interested in politics? Were there people in or outside the family who were available as political role models to them? Were there reasons why these particular women were more responsive than most women to political cues in their wider environment? These questions lead directly to a study of the political socialization experiences of women prior to their entry into politics.

The Political Socialization of
Women Activists:
Alternative Explanations

The basic outlines of the process by which individuals acquire political beliefs and behavior patterns are fairly well agreed upon among those who study the political socialization process. Much of the fundamental learning relating to politics has already taken place by the high school years as the culmination of a process originating far back in childhood. The attitudes and behavior patterns acquired in those years tend to stabilize by the high school years, and may undergo fairly limited change thereafter for many individuals.[1] Much of the work on political socialization has been concerned with weighing the relative influence of different types of variables that affect the process. That research, in general, continues to affirm the importance of the family's influence on the political beliefs and behavior of children. Some 80 percent of Americans, for example, support the political party of their parents—a finding that is often cited as evidence of the family's influence in the political socialization process.[2] Other agencies of socialization clearly play a critical role, however. Hess and Torney argue for the importance of the schools in reshaping basic political beliefs, for loosening some of the constraints set by the partisan views in the family unit.[3] Peer groups appear to play a similar role. Research done by Langton suggests that for children from high-status families, the peer group may be even more important than the family in shaping the beliefs of the young.[4] The work of Newcomb and others shows that the general setting to which youths are exposed during the college experience also functions to modify basic political beliefs.[5]

In addition to assessing the relative influence of the various agencies of socialization on the political beliefs and behavior of the young, researchers have attempted to study the actual

1. Robert D. Hess and Judith V. Torney, *The Development of Political Attitudes in Children* (Garden City, N.Y., 1968), p. 11. This assumption operates behind most studies, and is the basis for examining preadult political attitudes, party identification, and so on as a basis for investigating orientations toward citizenship, the legitimacy of major governmental institutions, and other adult "consequences" of earlier learning. See, for example, Jack Dennis and Donald J. McCrone, "Preadult Development of Political Party Identification in Western Democracies," in *Comparative Political Socialization*, ed. Jack Dennis and M. Kent Jennings (Beverly Hills, 1970), pp. 115–135; and Fred Greenstein, *Children and Politics* (New Haven, 1965), pp. 1–15.

2. For a summary of evidence on the transmission of political party preference, see Kenneth Langton, *Political Socialization*, p. 52–53.

3. Hess and Torney, *Political Attitudes in Children*, pp. 247–248.

4. Langton, *Political Socialization*, pp. 158–160.

5. Theodore Newcomb, *Personality and Social Change* (New York, 1943); Theodore Newcomb and K. Feldman, *The Impact of Colleges upon Their Students* (New York, 1969); William Hanna, ed., *University Students in Politics* (New York, 1971); Kenneth Keniston, *Young Radicals* (New York, 1968); Roberta Sigel, ed., *Learning About Politics* (New York, 1970), pp. 375–379.

process by which influence is transmitted. This work is at a much more preliminary stage, however.[6] Most of it has focused on the balance of conjugal power in the family, and has asked which of the two parents has more influence on their children in the area of politics. Much research in the past had simply assumed that the father played the more influential political role in the family. Recent studies have cast doubt on this conclusion, and have been working to develop a more comprehensive perspective on what roles the two parents play in such a subtle and complex process.[7]

Three propositions that emerge from research to date are especially relevant to this inquiry:

1. The family is a major—and probably, for at least the majority of the population, the foremost—agency in shaping the basic political attitudes and orientations of the individual, with other agencies functioning as mitigating influences on these main lines of influence.

2. To the extent that the individual is exposed to alternative agents of political socialization outside the family—such as the schools, the peer group, higher education, the wider social environment—basic political attitudes and orientations are likely to reflect the influences of these later agencies; conversely, those individuals less exposed to outside agencies are likely to remain closer to the family in basic political attitudes and orientations than those who are more exposed.

3. Within the family, there is every reason to believe that both parents play roles in shaping the political attitudes and behavior of children. Some type of political specialization appears to operate within the family, with each parent playing somewhat distinct roles in transmitting politically relevant influence.

These propositions provide a starting point for asking if

6. As Dawson and Prewitt observe, "A major gap in political socialization theory . . . concerns the actual learning mechanism." Richard E. Dawson and Kenneth Prewitt, *Political Socialization* (Boston, 1969), p. 80.

7. M. Kent Jennings and Kenneth P. Langton, "Mothers versus Fathers: The Formation of Political Orientations among Young Americans," *Journal of Politics*, 31 (May 1969): 329–357. Eleanor E. Maccoby, Richard Mathews, and Anton Morton, "Youth and Political Change," *Public Opinion Quarterly* 18 (Spring 1954): 23–39; M. Kent Jennings and Richard G. Niemi, "The Transmission of Political Values from Parent to Child," *American Political Science Review* 62 (March, 1960): 169–184; Langton, *Political Socialization*, pp. 21–51.

there was anything unusual about the political socialization of women who later became active in politics. The first two propositions direct attention to the key question of what role the family may have played in shaping their political beliefs, interest, and behavior. As hypotheses are developed to deal with this question it becomes apparent that the answer is in no way obvious. Available evidence points in directions that are diametrically opposed to one another. Some evidence suggests that the political socialization of activist women can best be explained by a *parental dependence model*, which would see them as especially responsive to political cues transmitted by the family. Supporting such an hypothesis, for example, is a great deal of research indicating that girls are socialized to be closer to the family than boys and are more dependent on their parents, emotionally and otherwise, than boys.[8] It is reasonable to go from there and speculate that women are somewhat more responsive to family political cues than are men, and that the same might hold for political women. Additional support for the hypothesis is provided by the

8. Hill, for example, in an early study, found that "boys, with age, show a declining identification with parents. However, girls continue to show a considerable idealization of parents." See P. S. Hill, "Personification of Ideals by Urban Children," *Journal of Social Psychology* (1930), p. 399. Allport and Gillespie found that girls in their sample placed greater emphasis on family values than did the boys. Gordon Allport and J. Gillespie, *Youth's Outlook on the Future*, 1955, p. 32, fn. A study of a national sample of college graduates showed that daughters defected from parental party preferences less often than sons. P. Salter West, Ph.D. dissertation, Columbia University, 1951, cited in Hyman, *Political Socialization*, p. 120. Various studies conducted by Fisher, Newcomb, and Svehla (cited in Hyman, p. 104) show a "consistent pattern" whereby "daughters resemble parents attitudinally more than sons do." A study conducted by Iisager in Denmark showed that women college students reported more parental influence in the formation of their views than males (Hyman, p. 105). The developmental bases for creating greater dependency in daughters than sons are explored in Mirra Komarovsky, "Functional Analysis of Sex Roles," *American Sociological Review*, 15 (1950): 508–516. She argued that women are raised to be dependent so that they will be able to switch over more easily from the family of orientation to a dependent role in the family of procreation. She cited evidence from her study of college-age females that parents sped the emancipation of sons from the family, but less so daughters (pp. 510–511). Vogel, in his study of middle-class, urban Japanese, almost precisely parallels her findings and her analysis where he contrasts the socialization of daughters and sons in the families he studied. Ezra F. Vogel, *Japan's New Middle Class* (Berkeley and Los Angeles, 1963), p. 109.

findings of various studies that women are more politically conservative than men and that they are more likely to support the values and orientation of traditional religious and social groupings than men of the same age group.[9] Since the family itself is widely considered to be the major transmitter in society of traditional values,[10] it would follow that women must learn their views in the home and retain them, despite outside influences, to a greater degree than men. Impressionistic evidence derived from reading about and observing the lives of a number of famous political women makes it reasonable to think that this might be true of them. Many conspicuous women leaders from Indira Gandhi to Eva Peron have famous political fathers, other male relatives, or husbands in their background.[11] Certainly this would apply to Japan, where a number of women in the Japanese Diet carry forward the political interests and basic political views of their own or their husband's famous political family.[12] If these "conspicuous" activists trace their politics back to the family, then the particular salience of the family's role in the political

9. Maurice Duverger, *The Political Role of Women* (Paris, 1955), pp. 143–147; Marcelle Stanislas Devaud, "Political Participation of Western European Women," *Annals of the American Academy* 372 (1968): 61; Herbert Tingsten, *Political Behavior: Studies in Election Statistics* (London, 1937); Harold F. Gosnell, *Democracy, the Threshold of Freedom,* (New York, 1948), chapter 4, all provide evidence that women in Europe have been more conservative politically than men. Evidence on women in the United States has been more contradictory. For findings pointing toward conservatism and, alternately, toward liberalism of women relative to men in the United States, see Jane S. Jaquette, "Introduction: Women in American Politics," in *Women in Politics,* ed. Jane S. Jaquette (New York, 1974), pp. xxi–xxii.

10. See S. N. Eisenstadt, *From Generation to Generation* (New York, 1964), pp. 37–45, who characterizes family relationships as ascriptive, particularistic, and diffuse, qualities which allow the family "to perform its socializing function and to be a mainstay of social solidarity and continuity" (p. 37). Settings outside the family teach the individual to act according to universalistic criteria and support his or her passage into modern roles (p. 45).

11. Gehlen, studying the background of women who have served in the U.S. Congress, found that 29 out of the 66 women who served in the House between 1916 and 1969 were "political widows," widows of congressmen who died in office. Frieda L. Gehlen, "Women Members of Congress," in *A Portrait of Marginality,* ed. Marianne Githens and Jewel L. Prestage (New York, 1977), p. 308.

12. Michael K. Blaker, ed., *Japan at the Polls* (Washington, D.C., 1976), pp. 96–97.

socialization of woman activists appears to be a reasonable possibility for investigation.

Other evidence, however, points to an opposite and contradictory theory of women's participation, which might be called a *parental independence model.* This model would hold that women who become active in politics adopt their political orientation less from the influence of family and more from that of outside agencies of socialization than is true for most Japanese. This hypothesis has its own kind of appeal in explaining the political socialization process as it affects activist women in a country such as Japan, where norms and values affirming women's place in political life have been introduced so recently. Because the changes are so new, many agencies of political socialization outside the family, such as the schools, the universities, and the youthful peer groups found in such settings, support the norms that see political interest and behavior as appropriate for women far more than do older-generation Japanese in the family. Parents' basic beliefs about women's roles and place were shaped in the prewar period, and thus of the various agents they are least likely to spur their daughters' entry into politics. It follows that political women must have developed their political orientations, interest, and desire to participate in politics independent of family political cues and must have turned elsewhere for support for their political interest and involvement. This hypothesis, it may be noted, takes into account the findings and interpretations of Krauss, Flanagan, and others, who argue that, in general, the family's role in political socialization is weak in Japan, for reasons that apply equally well to political women.[13] The hypothesis holds that to the extent the family's role is weak in the case of most Japanese, it is undoubtedly *even weaker* in the case of political women, for the gender-related reasons just cited. Testing these alternative hypotheses is an important first step in exploring how political women came to be where they are. The third proposition deals with a quite different issue. Whether the family's role is weak or strong in setting the directions of daughters who become politically active, certainly the family has some role to play. The question is, which parent plays the more significant role in the process, and how is the influence transmitted?

13. Ellis Krauss, *Japanese Radicals Revisited*, pp. 51–54.

Again, the answer is not obvious. Available data point in opposite directions. Some evidence suggests that the *father*
plays the key role. Not only is this view upheld by much early
research on political socialization, but it is supported by a
great deal of work on gender-role learning. Child development specialists and psychologists have long advanced the
proposition that children learn behavior associated with their
gender from the same-sex parent. That is, a girl learns female
gender-role behavior from her mother.[14] But when it comes
to learning behavior associated with the opposite sex—in this
case, the political role—she is thought to learn that from her
father.[15] It follows that political women may have had fathers
who presented themselves as strong models for political behavior, and who thus played the more significant role of the
two parents in influencing their daughters. This hypothesis is
also supported by the impressionistic evidence referred to
above on the special roles played by famous fathers, other
male relatives, or husbands in the lives of many well-known
political women. There is also support for an alternate
hypothesis that sees the *mother* as the key family agent. As
will be discussed shortly, recent research conducted in the
United States has found that mothers wield significantly
more influence than fathers in certain key areas of political
socialization. Testing these alternate hypotheses offers a basis

14. Although there are numerous areas of disagreement in the literature
on gender-role learning, the theory advanced by Kohlberg has many supporters. As far as gender-role identification is concerned, Kohlberg argues
that children first develop cognitions of gender-role stereotypes, which leads
in turn to the development of masculine and feminine values. After the latter
are acquired, children tend to identify with the same-sex parent. According
to present theorizing, the desire to be feminine or masculine thus leads to the
desire to imitate a model of those behaviors (the same-sex parent). See Lawrence Kohlberg, "A Cognitive-Developmental Analysis of Children's Sex-
Role Concepts and Attitudes," in *The Development of Sex Differences*, ed.
Eleanor Maccoby (Stanford, 1966), pp. 164–166.

15. Many writers accept this view; still, the process by which children
learn behaviors associated with the opposite-gender role is much disputed.
Brown argues strongly for the role of the father in teaching children of both
sexes various "instrumental" roles, since it is he who is "oriented towards
actively securing a relation between the [family] system and its environment." Miriam M. Johnson, "Sex Role Learning in the Nuclear Family,"
Child Development 34 (June 1963): 320. Clearly the political role would be such
an "instrumental" role.

for exploring the internal dynamics of the family as they operate in the political socialization of activist women.

Parental Dependence Model
versus Parental Independence Model

That the family has a major role to play in the political socialization of most people is a proposition that not everyone has seen as applicable to Japan. Indeed, in the popular press, this cornerstone of political socialization research conducted in the United States is openly challenged. A basic tenet of Japanese writing on youth and their political views is that a fundamental generation gap in Japan functions to limit the role of parents in influencing the beliefs of the young. Because of its support for a war that brought national disaster to Japan, the older generation is presumed to have lost its credibility with the young, and even the will, given its own record of defeat and disgrace, to teach them its values. This view, widely accepted in Japan, asserts that the family has surrendered its role in political socialization to other agents with more credibility for the young, such as the schools, peer groups, the universities, and the mass media.[16]

Political socialization research conducted in Japan so far presents an unclear picture of the degree to which this popular view is borne out in reality. Several studies suggest that the Japanese family may play a smaller role in the political socialization of children than does the American family, and that other agencies, such as the media and the university setting, may have particular mitigating influence on whatever

16. Mikio Sumiya, "The Function and Social Structure of Education," *Journal of Social and Political Ideas in Japan* 5 (December 1967): 129; Akira Kubota and Robert E. Ward, "Family Influence and Political Socialization in Japan," *Comparative Political Studies* 3 (July 1970): 142; Tsurumi Kazuko, "The Japanese Student Movement: Its Milieu," *Japan Quarterly* 15 (October–December 1968): 430–455, and "The Japanese Student Movement: Group Portraits," *Japan Quarterly* 16 (January–March 1969): 25–44; Takahashi Akira, "Nihon gakusei undō no shisō to kōdō" (Thought and behavior in the Japanese student movement), *Chūō Kōron* 5 (May 1968), 6 (June 1968), 8 (August 1968), and 9 (September 1968).

the child does learn in the home.[17] At the same time, however, a great deal of research affirms the importance of the family's role in the socialization process in Japan. Kubota and Ward, in an analysis of the voting behavior of matched pairs of parents and children drawn from a national probability sample, found that whichever party the parents supported, the children, in over 60 percent of the cases, agreed with them.[18] The children in that particular study were from fifteen to nineteen years old. A study by Massey based on a sample of 942 eighth-, tenth-, and twelfth-grade public school students and their parents reached a similar conclusion. Not only did Japanese youths share their parents' partisanship to nearly the same degree as Americans, but the congruence of political attitudes of parents and children actually increased as the children got older.[19] Most research to date has not adequately addressed the question of the influence of the family relative to other agencies of socialization, but certainly it has provided no basis for dismissing the family's role. Meanwhile, the data that are available for comparative purposes do make it possible to explore whether the role of the family in the experience of political women is greater or less than for most Japanese.

There are several ways to investigate this issue. The first is to look at data on the family's role in the transmission of basic political orientations. By comparing data on political women with data on the national probability sample of Japanese analyzed by Kubota and Ward, it is possible to search for any striking differences that may appear. The data presented in the Kubota and Ward study were reanalyzed to show the degree to which young people and their parents agreed in the matter of basic political orientation. "Basic political orientation" here refers to where the individual's allegiance lies in the confrontation characteristic of Japanese politics between

17. Scott C. Flanagan and Bradley M. Richardson, "Political Disaffection and Political Stability: A Comparison of Japanese and Western Findings," in *Comparative Social Research*, vol. 3, ed. Richard F. Tomasson (Greenwich, Conn., 1980), p. 23.

18. Kubota and Ward, "Family Influence," pp. 148–149. The percentage is derived from figures presented in tables 1 and 2, showing results of the first and second waves of the study.

19. Joseph A. Massey, *Youth and Politics in Japan* (Lexington, Mass., 1976), pp. 186, 188.

TABLE 9 *Basic Political Orientations of a National Probability Sample of Japanese Youth Compared with Political Orientations of Their Parents* (in percentage)

Political Orientation of Youth	Shared by One or Both Parents		Shared by Neither Parent		Total	
Conservative	80%	(28)	20%	(7)	100%	(35)
Progressive	55%	(17)	45%	(14)	100%	(31)
Totals	68%	(45)	32%	(21)	100%	(66)

SOURCE: Akira Kubota and Robert E. Ward, "Family Influence and Political Socialization in Japan," *Comparative Political Studies* 3, no. 2 (July 1970). Data are derived from table 1, p. 148. The Kubota and Ward study presented the data on parent-child identification by party. Here the parties are grouped. The designation of "conservative political orientation" applies to those who supported the Liberal Democratic Party (LDP), the party in power; "progressive political orientation" applies to those who supported the Clean Government Party (CGP), the Democratic Socialist Party (DSP), the Japan Socialist Party (JSP), or the Japan Communist Party (JCP), all of which are considered to be in the progressive camp. Kubota's and Ward's study involved two waves, before and after a national election. Figures for the first wave are presented above because it was theorized that data collected before an election would be more nearly comparable to my own, which is based on recall data. Kubota and Ward themselves note (p. 161) that the results of the first-wave study are more reflective of "normal" patterns of transmission than are those of the second wave, where testing is done in the wake of one particular electoral campaign.

the conservative and progressive camps.[20] The results appear in table 9. As it indicates, 68 percent of the Kubota and Ward sample shared the basic political orientation of one or both parents, a figure similar to that found in the case of the political women, of whom 64 percent shared their parents' views (see table 10). On the basis of this comparison, then, the influence of the parents in setting the basic political orientations of activist daughters appears to be little different from their presumed influence on most Japanese. When the age

20. See Jōji Watanuki, "Patterns of Politics in Present-Day Japan," in *Party Systems and Voter Alignments: Cross-National Perspectives*, ed. Seymour M. Lipset and Stein Rokkan (New York, 1967), pp. 456–460; Krauss, *Japanese Radicals Revisited*, pp. 3–4; Scott C. Flanagan, "The Japanese Party System in Transition," *Comparative Politics* 3 (January 1971): 231–254. Also see Appendix A for a discussion of Japan's polarized political system.

TABLE 10   *Basic Political Orientations of Activist Women Compared with Political Orientations of Their Parents* (in percentage)

Political Orientation of Activist Women	Shared by One or Both Parents		Shared by Neither Parent		Total	
Conservative	100%	(8)	0%	(0)	100%	(8)
Progressive	60%	(55)	40%	(36)	100%	(91)
Totals	64%	(63)	36%	(36)	100%	(99)*

*N does not equal 100 because one informant did not identify herself with either the conservative or the progressive camp.

difference between the two samples is taken into account, this statement can be made even more strongly. The children in the Kubota and Ward study were from fifteen to nineteen years old, whereas most of the political women were considerably older. Since the younger children are closer to the family, physically and emotionally, than the young adult women in the present study, it is reasonable to expect that the younger group would be much closer to parental views than the older group.[21] Yet the difference was not significant. This comparison, if it does not prove or disprove either hypothesis, offers little support for the view that the family's influence is significantly either weaker or stronger on political women than on most Japanese, at least in transmitting basic political orientations.

The next test is to look at the level of political interest in the home for its possible influence on women who later became involved in politics. Why and how political women develop their own high level of interest in political issues is obviously a key question for an understanding of why they—unlike most women—became active in politics. If it could be shown that a disproportionate number came from homes where the political interest was high, there would be a basis for a belief in links between their early socialization and experiences and their activism later on. Conversely, if it turned out that they were no more likely than usual Japanese to come from such homes, then family political cues could hardly be thought to

21. See Krauss, *Japanese Radicals Revisited*, p. 51.

explain their activism. To explore this question, the informants were asked to recall whether their parents were interested in politics. According to their reports, 49 percent had come from families in which one or both parents were politically interested (see table 11). The same question was asked of respondents in the 1967 Japanese Election Study. A secondary analysis of that data indicates that approximately 45 percent of a national probability sample reported at least one parent who was interested in politics—a figure that is not significantly different from the one for this study.[22]

What conclusions can be drawn from the comparisons so far of the experiences of political women with those of usual Japanese? It is fully recognized that comparisons of gross marginals across surveys are fraught with methodological problems and cannot provide a basis for making precise statements. However, in an area of research such as this one, where so little is known, such comparisons are valuable in establishing broad parameters for an investigation. In this study, the comparisons of data made thus far make it possible to rule out extremes of interpretation that would see the political socialization of activist women as different in fundamental ways from those of most Japanese. As a group, political women were no more likely or less likely to be responsive to family political cues than most Japanese, a finding that allows

22. The frequency distribution from their survey is:

	Father	Mother
very interested	443	102
somewhat interested	405	207
little interest	659	1168
don't know	532	547
no answer	12	26

Center for Japanese Studies, University of Michigan, *The 1967 Japanese National Election Study*, Robert E. Ward and Akira Kubota, principal investigators (Ann Arbor, Michigan: Inter-University Consortium for Political Research, 1972), pp. 93–94. If we add the "don't know" responses, hypothesizing that they reflect low socialization, with those reporting little interest, then 42 percent of the fathers and 15 percent of the mothers would be classified as interested. We can assume that at least some children would report interested mothers and uninterested fathers, which suggests that over 45 percent would have at least one interested parent. I am grateful to Scott Flanagan for bringing these data to my attention and for his help in interpreting them.

us to reject both of the models set out earlier as general explanations for how women might find their way into politics.

If this is the finding for the group as a whole, it is important to look more closely at the sample for any variations in the general pattern. It was hypothesized that one of the best tests of the alternative models designed to explain the influence of the family on women's political behavior would be the relation between the level of political interest in the family and the level of political activism of the informants. Why this is so requires elaboration. As chapter one indicated, the higher the level of a woman's activism, the greater the gender-related barriers that confront her when she becomes involved in politics. Lesser forms of participation, such as voting, involve few constraints; presumably women today engage in these lower-level activities from the same balance of forces that guide the behavior of most Japanese, and we would need neither a parental dependence nor a parental independence model to explain their behavior. On the other hand, women engaged in higher levels of activism do confront such barriers, and we need to look for special factors in the women's experience that may have helped them over these barriers. The parental dependence and independence models are really no more than alternative hypotheses concerning the origin of these "special factors." Coming from a home with politically interested and aware parents would clearly be one such special factor, for it would serve to legitimize politics as an appropriate subject of interest and concern, and would thereby smooth a woman's entry into a sphere of activity that otherwise would represent alien territory. Therefore, if the parental dependence model has any validity, it should hold best in the case of the women in the sample who were the most active in politics, and we should expect to find a positive relationship between the level of political interest in the family and the level of political involvement of the informants.

The informants were divided into three categories on the basis of their level of participation in group political activities: leaders, regular participants, and intermittent participants. The parents of the informants were classified according to whether they were interested in and discussed politics (based

TABLE 11   *Relationship between Level of Politicization of Parents and Level of Activism of Political Women* (in percentage)

Level of Activism	One or Both Parents Interested in Politics		Neither Parent Interested		Total	
Leaders	59%	(13)	41%	(9)	100%	(22)
Regular partici- pants	52%	(27)	48%	(25)	100%	(52)
Intermittent par- ticipants	35%	(9)	65%	(17)	100%	(26)
Totals	49%	(49)	51%	(51)	100%	(100)

Gamma = .29; x^2 = 3.14 (p < .20)

on their daughters' reports). The data were then tested to determine whether there was a positive relationship between the level of political interest of the parents and their daughters' level of political activism. The results, found in table 11, show that such a relationship does exist. Women who were leaders in their political groups were somewhat more likely to come from a home where political interest was present than were women who played less active roles.

This finding provides tentative support for the parental dependence model, as least as it applies to a portion of the sample, and illuminates some of the factors that may characterize the experiences of women who go on to increasingly high levels of political involvement. Before reaching that conclusion, however, it is necessary to consider alternative explanations for the finding. One such explanation is that the *real* relationship is not between levels of political interest in the family, but between the level of activism and other factors associated with coming from families with politically interested and aware parents. Most compelling of these factors is experience in higher education. In Japan, as in the United States, high political interest is disproportionately found in families that are well-off economically—precisely the kind of families that are able to send their children to college.[23] It is

23. Jōji Watanuki, "Social Structure and Political Participation in Japan."

possible, then, that the real relationship is between the informants' level of education and their level of political involvement.

This alternative explanation is especially compelling because it is consistent with the findings of a number of studies that suggest that the family may be a relatively weak agent of political socialization in Japan, and that agencies of later life experience play a more critical role in shaping the political perspectives and behavior of the young. In the identification of key agencies of later life experience, higher education has been singled out for particular attention.[24] "Higher education" is really a shorthand term for a number of variables that go along with increased educational exposure. Going to college gives the individual the opportunity to enter into new relationships with peers and with teachers whose ideas may be markedly different from those of the family, and the option, available in the university setting more than in almost any other major institutional setting in most societies, to try out new ideas and types of behavior in a subculture where experimentation is accepted and even valued. The university thus brings together a number of variables that maximize the possibility for individual change in many areas, including political beliefs and behavior. That higher education has a major influence on the political socialization of Japanese youth who attend universities has been upheld by many scholars, including Tsurumi, Takahashi, Lifton, Kuroda, and Krauss.[25] Krauss's work is of special interest because he focused on the socialization experiences of male activists. Studying fifty-three activists and nonactivists, he concluded that the family's direct role in their political socialization was relatively weak, and was less significant than the role of later agencies—the schools, the peer group, contact with wider social change, and institutions of higher education.[26] If

24. Flanagan and Richardson, "Political Disaffection and Political Stability," pp. 23–24.

25. Tsurumi, "Japanese Student Movement," vols. 15 and 16; Takahashi, "Nihon gakusei undō"; Robert Jay Lifton, "Individual Patterns in Historical Change," *Journal of Social Issues* 20 (October 1964): 96–111; "Youth and History," in *The Challenge of Youth*, ed. Erik H. Erikson (New York, 1963); Yasumasa Kuroda, "Agencies of Political Socialization and Political Change," *Human Organization* 24 (Winter 1965): 328–331; Krauss, *Japanese Radicals Revisited.*

higher education plays a key role in the political socialization of most Japanese young people who attend universities, and of male activists in particular, then it is reasonable to hypothesize that it plays an equally critical role in the experiences of political women, and that it may be positively related to their level of activism.

The importance of higher education in the gender-role socialization of women activists was discussed in the previous chapter. It is clear that for the sample as a whole, going to college was closely associated with their role experimentation in a number of areas, including politics. Although the sample was not a random one, it is remarkable that the effort to locate political women in Japan who were engaged in a wide variety of voluntary activities turned up a sample of whom 51 percent had attended four-year universities or colleges. A comparable figure for the general population of women in the age range of the informants would be well under 8 percent.[27] We must conclude that attendance at a university figures significantly among the factors that support women's political participation in a general sense.

To test for the more precise effects of the women's educational level on their political behavior, the experience in politics of those who had attended universities and colleges was compared with the experiences of those who had not. Given the presumed importance of higher education in political socialization in Japan, we expected to find that women in leadership roles would have had disproportionate exposure to the type of experience represented by higher education, and that there would be a positive and significant relationship between the level of activism and the level of education of the informants. This was not the case, however (see table 12). Having a university education made a slight difference in distinguishing women at higher levels of activism from the women whose participation was more sporadic, but there was no overall positive relationship between educational level and level of activism.

26. Krauss, *Japanese Radicals Revisited*, pp. 43, 53.

27. This is an estimate based on educational data provided in Ministry of Labor, Women's and Minor's Bureau, *The Status of Women in Japan* (Tokyo, 1972), pp. 6–7. Out of the total population of women of college age over the period from 1957 to 1972 when my sample was of college age, roughly 3–10 percent were in four-year institutions, depending on the year.

TABLE 12 *Relationship between Level of Activism of Political Women and Educational Level* (in percentage)

Level of Activism	Four-year University or College		Two-year College or Less		Total	
Leaders	50%	(11)	50%	(11)	= 100%	(22)
Regular partic-ipants	56%	(29)	44%	(23)	= 100%	(52)
Intermittent par-ticipants	42%	(11)	58%	(15)	= 100%	(26)
Totals	51%	(51)	49%	(49)	= 100%	(100)

The data presented so far raise the distinct possibility that the level of political interest in the family may be somewhat more important than higher education in explaining women's level of involvement in politics. This conclusion is further supported when we look again at the relationship between family politicization and level of activism, controlling for education (see table 13). The results tend to show that the most active women were somewhat more likely to come from politically interested and aware families, whatever their educational background.

The findings in this section represent but the first steps on the way toward explaining how and why political women—unlike most women—become politically active. As was noted earlier, the balance of forces that shape the political orientations, interest, and behavior of most Japanese is as yet not well understood. More definitive statements comparing the experiences of political women with those of most Japanese await a more comprehensive study with a larger sample that includes activists and nonactivists, and both men and women. This study lays the groundwork, however, by allowing us to rule out various extremes of interpretation and to point out promising areas for further research.

For the group of political women as a whole, there is limited support for either the parental dependence model or the parental independence model as a general explanation for how the women found their way into politics. For the sample as a whole, higher education appears to have figured promi-

TABLE 13 *Relationship between Level of Politicization of Parents and Level of Activism of Political Women, Controlling for Education (in percentage)*

	University-educated			Less-educated*		
Level of Activism	One or Both Parents Interested In Politics	Neither Parent Interested	Total	One or Both Parents Interested in Politics	Neither Parent Interested	Total
Leaders	64%(7)	36%(4)	100%(11)	55%(6)	45%(5)	100%(11)
Regular participants	52%(15)	48%(14)	100%(29)	52%(12)	48%(11)	100%(23)
Intermittent participants	18%(2)	82%(9)	100%(11)	47%(7)	53%(8)	100%(15)
Totals	47%(24)	53%(27)	100%(51)	51%(25)	49%(24)	100%(49)

*Two years of college or less

hently as a factor supporting their entry into political activities, as evidenced by the fact that the overall educational level of the group was extraordinarily high. But there was some evidence to suggest that educational level figured less prominently in shaping the nature of their political involvement than did the family political atmosphere, and this raises serious doubts that their behavior can be explained in the framework of a parental independence model. This in itself is a significant finding, given the importance that a number of scholars attribute to agencies outside the family in the socialization of Japanese people in general and of male activists in particular. On the other hand, the findings at best lend only the most tentative support to the parental dependence model. Half the sample did not have even one parent who was interested in politics, and yet they had somehow found their way into voluntary political activities. Therefore the parental dependence model cannot be offered as a framework for explaining the experiences of the sample as a whole.

What the findings do suggest, however, is that once women make their way into the political arena, the political atmosphere in their homes when they were growing up may have some influence on how far they will go with their activism. Like the conspicuous women activists referred to earlier—the Indira Gandhis, the Eva Perons, and the women legislators in Japan who come from political families—the leaders in the sample appear to have been influenced by a family atmosphere in which political interest and concern was accepted as appropriate and legitimate. In combination with other influences and experiences, their exposure to political cues in the home may have functioned as one type of "special factor" that helped them overcome the numerous constraints that bar most women's passage to higher levels of political activism. This conclusion, it may be added, is consistent with the findings of Jeane Kirkpatrick in her study of political women in the United States. Looking at the parents of women who later became state legislators, she noted that while few had been politicians, their level of political interest and community concern had been high, and that this factor had been significant in setting the stage for their daughters' later political involvement.[28]

28. Kirkpatrick, *Political Woman*, pp. 34–36.

The analysis so far has been concerned with the influence of the family, relative to other agents, in shaping the basic political orientation and behavior of political women. To the extent that the family's role is important in the political socialization experience of the informants, it becomes all the more essential to explore the dynamics within the family by which this influence is transmitted.

The Dynamics of the Family:
Fathers versus Mothers

Studies on political participation in Japan consistently show that political interest is lower among women than men for any given class and geographical background. Because men express greater interest in politics, discuss politics more frequently, and engage in political behavior more frequently, most writers, including Blood, Vogel, Dore, and others who have conducted research on the family in Japan, have concluded that, of the two parents, the father plays the more significant political role.[29] It is easy to go on from there and assume that the father is the primary model for political behavior to a child learning the political role. Since we know that children ordinarily do much of their role learning by observing the same-sex parent, it is especially easy within this framework to understand how a son might learn the political role. For daughters, however, the dynamic is less clear. Do politically active daughters, to the extent that they learn their political orientation and behavioral style within the family, learn them from the more politically aware parent, the father? Or could it be that in the families of daughters who become politically active, the family structure itself is atypical, and that the mother is the more politically interested and aware of the two parents?

To explore this question, the relative levels of political

29. Robert O. Blood, *Love Match and Arranged Marriage* (New York, 1967), pp. 105–107, treats politics as a male specialty area; Vogel, *Japan's New Middle Class*, pp. 96–100, describes wives as less efficacious and less informed than husbands; Ronald P. Dore, *City Life in Japan* (Berkeley and Los Angeles, 1958), pp. 221–228, records women's low level of information relative to men's.

interest and discussion for fathers and mothers were examined. This test made it possible to dismiss the proposition that, overall, the informants' families might be atypical in family structure when it came to politics. According to the reports of the informants, twice as many fathers as mothers were interested in and discussed politics. Next the investigation focused on those cases in which family political influence might be thought highest: where a daughter had adopted the political orientation (conservative or progressive) shared by both her parents. Could it be that in these families, of which there were fifty in the sample, the mother was the more politically interested parent? The answer once again appeared to be negative. In these families, the fathers were almost twice as likely to be interested in politics as the mothers. These findings on the relative levels of political interest for the two parents generally confirmed the father's more conspicuous political role relative to that of the mother. The data, then, initially upheld the view of Vogel, Dore, Blood, and others that politics is a specialty area for fathers within the family unit in Japan and indicated that this is so even in families that produce a politically active daughter.

So far, however, the data have shown nothing about the actual relative *influence* of the two parents on their daughter's political beliefs and behavior. The analysis has dealt only with how daughters perceived their own parents' relative level of political interest. To test for influence, the political orientations of daughters were compared with those of the parents where parents disagreed with each other. There were thirteen sets of such parents in the sample. Here it was found that *in every single case, when parents disagreed over politics, the daughter had sided with the mother.*

To see whether these particular families were different from the others in the relative level of political interest of the parents, the interest levels for mothers and fathers were compared. Despite the fact that daughters had adopted their mother's political orientation over their father's in all thirteen cases, they still reported twice as many fathers as mothers interested in politics. The close parallel between the data in these thirteen cases in which daughters overwhelmingly adopted the mother's orientation over the father's and data for the whole sample indicates, first of all, that these families, at least superficially, do not appear to deviate in major ways from the general pattern. That is, they certainly do not seem to be families in which roles are reversed, with the mother becoming the more politically aware parent. Furthermore, there is the strong suggestion in the data that the father's greater level of political interest and awareness may not have given him the more powerful role when it came to influencing the children, at least his daughters. Finally, there is the possibility that the mother, even when she expresses little overt interest in political matters, may have more direct political influence over her daughters than a more politically aware father.

The general findings of this study on the mother's role in influencing the politics of the young are upheld by recent research conducted on the conjugal power relation in the United States and its effect on politics. Maccoby, Mathews, and Morton in a study issued in 1954 pointed out the importance of the mother's role in influencing the party identification of the offspring, a finding that was recently verified by Langton and Jennings.[30] In a study based on a national probability sample of 1,669 high school seniors in the United States, Langton and Jennings found that when parents disagreed over party affiliation, the children tended to adopt the political orientation of the same-sex parent, but that the tendency was even stronger for girls than for boys. Forty-seven percent of the girls in their sample shared the mother's view, whereas only 39 percent of the boys had adopted the father's orientation.[31] Since the mother's apparent influence on daughters was so noticeably greater than the father's influence on either his daughters or his sons, Langton and Jennings concluded that the mother appeared to be the parent with the edge in influencing the political orientation of the children. The explanation they advanced for this phenomenon is relevant to the present study, for it seems to apply particularly well to Japan, perhaps even more than to the United States. They attributed their result primarily to the psychological makeup of the nuclear family in modern

30. Maccoby, Mathews, and Morton, "Youth and Political Change"; Jennings and Langton, "Mothers versus Fathers."
31. Jennings and Langton, p. 343.

societies, within which children of both sexes spend more time with and feel closer to the mother than the father.[32]

Kubota's and Ward's study, referred to earlier, began the work of investigating whether the same pattern is to be found in Japan. In their two-wave study, they found that the mother's influence was greater in the first wave of the study, but that the father's political orientation tended to prevail in the second wave, conducted just after an election. Kubota and Ward concluded that the father's influence, because of the particular pattern of Japanese politics where *kankei*, or family-determined relations, are important, may be greater at election time, but that in ordinary times the mother's nurturant role in the family may give her somewhat more influence over the politics of young Japanese.[33] Unfortunately, since they did not present their results separately according to the sex of the offspring, their data do not indicate whether daughters, as Langton and Jennings found, were especially close to the political orientation of their mothers. But it can be concluded that within the average Japanese family, as in the American family, the mother's role in influencing the politics of the young probably is much more significant than other indicators (such as her level of political interest) would suggest.

This section has only begun to scratch the surface in exploring the dynamics by which political influence is transmitted within the families of women activists. Research in this important area of inquiry is relatively new. In the absence of data on how the process operates within the usual Japanese family, it is not possible to pursue the investigation on a comparative basis. What is called for is a close examination of the experiences of political women, using case materials collected in Japan. In this way, an attempt will be made in the next chapter to integrate the findings of the study so far, and to offer a more comprehensive view of how and why certain women in Japan become involved in politics.

32. Ibid.
33. Kubota and Ward, "Family Influence," pp. 160–161.

5

Becoming Politically Active:
The Dynamics of Change

A variety of influences in the life of the individual woman affect her adult political behavior. The basic political orientation of the parents, the level of political interest in the family, and many other variables directly related to political behavior and belief bear on the process of becoming a political being in adulthood, as do many influences that operate more indirectly.[1] How any given variable operates alone or in

1. For the distinction between direct and indirect influences in the process of acquiring political behavior patterns and attitudes, see Richard E. Dawson and Kenneth Prewitt, *Political Socialization* (Boston, 1969), pp. 63–80. Direct influences transmit learning that is specifically political (e.g., family political orientations and attitudes are transmitted to the child). Indirect influences lead to attitudes and behaviors that are not explicitly political, but that later on may influence political behavior and attitudes (e.g., family structure variables may affect a person's adult political style).

concert with others—that is, the dynamics of the process—is little understood. How the myriad influences that bear on political socialization combine in the experience of the individual is understood even less. Using interview data, the task of this chapter is to piece together the process by which political women, unlike most women, emerged from childhood and adolescence into young adulthood as political activists, and to offer a theory of growth and change to explain why they came to be different from most women.

The analysis offered in the two preceding chapters has laid the groundwork for the inquiry. Chapter four explored a number of variables that operate more directly on women's choice of politics as an outlet for self-expression. Generally speaking, the chapter turned up little evidence to indicate that political women acquire their interest in politics from a balance of forces different in fundamental ways from the one that operates in the lives of most young Japanese and in the lives of male activists studied to date. Distinguishing factors appeared to operate primarily in the experience of those women who had sought higher levels of political involvement. Like the political women in the United States studied by Kirkpatrick,[2] the leaders in the sample had come disproportionately from a family environment marked by a concern for social and political issues. For the sample as a whole, there was also evidence that pointed to a particularly important role that mothers may play in the political socialization of activist daughters, even when those same mothers are thought by their daughters to have little interest in politics. Perhaps the larger finding of the chapter, however, is that for understanding how and why individual women—unlike most women—make their way into political life, the kinds of questions asked by those who study political socialization do not offer more than a preliminary glimpse into a complex process of personal change.

Focusing on influences that operate more indirectly in the experience of political women, chapter three dealt with some of the larger social forces at work in postwar Japan that support role change in women. New opportunities in higher education, greater flexibility in male-female relations, various new work options, and other new life possibilities create a

2. Jeane Kirkpatrick, *Political Woman* (New York, 1974), pp. 34–36.

setting in which change in women's notions of self and role can occur. As chapter three showed, 80 percent of the political women in the study had moved toward new conceptions of woman's role and had engaged in various forms of role experimentation before becoming politically active. Role change, then, loomed as a major step in the process by which certain women, unlike most women, became open to the possibility of becoming involved in politics.

How these various factors combine in the experience of political women will be explored shortly. In the analysis, the relation between role change and other, more immediate factors that direct women's entry into politics is the central focus. However, before proceeding with the analysis, I must clarify a major point. Although role change was a key step in the process in 80 percent of the sample, 20 percent, it will be recalled, had views of woman's role that had not changed prior to their entry into politics. These latter women continued to support a Neotraditional role ideology that most Japanese women see as precluding the possibility of becoming involved in politics, at least for women in the age range for this study. Before proceeding with the analysis of the experiences of the majority of the sample, it is important that I take up the unfinished business of chapter three and explain how these Neotraditionalist women had found their way into politics.

Neotraditional Activism: Politics without Role Change

Some of the best spokeswomen for the Neotraditionalist view were to be found in the ranks of the Liberal Democratic Party, the conservative party in power in Japan today. This should come as no surprise. The LDP in its philosophy and in its policy pronouncements has stood in proud and open support of traditional Japanese strengths and virtues as represented in the family system at whose center is the nurturing wife and mother. The LDP view of woman's role was stated eloquently and unequivocally in an interview with a policy spokesman at party headquarters in Tokyo.

Asked what were the main problems Japanese women face today, he replied as follows:

> Women today really face four different problems, depending on the stage of their lives. A woman's first problem comes when she is pregnant: how to protect her health so that her baby will be strong and healthy. The second problem comes in the years before the child enters school: she must make sure that the child gets good training in his early years. The third problem is the one that arises once the child is in school: she must educate him at home so that he can succeed in the entrance examinations. Her last big problem comes when her child grows up. She must make sure that her son finds a good job and a wife to take care of him, and that her daughter becomes a good *oyome-san* [bride].[3]

These words, so reminiscent of the traditional view that women function in this world primarily to bear the future generation, constitute an eloquent statement of the Neotraditional view of woman's role as set out earlier. Little wonder that a party with such a strong commitment to the traditional view of woman's role should provide a comfortable environment for women who see child bearing and nurturing as their main life function. But to say this begs the question. Why is it that Neotraditional women are attracted to politics at all? Most women in today's Japan who hold a Neotraditional view of woman's role define that role in a way that excludes the possibility of such "unfeminine" ventures as active political participation. Traditional party organizations like the LDP themselves support an ideology of woman's role that would seem to exclude a woman's active political participation. And yet women take part in their activities. Under what circumstances *do* women become active in such organizations?

A woman whose experience provided a basis for answering all these questions was Takenaka Keiko, an LDP follower who was the twenty-seven-year-old wife of an elected representative to the city council of a medium-sized city near Osaka. Impeccably dressed in a pink knit suit, Keiko was accompanied to the interview, which took place in a quiet corner of the lobby of a major Osaka hotel, by her politician

3. Interview with Murakawa Ichirō, staff member, Policy Board, Liberal Democratic Party, Party Headquarters, Tokyo, March 17, 1972.

husband, a heavy-set man some ten years her senior, and by a woman well into her fifties whom the husband introduced as the head of his support group *(kōenkai)*. Councilman Takenaka told me amiably that he had come along to answer any "hard political questions" I might put to his wife. He assured me that Keiko followed him completely in matters of policy. She softly concurred and was preparing to settle into a role as spectator when I stated my desire to talk to her alone. The councilman and both of the women were dismayed. Keiko searched her husband's face anxiously, awaiting his decision. Then, after a pause, the politician agreed to my request, under the condition that Mrs. Matsumura, the *kōenkai* head, be allowed to remain to help out. He then retired to the hotel bar from which he occasionally emerged during the interview, gazing over at the three of us with undisguised curiosity and concern.

Keiko said that she had met her husband in Tokyo while working as a secretary for a noted LDP politician, a job she had obtained through family political connections. Keiko herself was the daughter of an LDP official prominent in her area of the country far from Tokyo. Now, six years and two children after her marriage, she was first and foremost a politician's wife, actively engaged in politics for the man she married. The year before the interview, when her husband had come up for reelection, she had made the rounds of constituents' houses during the day, cultivating the good relations that lead to success in the electoral politics of Japan; she had accompanied her husband when he made speeches, and had herself given numerous speeches in his support. With the election behind her, she had become active in the national and local branches of the Women's Bureau of the LDP.

There is no question that by any objective standards, Takenaka Keiko was a political activist. But it is clear that her political participation, like that of most other Neotraditionalists interviewed, had unique elements. Her activism was circumscribed by numerous conditions that do not apply under most people's definition of a political activist. First, while most people think of a political activist as an individual who has entered politics out of his or her personal convictions as an autonomous entity, the Neotraditional activist was usually in politics with the explicit approval of an individual or individuals she regarded as authority figures in her life, almost always male. Furthermore, all evidence suggested that this approval was a precondition of her entry into the political sphere. In some cases, like that of Keiko, the authority figure was a husband; in others, he was a father, a brother, or in several cases, a boyfriend. But almost every woman holding a Neotraditional view of woman's role appeared to have entered politics only where her entry was "legitimized" by such an authority figure.

Second, the Neotraditionalist activist tended to treat her political activism as an extension of other kinds of obligations she felt toward this individual, which were dictated by the terms of the dominant definition of woman's role. Typically, the Neotraditional woman had become involved in politics only when a man who was politically active urged that she participate. Her political activity was then wholly acceptable under the traditional formula for being a good wife, a good daughter, or a loyal follower. This is not to say that Neotraditionalists themselves were not interested in politics. There was no doubt that many were, whatever their original motives for becoming active. But it was highly characteristic of the Neotraditionalists who were interviewed for the study that they saw political activism as normally out of bounds for women and permissible for them only because it was consonant with the role demands placed on them by the principal males in their lives.

Finally, since most Neotraditionalists had entered politics at their husband's or father's bidding and saw their political duties mainly as an extension of wifely or daughterly duties, it followed that their primary political loyalty was attached to individuals rather than to ideologies or causes. Sometimes the Neotraditionalist woman gave her allegiance directly to the individual concerned, as did Mrs. Takenaka. Many other women's loyalty might extend, at least for a time, to the political cause, party, or ideology the male supported. However, because of the personal nature of the allegiance, it followed that the political commitment itself was closely tied to the changing political position or ideology of the person who served as a legitimizing agent for her own political involvement. If his political views changed, it was very likely that she would follow him to the new position and see it as incumbent upon herself to do so. If he terminated his political affiliations or involvement and urged her to do likewise, the Neotraditionalist generally saw her decision as a foregone conclusion.

Most Neotraditionalists participated in politics more or less under the conditions just described. A few denied that they obtained, or downgraded their importance, but most defended the conditions as natural and legitimate. Several of the latter were surprised when I told them of married American women who joined in political party activities on their own. Mrs. Matsumura remarked, shaking her head, "Japanese husbands haven't gotten to that stage yet." She told me that the membership of the candidate support group she headed was made up exclusively of family units. Often wives took part in political functions as representatives of their family. But a married woman would never join on her own. Most Neotraditionalists did not hesitate to say that they were in politics to serve the interests of politically active husbands or fathers, or to further a political cause to which their family as a unit was committed. Since they legitimized their political participation under traditional definitions of woman's role, their notions of that role itself remained unchanged. That husbands and fathers of Neotraditionalists saw things the same way was indicated in a comment of Mrs. Takenaka. Asked how Councilman Takenaka would feel if she took part in other kinds of activities outside the home beside those relating to politics, her answer came matter-of-factly: "He'd be opposed. If I do things outside the home to help him politically, then he's very pleased. But if I did things out of my own interest, he'd object."

Keiko appeared to derive considerable satisfaction from political activity through which she expressed her loyalty to her husband. Asked about her future, she talked of her husband's future plans and ambitions rather than any plans of her own. Her ambitions for her daughter were in the same vein. She expressed the hope that her daughter, five years old at the time of the interview, would someday become her husband's secretary.

Neotraditional activists tended to be concentrated in the political parties and unions of Japan, rather than in newer and more informal political groups that have appeared in postwar Japanese society. Structural barriers within such organizations constrain women's possibilities for participation on an equal basis and press women toward the performance of support functions that are more compatible with the dominant view of woman's role. This is true, although to a lesser extent, even within parties and unions with a guiding ideology of Marxism, with its emphasis on egalitarianism.[4] Although such organizations acknowledge, even herald, woman's equality in principle, in practice the leadership generally assumes that key positions of any kind will be held by men, unless the position specifically falls in the domain of "women's affairs."[5] A number of structural features of large organizations dictate this pattern: a hierarchical structure, a leadership core usually made up of older-generation men who hold the Neotraditional—or even a more traditional—view of woman's role, and the greater stakes (in terms of money or power) attached to holding positions of power in large organizations.[6]

All these features of large organizations combine to make them a comfortable haven for Neotraditional activists. However, since the Neotraditional activist's political commitment is almost always tied to her allegiance to a male, she can also be found in other types of political groups in Japan, including groups in which her role ideology is challenged by many of the other members, male and female. A good example is provided in the experiences of Masuda Yōko, one of the two

4. The greater support of parties of the Left for women's political roles was noted long ago by Duverger. Maurice Duverger, *The Political Role of Women* (Paris, 1955). A nine-nation study conducted in Europe in 1975 has upheld this view. Overall, electorates of the Left were much more favorable to women's participation in politics than were supporters of middle-of-the-road or conservative parties. The study concluded that "the Left tends to be change-oriented in this, as in other respects." Margaret Inglehart and Ronald Inglehart, "Women's Role in Society: Public Attitudes in the European Community," unpublished paper, n.d., p. 14.

5. At LDP headquarters in Tokyo in 1972, however, even the Women's Division was headed by a man.

6. Such structural variables have been found to dictate division of labor by sex in many large organization settings. Rosabeth Moss Kanter, "Women and Hierarchies," paper presented at the Annual Meeting of the American Sociological Association, San Francisco, 1975. Also see her *Women and Organizations* (Englewood Cliffs, N.J., 1976). The effects of group structural characteristics on women's political participation in Japan are discussed further in Appendix A.

Neotraditional activists in the study who had joined sects in the highly radical, ideologically oriented student movement. Yōko, a delicately built woman of twenty-four, was a full-time housewife at the time she was interviewed for the study. Three years earlier, she had been a student at a prominent, conservative women's college in Tokyo, which is attended by many young women from upper-middle-class families. In the excitement of the 1968 period in Tokyo when the student movement was at its height, Yōko had accompanied some classmates to a rally organized by the Revolutionary Faction (Kakumaru-ha) at Tokyo University.[7] There she met Shimura Hajime, a young law major of Tōdai who was a leader of the radical sect. She was overwhelmed by his dynamism and sincerity, she told me, reminiscing. He took her out, and she listened many hours to his account of what was happening at the University and of what his sect was attempting to achieve. He urged her to come to meetings. The Revolutionary Faction, he told her, was going to unite the students and the workers, and there was a place for her in the group.

Soon Yōko was attending meetings, pouring the tea, and preparing rice balls for the next day's demonstrations.[8] She was uncomfortable in the presence of the many women in the sect who spurned these tasks and who joined in discussions of ideology and tactics. Yōko felt a dread of physical combat, but once, at Hajime's insistence, she took part in the charge against the riot police. She was well on the inside of the charge, protected on every side by the group's male members, but she was terrified and felt physically ill afterwards. She never again took part in demonstrations, but continued

7. For accounts of the student struggle at the University of Tokyo in the period 1968–69, see Kazuko Tsurumi, "Student Movements in 1960 and 1969," *Research Papers of the Institute of International Relations*, Sophia University, Series A-5 (Tokyo, 1972) and Institute of Newspaper Research of the University of Tokyo, *Tōdai funsō no kiroku* (Record of struggle at University of Tokyo) (Tokyo, 1969).

8. Although sandwiches are popular for lunches and snacks in Japan, many Japanese prefer rice balls made of sticky rice that has been molded into oblong, thumb-sized shapes and stuffed with bits of pickles or fish. Political groups that are taking part in demonstrations frequently subsist on such snacks, the preparation of which typically falls to the women members. A number of informants in student political sects said that they resented being asked to perform this time-consuming task, especially when the group was in the midst of preparing psychologically for a demonstration.

to cook, sweep, and clean behind the barricades of Tokyo University for the rest of the long dispute.

Yōko's upper-middle-class, affluent parents attempted to persuade her to give up her relationship with Hajime. Their objections were not so much to his politics or to their daughter's political involvement. Indeed, they felt that a Tokyo law major from a good family had much to recommend him, and they did not take their daughter's new political allegiance seriously. Their objections were the traditional ones that concern many parents in modern Japan, and in most societies today. They feared that the young man, having "used" their daughter sexually, would back out when it came to marriage and leave her with a bad reputation.

Faced with her parents' objections and warnings, Yōko pressed Hajime into marriage. At the time she was interviewed, she was keeping their tiny apartment full time. Her husband remained active in his group and committed to its ideology. Scorning his Tokyo University law degree and the successful career it guarantees so many men in Japanese society, he had joined the counterculture and had become a blue-collar worker. As a married man, following the traditional view of marriage, he no longer insisted that Yōko take part in his political activities. Thus with some relief Yōko had retired from a movement to which she had given much of her time and energies over a two-year period, but in which she had little personal interest and to which she had virtually no ideological commitment.[9]

To describe a Neotraditional activist like Keiko or Yōko as an individual who blindly follows a primary figure in her life into political activities and continues to participate in politics only at his bidding is, of course, an overstatement that distorts the reality of the complex set of psychological and sociological factors that guide human behavior. Many Neotraditional informants who had taken up a political role were

9. Neotraditional political women in radical sects have drawn much attention in the press. One popular story in 1972 was that of Mochihara Yoshiko, a former geisha who met a prominent Red Army activist. She worked in the kitchen of the group's hideout, scouted banks that were to be held up by the Red Army, and transported weapons. Arrested, she was an obedient prisoner who was "deeply repentant for her past actions." "Sekigun geisha" (Red Army geisha), *Josei Jishin*, 1 (May 1972): 29–31.

obviously deriving satisfactions from political participation above and beyond the satisfactions of meeting the expectations of a husband, a boyfriend, or a father. It was clear that the promptings of a husband or a father had propelled several Neotraditional women into a type of activity that had strong attractions for them. Indeed, one could ask an even more fundamental question, when a woman had gone into politics at the instigation of a boyfriend or a husband, of why people are attracted to certain individuals as love objects. Perhaps part of the original attraction Yōko and other Neotraditional activists felt for the men in their lives lay in the demands the men placed on them to share their activities, which made it possible for these women to enter forms of activity that they would not have had the courage to undertake alone. With his support and urgings, this husband, brother, or lover gave them an unassailable traditional rationale for their political activism. It is not assumed here that the Neotraditionalists' motives for political participation are simple ones.

In distinguishing the political experience of the Neotraditionalist activists from that of the majority of women in the sample who articulated new views of woman's role, the key factor is the highly conditional nature of the political role they adopt. Whatever unconscious needs may have been satisfied by their entry into politics, the Neotraditionalist participated only when certain conditions were met, conditions that did not obtain for informants with the other two role ideologies described earlier and, significant for our purposes, conditions that are only rarely met in Japan. Relatively few women are from political families that might urge a daughter to help her father with his campaign for elective office. Relatively few Japanese women marry career politicians who need their help. Only a few women become involved with student activists or other men who are so committed to a political cause that they cannot rest until those close to them join it also. Furthermore, among women in the age range for this study, few would be asked by their husbands to play a "family delegate role" that brings many older Neotraditionalists into politics. As chapter six will show, the role expectations brought to bear on women in the early adult years normally preclude that possibility, even though they may permit it later on in a woman's life cycle.

Political science theory to date provides relatively little basis for understanding the political participation of the Neotraditionalist activist. Most writers take into account personal loyalty bonds between leaders and followers and acknowledge the importance of charisma as a force in politics. But the starting point of most analyses of why individuals participate in politics is the autonomous actor whose political behavior and ideology can be analyzed using variables relating to personality, life experiences, and intrapsychic processes. It is possible, of course, to offer a psychological explanation for the conduct of the Neotraditional woman in politics. Some might argue that her political participation satisfies dependency needs. Certainly the same behavior in a man would probably be interpreted as overdependent and possibly neurotic. It should be borne in mind, however, that for women in Japan, dependent conduct is the behavioral norm in all the roles they play vis-a-vis men.[10] A psychological explanation for the conduct of a woman who follows her brother, husband, lover, or father into politics and gives herself over to a political cause in the name of personal loyalty appears less useful than a sociological explanation that takes into account traditional role expectations for woman's behavior. The political activism of the Neotraditional woman traces its roots back to the nature of the male-female relationship in Japan and its particular requisites.

It is possible, then, for women to become involved in politics without changing their view of woman's role before or after entering politics. But as was shown, the Neotraditional woman's activism entails special conditions that do not obtain for most women. Indeed, the conditions are so special and extraordinary that it is little wonder that so few Neotraditionalists in Japan are active in politics. The analysis just offered explains the non-participation as well as it explains the participation of the great majority of women today who hold the Neotraditional view.

10. Research findings on a U.S. sample by Kagan and Moss support the view that dependent behavior not only is more common in women than in men, but is less likely in women to be linked with neurotic symptoms. Jerome Kagan and Howard A. Moss, "The Stability of Passive and Dependent Behavior from Childhood through Adulthood," *Child Development* 31 (September 1960): 577–591, especially p. 581.

Role Change and Activism:
Toward a Two-Stage Theory of Change

For the majority of political women included in the study, the "special conditions" discussed above were not in effect. These women had adopted alternative ideologies of woman's role that rejected the notion that women's active political participation had to be legitimized in that way. Unlike most of the Neotraditionalists in the sample, New Women and Radical Egalitarians were indignant or angered at the notion that a woman might alter her political views to follow a man's because of her personal loyalty to him. They saw their political commitment, not as an extension of their duties as women to primary figures in their lives, but as a separate category of activity that they had undertaken as adults.

From the discussion by these women of how and why they had become politically active, it gradually became clear that two distinct stages in an overall process were involved. During one stage, the women had become attracted to politics and had taken steps toward active political involvement. This stage, however, was preceded by a stage during which role change, the fundamental precondition to their activism, had occurred. These processes were clearly interrelated, and at different points had been affected by identical agencies and experiences. In certain cases, the processes proceeded simultaneously rather than sequentially. The contribution of each, however, was distinct. The first process, involving role change, culminated in the emergence of an adult woman who was open to the possibility of engaging in behavior outside the normal bounds of appropriate female behavior. Through gradual changes in her conception of self and role, she had become receptive to, and in fact had engaged in, role experimentation in areas other than politics prior to her entry into politics. Here the reference is to the many different types of role experimentation discussed in chapter three: attending a four-year university, majoring in a "men's" field, continuing a job after marriage, seeking a part-time job (a married woman with small children in a family that did not need the money), living with a man outside marriage, and so on.

The end product of the second process is a woman who is

attracted to politics per se as a forum for self-expression. Unlike the majority of women in Japan, who see active political participation as out of bounds for them, this woman has come to view politics as a viable option. The dynamics of each process will now be explored in turn.

Steps Toward Role Change / In the mind's eye of most Japanese parents, boys file into the work world, and girls, into the home, just as surely as if a great wall divided their adult spheres. When it became apparent, from interviewing women activists, that some degree of role change generally had preceded their entry into politics, a major question was whether their parents' attitudes toward woman's role might have been different from those of the majority of parents. The logical place to begin an investigation of this matter was with the activists' mothers. Few mothers were politically active themselves, but it was possible that they were unusual in some other way and that they had engaged in their own types of role experimentation in areas of activity other than politics. Were they women who, even in growing up in a prewar world of limited opportunities for women, had become career women, had traveled extensively, or had been among the select few to attend college? Since the mother is a daughter's model for so much behavior relating to woman's role, any such pattern in the life experiences of activists' mothers would go a long way toward explaining the learning process behind activists' adoption of an alternative view of woman's role.[11]

The search for such a pattern was soon abandoned, however. In the majority of cases, the informants' mothers had led lives that were singularly unmarked by noteworthy or unusual events. Only a few mothers had attended college; none had graduated. Except for a few elementary-school

11. The findings of a number of studies point toward a close relationship between characteristics of mothers (e.g., work experience) and gender-role attitudes and behavior on the part of daughters. See A. E. Siegel, et al., "Dependence and Independence in the Children of Working Mothers," *Child Development* 4 (1959); Per Olav Tiller, "Parental Role Division and the Child's Personality Development," in *The Changing Roles of Men and Women*, ed. Edmund Dahlstrom (Boston, 1962), p. 99. Both studies suggest that daughters of working mothers show greater independence and have greater freedom to experiment with nontraditional female behavior.

teachers and nurses among them, the mothers who had worked had thought of their job in a way that was consistent with the traditional or Neotraditional woman's view of work. They had sought work only when the income was needed and when their husband or father had approved. Not a single political woman had a mother who could be considered a "career woman." Few mothers had ever traveled outside Japan. Objectively, then, there was little about the mothers to suggest that they presented themselves as unusual role models to activist daughters.[12]

Furthermore, when asked directly whether their mother had challenged dominant prescriptions for how women should conduct their lives, political women in most cases said no. Asked what ambitions their mothers had had for them, most activists gave similar replies. Their mothers had wanted them to follow "the usual course" (heibon), and to become wives and mothers. Few mothers, as described by their daughters, would be regarded as social critics, outspoken dissenters from current social prescriptions for what life should hold in store for the adult woman. Nor had they urged daughters toward the single life, spurred them toward adopting a career, or encouraged them to believe that a woman could be anything she wanted to be—wife, mother, and worker in a happy and successful combination. On the whole, they were mothers who accepted current social prescriptions.

Attention then focused on the activists' fathers. If their mothers had not served as role models for new styles of behavior, it was possible that the father had been the parent who was supportive of role change. Could it be that activists' fathers were men who were unusually close to their daughters and who might have been supporters of an alternative ideology of woman's role? Although, as will be explored shortly, it was clear that the fathers had played important roles in an overall process of change and were often the role

12. This finding parallels Kirkpatrick's on women state legislators in the United States. Only a relatively small percentage (13 percent) of their mothers were college graduates; economic need had been the primary motivation when they had worked; and few mothers had "provided their daughters with a model of feminine professional achievement." Kirkpatrick, *Political Woman*, p. 32.

model for their daughters' political behavior, there generally was little evidence that they had been active sponsors of their daughters' role experimentation. Nor was there any obvious basis for concluding that the typical political woman had had an unusually close relationship with her father. Overwhelmingly, political women reported that they felt closer to their mothers than to their fathers. Asked whom they had talked to in their teens about school-work, boyfriends and sex, money that they needed, future educational plans, and other plans for the future, most reported that the mother was the parent to whom they had taken all these problems. Any speculation that there might have been some type of specialization in the family, with daughters going to their mothers to discuss "women's matters" (boyfriends and sex, marriage plans) and to their fathers to discuss problems and decisions that were linked to role experimentation (educational plans, work options, and plans relating to political participation), was not borne out. Political women had gone to their mothers rather than their fathers, regardless of the nature of the issue or problem. Most fathers, according to political women's accounts, either were harder to talk to or were not around when their daughters had problems that they wanted to take to a parent.

It was still possible, of course, that political women's fathers might have been critical of the dominant view of woman's role and might have provided support from the sidelines as their daughters began to challenge that view, even if they were consulted less often than mothers. Several such fathers did surface in the interviews. One activist initially reported that her father had wanted her to follow "the usual course." But when asked what "the usual course" consisted of, she answered in surprise, "Why, to succeed on the entrance exams, to get into Tokyo University, and then to get a good job in a company." This father, however, was the exception. Overall, the activists reported that their fathers had had traditional expectations for them as women. When the political women were asked to describe what each parent had felt about a whole range of conduct relating to women's role performance (e.g., whether it was all right for a woman to continue working after she married; whether it was all right for her to have outside interests if she had small children),

their responses indicated that their mother had had views
that were more flexible. Most parents had upheld the Neotraditional ideology of woman's role, but the fathers had been
stricter constructionists than the mothers. It was difficult,
then, to find the source of support for role change either in
the role attitudes of the father or in an unusually close
father-daughter relationship that might have led activists to
turn away from the feminine role model offered by their
mothers.

As the investigation proceeded, however, two key patterns
began to emerge in the relations between daughters and parents, which bore closely on the type of women their
daughters later became, and that appeared to function in
support of role change. First, it was apparent that many parents, despite their verbal disapproval of many types of role
experimentation engaged in by their daughters, had indirectly conveyed a contradictory message to their daughters
that in effect had encouraged role experimentation. The parent offering this support was usually the mother, and the
support itself arose in the context of an extraordinarily close
affective tie between mother and daughter. The dynamics
through which the support was conveyed will be discussed
shortly. A second pattern was one whereby the parents of
political women had offered a wide degree of latitude to their
daughters for personal growth and change, even though they
had not actively directed the change. In the literature of political socialization, the pattern referred to here is one of parental permissiveness, which has frequently been found to be
associated with political activism among young people.[13] But
the term "permissiveness" does not convey the content of the
possible outcomes of permissiveness in the case of daughters.
In a society in which there are several competing views for
how women should behave, "parental permissiveness"
makes it possible for women to experiment with the role op-

13. See Richard Flacks, "The Revolt of the Advantaged: Exploration of the
Roots of Student Protest," in *Learning About Politics*, ed. Roberta S. Sigel
(New York, 1970), pp. 186–188; Kenneth Keniston, *Young Radicals* (New
York, 1968), pp. 306–310. Krauss found that permissiveness also characterized the family backgrounds (and especially the mothers' orientation) of
male activists in Japan. Ellis S. Krauss, *Japanese Radicals Revisited* (Berkeley
and Los Angeles, 1974), pp. 40–41.

tions before them and to challenge the dominant prescription for feminine behavior. Parental permissiveness thus may function specifically in support of role change for women.

These two patterns provided a psychological basis for role experimentation. But a third factor enters here. For the existence of such patterns hardly means that role change will take place automatically. They provide the dynamic, not the opportunity. If society had not offered political women multiple outlets for experimenting with woman's role, it is unlikely that change of a magnitude sufficient to propel them into politics would have occurred. But as chapter three indicated, the occupation, urbanization, prosperity, and other forces have combined to produce a setting in postwar Japan in which a wide range of options and possibilities are available to women. Even if customs and attitudes are not fully in support of women's entry into new areas, there are legal guarantees that permit role experimentation. Contemporary Japan thus provides the laboratory in which role change for women can occur.

In combination, the three factors discussed in this section go a long way toward explaining the conditions under which political women's views of woman's role had changed. The next step is to show how the process of role experimentation, once set in motion, led ultimately to the political arena.

Steps Toward Activism / Many of the steps in the process by which individuals become attracted to political groups or causes are the same for all activists, male or female. The influence of admired and respected friends, personal contact with a political event, candidate, or leader, and other situational variables could be seen at work in the process by which political women had become active in politics.[14] Their entry into politics had often been supported by historical accident—being in the right place at the right time. De-

14. See Davies for a discussion of the importance of situational factors as a context for political activism. He distinguishes between "mediated, distal influences" (i.e., influences in the wider environment) and "proximal mediating influences" (i.e., "direct, affect-laden contacts with specific events and specific individuals"), which, in combination, create the setting in which a person may become politically active. James C. Davies, "Where From and Where To?" in *Handbook of Political Psychology* (San Francisco, 1973), p. 14.

velopments in postwar Japan provided many settings that have swept up substantial numbers of people into political causes. Women who were on university campuses during peak periods of the student movement, who were working in companies during periods when unions were being formed or were especially active, who as young married women moved into neighborhoods in which many housewives were involved in antipollution groups or consumer protection movements, or who were coming into young adulthood in the early 1970s when women's movements in Japan and abroad were attracting considerable attention in the press, all were exposed to strong situational cues in support of their activism. Similarly, the political interest of these women —like that of political men exposed to a similar home environment—was supported by whatever level of political interest existed in their particular families.

None of these factors in the more immediate home environment or in the wider social and political environment of Japan explain why a woman would respond to these cues, however, when doing so would require her to cross into an area of activity regarded as the preserve of men.

How society views women's active participation in political groups can be seen in the objections that political women's parents had raised before, during, or after their entry into politics, all of which were rooted in the dominant view of woman's role. For unmarried women, the most common objection was that involvement in politics compromised their femininity and would hurt their marriage chances.

Specific parental objections on these grounds were numerous. One aspect was a feeling that their daughters were becoming too serious. Several political women reported that their parents—generally their fathers—had seen their interest in politics and liking for political discussion and debate as *kawaisō, or pitiful.* Women, according to this view, should be soft and romantic, not hard and serious. Another related objection was that their daughters would become too self-assertive and thus be deemed unmanageable by a prospective mate. Self-assertiveness in unmarried women was objected to on other grounds as well. A number of parents—again, more commonly the father—appeared to see a daughter's entry into politics as a challenge to his authority as family head to dictate the family's political positions. When political women had become leaders of their groups, they were sometimes criticized by their fathers for becoming conceited or self-centered; they were urged to be more modest and self-deprecating. As one father reportedly told his daughter, a leader of a student sect: "Don't become so prominent (*erai*), otherwise you'll get further and further away from me. You're a woman, and it's much better for you to play yourself down and to act more humble."

For married women, the objections were in a different vein. Even when married women did not have children and had substantial amounts of free time, their parents expressed concern that their daughter's involvement in activities outside marriage would be taken as a sign of marital discontent and that marriage was not enough to satisfy her. Parents of unmarried and married political women alike had voiced still another type of objection, which grew out of the Neotraditional belief that because of fundamental biological differences between men and women, women lack the stamina to be politically active. Thus parents warned their daughters that women were too weak to take part in electoral campaigning or demonstrations, that political involvement was too tiring for a woman, and that they would ruin their health. One mother's comment to her daughter, a union activist in her mid-twenties, was typical: "You'll exhaust yourself. You'd better stop."

Political women consistently reported that these types of objections had been raised by their parents—as well as by many other people—at some stage of their becoming politically active. Faced with such objections, most women, even if they were exposed to types of situational cues referred to earlier, would hardly be prepared to venture into politics. Why, then, were the informants different? Two questions loomed large. First, it was important to locate the sources of support for a woman's entry into such a forbidden area of activity. Second, if the behavior required of women who play a political role is so antithetical to the attributes associated with woman's role—as the parental objections discussed above indicated—where had the political women in the study learned it? Who had been their role models?

From the outset of the interviews it was apparent that parental attitudes toward a daughter's political activism were extremely complex. On the one hand, again and again they were reported to have raised verbal objections to their daughters' political involvement. On the other hand, they appeared to be communicating a different message, expressed much more subtly and indirectly, which extended *support* support to their daughters' experimentation with political roles. Typically, the mother had provided the support, although in a small number of cases it had come from the father, an older sibling, or a grandparent. For a few women several family members had provided the support. However, almost all political women had had at least tacit support for their activism communicated to them in the family circle. The dynamic underlying this will be discussed shortly.

In addition, a role model for the women's creation of a political self generally could be found in the family. Usually the model was the father. Sometimes it was an older brother. In a very few cases, it was a person outside the family, such as a high school teacher or a respected older classmate. Typically, the role model was a male who enjoyed leading others, who liked discussing or debating issues, political or nonpolitical, who felt a strong sense of outrage at social injustice, or who, in some way, had particular characteristics that were repeated in the political woman's own style of political behavior or in her type of political concerns.

The male had not usually been an active teacher of the political role. As was indicated earlier, fathers were typically more conservative constructionists of appropriate female behavior than mothers, and thus they appeared to be less willing to encourage their daughters' experimentation in the political role or outside of it. When the father had played a more active role in sponsoring role change or encouraging her interest in politics, there were often special family structural *fam.* characteristics. Relevant to all the support patterns discussed so far, it was remarkable to find that a substantial number of political women in the sample were from families in which there were no sons. Twenty-six out of one hundred political women had come from such families, which is well above the expected rate. In families like these, daughters fell heir to the kind of support for achievement that normally would have been conferred on a son.[15] In these "son-less" families, both parents had encouraged role change, and the father was much more likely to be an active teacher of the political role than in families in which there were sons. Other families in which fathers had played a more active sponsoring or teaching role were those of political women whose natural mother had died and whose father, after remarriage, had forged a close relation with his daughter, which functioned in support of role change.

It may be added that although most role models were male, many political women expressed strong feelings of esteem for and identification with women political leaders in Japan or abroad who may have served as secondary role models in an overall learning process. Noted Japanese women, such as Ichikawa Fusae, Hiratsuka Raichō, Tanaka Sumiko, and foreign women, such as Agnes Smedley, Eleanor Roosevelt, Gloria Steinem, Angela Davis, and Simone de Beauvoir were deeply admired by many of the informants, who were faithful readers of their books and biographies.[16]

MENTION FEM JPN WOMEN As ROLE MODELS.

15. Any number of studies conducted in the United States point up the importance of variables in family structure in shaping women's career and life expectations. See Alice Rossi, "Naming Children in Middle-Class Families," *American Sociological Review* 30 (August 1965): 499–513; also see Kenneth Kammeyer, "Birth Order and the Feminine Sex Role Among College Women," *American Sociological Review* 31 (August 1966): 508–515. Epstein also treats that subject: see Cynthia Fuchs Epstein, *Woman's Place: Options and Limits in Professional Careers* (Berkeley and Los Angeles, 1970). Most of the work so far has explored the effects on women from (a) being an only child (see Epstein, p. 78) or (b) being a first-born as opposed to a second-born female child in families where there are also sons (see Rossi and Kammeyer). Their findings, then, are not precisely applicable to the cases of daughters in families where there are other children but no sons. However, the implication of most of these studies is that when there are no sons for parents to look to for achievement, there is a greater likelihood that daughters will be pushed toward achievement. Note, for example, Rossi's finding that "[a] first-born girl may develop the same characteristics as a first-born boy—the social-psychological traits of a relatively dominant, responsible, highly motivated person, predisposed to educational success" (p. 507).

16. Ichikawa Fusae and Hiratsuka Raichō are discussed in chapter two; Tanaka Sumiko is a prominent Socialist member of the Diet (see Appendix A). Agnes Smedley (1892–1950), Missouri-born journalist and author from a poor family who took part in both the Indian nationalist movement and the Chinese revolution, is perhaps better known in Japan than in the United States. The only major biography of her life was written by a Japanese:

The process of imitating role models other than the mother for significant aspects of their adult behavior was complex. The typical pattern was one in which political women's mothers, for reasons to be discussed shortly, appeared to have de-selected themselves as role models for much of their daughters' behavior, conveying indirectly what one mother said openly to her activist daughter: "Don't imitate me." Typically, however, this de-selection occurred in the context of an extremely close mother-daughter relationship.

This section has described two separate but interrelated processes that direct women toward new styles of behavior and that eventually provide them with a psychological basis for crossing the threshold into political activism. How these processes operate and some of the dynamics underlying them will now be explored more fully in the examination of a case history.

Suzuki Kimiko:
Portrait of a Political Woman

Most major Japanese universities have within them a special breed of highly committed student activists who linger on long past the normal four years it takes to graduate in Japan. For most such activists, their political faction has become the pivot of their daily life at school, the center of their interests and concerns. Many eschew classes or drop in only occasionally to challenge the professor's lecture. Seated in a favored coffee shop, the group's campus meeting room, or occasionally in a member's small apartment, these doyens of activism groom the younger members of the faction, lead the discussion, and map the group's strategy. They are the driving force behind the faction's undertakings, and their commitment becomes a model for younger members.

Ishigaki Ayako, *Kaisō no Sumedorē* (Remembering Smedley) (Tokyo, 1967). Among Japanese women participating in progressive political causes, Agnes Smedley was admired as a socialist from humble origins who had grown up in a capitalist society, as a person who had spent her lifetime fighting oppression, as an adventurous woman, as a feminist, and as a foreigner who sympathized with the struggles of oppressed peoples in Asia.

When those who are less committed phase out of the group's activities in their junior or senior year and prepare for a usual job and marriage after graduation, it is these senior activists who keep the group alive and carry its work forward. The number of women who play such a role is small but probably increasing. In general, the more politically radical the sect, the more prominent the role that women play in its activities. Here the force of Marxist ideology, with its principles of egalitarianism, appears to be the best explanation: it is in those radical groups where the greatest efforts are made to reorient one's life according to new values that women are most apt to be found playing new roles.

Although several of these "senior" activists were among the informants in this study, one in particular stands out. At the time of the interview, Suzuki Kimiko was a fifth-year student at a prestigious coeducational university in Tokyo, where she was in the leadership corps of one of the most radical of the New Left factions of the Japanese student movement. The interview took place in a tiny, crowded coffee shop near the university. A slender young woman with an angular, intelligent face, Kimiko's eyes wandered around the room as we talked, particularly when she made a point well. Like a number of political women, particular those in Marxist groups, she was restless for a wider audience. The faction she led was absolutely central to her life. It is common among Japanese people, when explaining some aspect of the culture to a foreigner, to begin statements with the pronoun "we," or "we, the Japanese people," and thereby step into the role of cultural interpreter. Kimiko's "we," which she used often, referred not to the Japanese people, but to the tiny segment of it that defined her world, the faction members with whom she spent most of her waking hours.[17] Questions of ideology were similarly central in her thinking. In the interview she often left the specific question she had been asked, in order to explore its ideological implications. When she had moved a question to an appropriate level of abstraction, she put her full energy into trying to win the interviewer to her argu-

17. The tendency of groups and organizations in Japan to develop a strong sense of solidarity vis-à-vis the outside world is a much-observed characteristic of the social structure. See Chie Nakane, *Japanese Society* (Berkeley and Los Angeles, 1970).

ment. Her tone sometimes slipped into the cadence of someone addressing a large gathering through a bullhorn. Jabbing the air fiercely with a cigarette as she ticked off the points of her argument with great logical precision, she spoke with such animation that she drew many eyes in the coffee shop. Other questions, personal ones that had no links to wider social problems, obviously bored her. The light faded from her eyes, her voice dropped, and she shuffled restlessly in the uncomfortable wooden chair in the coffee shop.

Anti-Stalin, anti-Trotsky, Kimiko shared her group's view that revolution will come only when it is brought on by a proletariat committed to that end. Her personal plans were closely tied to her ideological view:

> Japan is a capitalist society rigidly divided into labor and the bourgeoisie. That means that I will have to align myself clearly with labor. The best way, it seems to me, is to take a job as a blue-collar worker after graduation, get into the union, and gradually take over the leadership. Some of us are talking about doing that.

When she was asked whether a woman would have difficulty achieving a leadership position in a union in Japan, her reply, like that of many women in the student movement to similar questions, suggests the degree to which she saw her personal destiny as a woman within an ideological framework:

> INFORMANT: Being a leader has nothing to do with whether a person is a man or woman.

> INTERVIEWER: Yes, I wonder, though . . . many people say it's difficult for a woman in Japan. They say that women have an inferior position, even in unions, that their wages are lower and so on. What do you think?

> INFORMANT: It's true that women are equal to men and should get equal wages. But all the things you're talking about are unimportant. The problem isn't one of equality or inequality. Even if wages were the same for men and women the real problems would remain. What we have to fight is the problem of wages in a capitalist system. Improvements in the system as it stands have no meaning. After the revolution, the kinds of superficial problems you're talking about will right themselves.

Kimiko's actual entry into radical student politics had come in much the same way as it had for many Japanese activists, male or female. Her interest, she said, could be traced to an incident that had occurred early in her first year at the university and was still deeply etched in her memory. In 1967 former Prime Minister Satō had been leaving Japan for a trip to South Vietnam, and a large group of students had gathered to demonstrate at the Tokyo airport. Because her home was nearby, Kimiko had gone out to watch the demonstration. Then suddenly, quite near where she was standing, one activist was killed, trampled in the confusion.[18] To Kimiko, at least in retrospect, the interpretation of this event was clear: Satō, supporting an unjust war to keep his military alliance with the United States, was responsible for this death and for a great many other injustices in Japanese society. The conclusion she drew, as she remembers it, was that all people who opposed the war had to organize and fight until Satō and those like him were forced aside.

In a state of shock from what she had seen, Kimiko talked to fellow classmates at school in the days following the airport demonstration. Most of her friends were in the drama club she had joined early in the school year, and among them were several members of the faction she was soon to join. Listening to them and reading the pamphlets they gave her on the faction's analysis of the Satō visit, she felt they were right. The other major faction on her campus, she noted, had scheduled a social event for the day of Satō's departure for South Vietnam. Though members of that group were on hand the next day to distribute on campus their pamphlets interpreting the visit, they had not been present at the demonstration. Kimiko was shocked at the seeming flippancy of their behavior. Her attraction to the faction she soon joined was intensified.

These events in Kimiko's experience, which had led her into the movement, parallel those in the lives of many indi-

18. An account of this demonstration near Haneda airport is in Tsurumi, "Student Movements in 1960 and 1969," p. 28. There were actually two major demonstrations at the airport, on October 8 and November 12, aimed at preventing Prime Minister Eisaku Satō's visit to South Vietnam. The trip was widely interpreted as a gesture of Japan's support for the U.S. position in the war.

viduals who become involved in political causes. A peak experience, the influence of friends, other events that affirm the rightness of one's own choice of a group or cause—these elements in various combination are to be found in the experience of many individuals drawn to politics. There were also less immediate but equally important situational factors in the background of her decision to join her faction: she was on the campus of a major coeducational university where radical factions were an accepted part of campus life; the university was in Tokyo where student activism is centered; she entered school at a time when the student movement was going through one of its peak periods of the postwar era. These circumstances had shaped a context within which radical political involvement was regarded as acceptable activity. If it was not the norm or even a "usual" activity for a woman, her entry into politics was not the unheard-of aberration it would have been in many women's colleges or junior colleges in Japan. These experiences in late youth could not explain, however, why Kimiko, unlike most women who were exposed to the same situational cues, was drawn to join and, eventually, to lead a political group. The investigation focused on earlier experiences that might have shaped her response to the setting she found herself in upon entering the university.

Given the degree of her absorption in and commitment to the activities of her sect, it came as a shock to learn that she was living at home with her family in a well-to-do suburb. This zealous activist planning to work her way up in the labor movement, this determined opponent of bourgeois capitalism, was supported financially at the university by a well-to-do physician father and continued to live under the roof he provided. Returning from a day of pamphleteering for radical change and revolution, she took her place in the evenings at the family dinner table and waited as her mother, who had never held a job and who had never joined a political movement of any kind, served the rice.

In the interview, Kimiko's parents took shape as stereotypical upper-middle-class Japanese. She described a father who was a model of those virtues for which Japanese are noted in the world: perseverence, industry, and dedication to his work. His life revolved around a clinic he had started himself. His days began early and ended late as he gave himself over to the care of his patients. Other things Kimiko said about her father placed him as a man of science. He was without any religious convictions, and above all, she noted, he was "a rational man" who expressed himself with great logic and precision. If there was an element that appeared to be missing in his makeup compared with that of many hardworking and successful Japanese men, it was a more frivolous side. Unlike many informants, daughters of businessmen or professionals, who reported that their generally hardworking fathers "loved *asobi*" (fun, meaning here carousing with fellow workers after hours), Kimiko described a father who gave himself over rather completely to his responsibilities at the clinic, with little time for family, friends, or even co-workers outside the clinic setting. Kimiko's actual contact with her father was rather limited, she said. Their daily routine was different, so they seldom saw each other. Sometimes he came home to dinner, but often not. The life of the family went on with Kimiko, her mother, and two younger sisters, both in their teens.

Kimiko's mother, at least from the initial description, was another stereotypical figure of today's Japan: the Japanese wife whose life centered on her children, fully accepting her husband's absence as a fact of her life. Her personal background was similar to that of many other informants' mothers who had married successful professionals or businessmen. She had grown up in a well-to-do family, attended a prewar girls' high school, and prepared for marriage in the traditional way by learning tea ceremony and flower arranging from her mother and private teachers. Like the mothers of many of the younger informants, her plans to marry had been disrupted by the war. As she neared her mid-twenties without a marriage prospect, her family at last hastened to arrange her marriage to a young military officer then in the field, far from Japan. The marriage was arranged in letters with an exchange of photographs. After the war, when he returned to Japan, the couple met for the first time at the wedding ceremony. He was thirty-five, and she, twenty-six. Marriage to a doctor eager to make up for lost time in his career was very much what his wife had expected it to be. His work was at the clinic; hers was in the home. Kimiko, critical of so many things she saw around her at the university and in society at large, volunteered that her parents were quite suited and got along well together.

Superficially her account of neither parent, either in personal background or attitude, shed much light on why Kimiko had become a political woman, and it was apparent that neither parent had actively sponsored her political involvement. Unlike the parents of many leaders in the sample, these parents were not people who had much interest in politics. Her father voted for LDP candidates most of the time, but with no particular enthusiasm or conviction. Her mother leaned more toward the Japan Socialist Party, but according to her daughter she had little interest in candidates or issues. When it came to the question of how her parents felt about woman's role, again there were no obvious signs of either parent's support for Kimiko's role experimentation. According to Kimiko, her mother had hopes that her daughter—leader of a radical, militant political faction—eventually would settle down into an arranged marriage. In her own life Mrs. Suzuki hardly offered a model of a postwar woman eager to try new things. She had never worked, never traveled outside Japan, and in fact had really seen very little of life outside the two homes where she had spent most of her days. As for Doctor Suzuki, his career appeared to have left him little time to guide his daughter toward a particular set of life goals. When Kimiko was asked what her father hoped she would do after graduation from the university, she was clearly at a loss. They had never discussed it.

As the interview proceeded, the attention focused on the two interrelated processes discussed earlier as they had operated within Kimiko's experience. The first question was what influences or dynamics within the family might have contributed to her political involvement. The parents' low level of interest in politics suggested that there had been few direct political influences operating in the immediate family environment. Although situational cues were useful in explaining her actual entry into the group, they could not explain why Kimiko, unlike most women students exposed to the same environmental stimuli, had decided to join. A beginning step, however, was to identify the person or persons Kimiko had looked to as models for the behavior required in her new political role. An additional aim was to explore the dynamic operating behind the role change that had occurred to make Kimiko open to the option of joining a political group.

In the search for a role model for Kimiko's activism, attention fell first on the obvious model for a daughter, her mother. Although there was nothing in Mrs. Suzuki's life experiences, as described by her daughter, to indicate why she might have supported Kimiko's entry into politics, much less have been a role model for political activism, the focus came to rest on a mother-daughter relationship that appeared often in political women's descriptions of their home. The relationship, first of all, was one of extraordinary closeness. Asked with whom she had discussed school, plans, marriage, and so on, Kimiko's answer, like that of most of the informants, was "Mother." In contrast, the father, however important he might have been in their lives in other ways, typically was a remote figure. Even when daughters had strong affectionate feelings toward him, he was simply not present when things that mattered to them were discussed at home.[19] Much writing on the Japanese family has stressed the importance of the mother-son relationship, with its enduring psychological ties that appear to replicate themselves in other forms again and again in Japanese culture.[20] Few writers have dealt with the

19. The limited role of Japanese fathers in child rearing has been noted in virtually all major studies of the Japanese family. See Ezra F. Vogel, *Japan's New Middle Class* (Berkeley and Los Angeles, 1963); Ronald P. Dore, *City Life in Japan* (Berkeley and Los Angeles, 1958); Linda L. Perry, "Mothers, Wives, and Daughters in Osaka," Ph.D. dissertation, University of Pittsburgh, 1976; Koyama Takashi, *Gendai kazoku no oyako kankei* (Parent-child relations in the contemporary family) (Tokyo, 1973). As Perry notes, even disciplinary responsibility is generally left to the wife. Middle-class fathers are seldom at home in time to eat with the children. This does not mean fathers play no role. They expect to be consulted when major decisions affecting the children are made, and find ways to be with the children, even if they do not eat with them. Perry found, for example, that many fathers made a special effort to be home in time to bathe with their young children (pp. 185–188).

20. Vogel, *Japan's New Middle Class*; Christie W. Kiefer, "The Psychological Interdependence of Family, School, and Bureaucracy in Japan," *American Anthropologist* 72 (1970): 66–75; George DeVos, "The Relation of Guilt toward Parents to Achievement and Arranged Marriage among the Japanese," *Psychiatry* 23 (1960): 287–301; William Caudill, "Anthropology and Psychoanalysis: Some Theoretical Issues," in *Anthropology and Human Behavior*, ed. Thomas Gladwin and William C. Sturtevant (Washington, D.C., 1962); William Caudill, "Thoughts on the Comparison of Emotional Life in Japan and the United States," *Seishinigaku* 6 (February 1964): 29–33; Doi Takeo, *Amae no kōzō* (The structure of *amae*) (Tokyo, 1971).

Japanese mother's relation with her female offspring.[21] Since this particular study did not include male informants, the two sets of relationships cannot be compared here for relative intensity. What was notable, however, was to observe, from political women's accounts of their family life and their mother's role in it, how deeply the informants' mothers appeared to be involved in the lives of *all* their children, rank order and sex of the child aside.[22] The mothers of political women who had grown up in an urban nuclear family appeared to have led lives focused almost exclusively on the comings and goings of their two or three offspring. With few outside interests, with a small circle of women friends, with a husband frequently absent from the home because of the demands of his job, with almost no social life with their husband or without him, these urban mothers were remarkably absorbed in the smallest details of their children's lives.

When Kimiko had decided to join her radical faction in her first year in the university, she had not told her father. But it would have been difficult, she said, to keep the information from her mother. In a somewhat simplified form, minus much of her Marxist rhetoric, Kimiko recounted each day's events when she reached home, and discussed with her mother plans for demonstrations, the issues her faction was debating, and new ideas on revolutionary tactics. Sitting together on the *tatami* mat, the daughter in her jeans and blazer, the mother in the traditional kimono, the two relived Kimiko's adventures each evening, in a family life in which Dr. Suzuki was little more than an occasional guest.

The mother-daughter relation had conspiratorial overtones. Like many of the mothers of political women, Mrs. Suzuki told her husband relatively little of what Kimiko reported to her about the radical group. Kimiko thus knew that what she passed on to her mother would be treated as

21. An excellent, recent exception is Perry, "Mothers, Wives, and Daughters in Osaka."

22. Perry's findings support this view (ibid., p. 11). It may be noted, too, that comparative data on child rearing practices in Japan offer further support for it. In a study comparing the maternal behavior of Japanese and American mothers, American mothers were found to give somewhat more attention and affection to boy babies than to girl babies; there was no difference according to sex of infant among the Japanese mothers, however. William Caudill and Helen Weinstein, "Maternal Care and Infant Behavior in Japan and America," *Psychiatry* 32 (1969): 12–43.

privileged information. Even if it was repeated to her father, it would be conveyed in the most favorable light possible. In the thinking of most Japanese families, failures in the training of children are laid firmly at the door of the mother. Reports by a mother of a child's adventures or misadventures may arouse the criticism of a husband who prefers not to get involved, or who, if he does intervene, may usurp her authority over the lives of her children.

The tremendous importance that mothers like Mrs. Suzuki attached to their relationship with their children was obviously a key factor in keeping the lines of communication open, even when their daughters were engaged in activities of which they disapproved. The mothers often offered strong direction to their daughters and criticized them on occasion. But when a daughter strayed far from conduct approved by the mother, at a certain point the mother's criticism was likely to soften. If she pressed too far, there was the ultimate danger that her daughter would turn away from her and no longer confide. Because the relation itself was so important to a great many mothers, they acquiesced, tacitly, to conduct they did not approve of or understand rather than lose a highly valued line of communication.[23]

It might be pointed out that certain changes in postwar Japan have made the pattern described above more common than before the war. In the extended family more typical of the prewar period, a child's misconduct or deviance from accepted norms was observed not only by other relatives, including the mother-in-law, but by a father who was far more likely to be working nearer home. There was hardly the potential in that situation for a mother to screen a child's conduct from the family for long. Nor, in the pattern of life of the family-run farms and small businesses of the prewar period, was the child her single, absorbing interest. Not only the mother, but the children too, had institutionalized contacts with other family members, as well as work or housekeeping

23. The mother-daughter relation that Perry found among her Osaka informants closely parallels the one described by political women. Perry has characterized the relation as an "alliance" in which mothers mediate between father and child and control the father's access to information. Perry, "Mothers, Wives, and Daughters in Osaka," pp. 185–187. Also see Vogel, *Japan's New Middle Class*, pp. 184–189.

responsibilities, that functioned to reduce the intensity of the mother-child interaction. But in the nuclear family of urban Japan, with a father often away from the dinner table and no other relatives present, many mothers rely primarily on the children for companionship. Moreover, they can choose, without interference from their husband or other family members, how they will act on any information the child conveys to them. What a wife does not report to her husband, harassed as he is by work responsibilities, he will probably not find out on his own. Intuitively, many informants such as Kimiko recognized the unspoken terms of their close relation with their mother. They told all, or most, knowing it would go no further. When they had said all they intended to say, they knew that their mother would usually press no further. There were some things—aspects of the daughter's conduct that might jeopardize the family reputation—that mothers preferred not to hear, lest they be forced to betray their child's confidence by going to their husbands.

The pattern of mother-daughter interaction described above functions in strong support of role change in women. It appears to provide a central dynamic behind the process by which political women began to experiment with woman's role. It could also be seen at work in the response of many mothers to their daughters' activism, even when the daughter's behavior was far beyond the mother's own experience or understanding. A good example was provided by Kimiko's description of her mother's response to her single experience with arrest. At a demonstration at the Soviet Embassy following the Soviet invasion of Czechoslovakia, Kimiko had hurled a rock and had found herself under arrest with several other members of her group. After three days in jail, she was at last released. When her mother found out about the arrest, she was, in her daughter's words, "hysterical, shocked." Upon Kimiko's return home after the sect had secured her release, Mrs. Suzuki expressed anger at her daughter's conduct. But at no point did she really urge her daughter to give up the political activities. Even after the arrest of her daughter, Mrs. Suzuki had not threatened or cajoled: "Mother is always anxious about her children. When she saw that I had returned home safely, that was enough. She didn't tell me to quit." What made Mrs. Suzuki angry, Kimiko said, was her not keeping her mother informed about where she was and what she was doing. "As long as she knows, it's all right."

The interest of mothers like Mrs. Suzuki in their daughters' activities appears to go beyond their need to keep good communications with their children, the explanation advanced so far for these mothers' extraordinary tolerance for their daughters' role experimentation in areas of activity like politics. There are signs of a subtle dynamic in operation, whereby mothers such as Mrs. Suzuki enrich their own lives with the exciting comings and goings of activist daughters. With a daughter like Kimiko, engaged in pursuits that were almost unthinkable for women before the war, the mother's combination of fear and fascination, horror and admiration, at her daughter's exploits reflects her own subconscious longings to engage in these activities herself. In a prewar world, women like Mrs. Suzuki faced limited life options and, if the accounts of many informants are accurate, accepted their lot without rancor or bitterness. But in a postwar world in which new freedoms and possibilities have opened up to women, these women may feel a certain distant longing for experiences they can never have, for opportunities available to young women of today that came too late in their own lives. Because many of the new activities for women—whether dating, premarital sex, educational or job opportunities, travel abroad, or active political participation—are outside their own realm of experience, they express their own inner fear when they warn their daughters about the possible dangers of what they are doing. But there is also admiration, even envy, of their daughter's courage. If the explicit message conveyed to daughters is to be careful, to stay out of trouble, to think of the damage their present political or other activities might do to their marriage prospects or to their marriage, the implicit message communicated to a great number of political women by their mothers in a variety of subtle ways was "Go, girl, go."[24] To the extent that such a dynamic was at work in the relation between political women and their mothers, it was a force that operated in support of women's entry into

24. I am grateful to Dr. Walter Slote, a clinical psychologist and Adjunct Professor of Sociology at Columbia University with extensive field experience in Asia, who in several valuable discussions greatly aided my understanding of this important dynamic.

politics. However many protestations a mother might make over a daughter's wayward conduct, however many times she might express fear that her daughter would lose out on marriage because of her behavior, daughters were deeply aware of other, contradictory currents in messages communicated by their mothers, and sustained themselves on the support extended to them. Political women appeared to know, at some level, of the satisfaction their mothers derived from their adventures. Their experimentation with political roles was something that they did not only for themselves, but for their mothers as well. They were her emissaries, dispatched into the postwar world of greater opportunity for women.

There is a final dimension to the same pattern that should be considered. As was discussed earlier, girls growing up learn the female-gender role from their mothers. Certainly the political women in this study had emulated and acquired many of the "womanly" behaviors through observing their mothers in the early years.[25] However, to the extent that mothers feel a vague dissatisfaction with what their own lives hold for them as women, they become reluctant to offer themselves as role models to their daughters. How this dynamic operates today was spelled out in the remarks of another student activist, a twenty-two-year-old student of design from a small city outside Tokyo, whose mother sounded very much like Kimiko's:

> My parents had an arranged marriage. My father had been away in the war. He returned and they married. For three years after the war they lived with relatives. Their marriage has been happy and they have been pretty well off, especially in the last few years. But once my mother said to me, if a woman lives without any purpose, without following what she wants to do, that must be a sad thing. She's willing to let me do what I want to do.

25. See Kirkpatrick, *Political Woman*, pp. 46–48, for a discussion of the importance of strong feminine identifications for political women. The data for this study support the same conclusion. Political women in Japan appear to identify strongly with their mothers, to adopt many feminine behaviors from them, and to rely on the support and sense of self-esteem they derive from them as a basis for role experimentation. Research on upwardly mobile women in the United States also confirms the existence of a strong identification with the mother among such women. Elizabeth Douvan and Joseph Adelson, *The Adolescent Experience* (New York, 1966), pp. 72–77.

When mothers hold back in this way from presenting themselves as role models for their daughters, they support their daughter's search for alternative role models.

In the search for the person or persons Kimiko might have turned to as a model for her behavior in the political role she had adopted, the attention quickly came to rest on her father. Given Dr. Suzuki's apparent indifference to his daughter's extraordinary political activities at school, the degree to which he appeared to have served as a model for Kimiko's political style in her faction was noteworthy. Her dedication to the work of the group and the long hours she put into its activities mirrored the fervor and devotion Kimiko's father gave to his medical practice. In her own approach to ideology, she spurned intuition and the human dimension in favor of the logic and rationality that were her father's guiding principles. Like her father, Kimiko was not a follower. She presided over her group with the same single-minded determination and sense of responsibility for younger, more inexperienced members that characterized his direction over the life of the clinic. And in Kimiko's account of her own life, plans, and beliefs, there was the same singular absence of humor and frivolity. Her commitment, like his, was sober, reasoned, total.

If her father had served as a model at some level for the political role she had adopted, there were other ways he had functioned in her life that were equally important in explaining how she had maintained her political commitment in the face of strong disapproval from many people around her outside the home. Unlike many busy Japanese fathers who delegate most child-rearing responsibilities to their wives and who break that pattern mainly in the case of a child's aberrant behavior, Dr. Suzuki was permissive in a way that had given his daughter growing space, a chance to move independently in new directions. Unlike many fathers who would threaten to cut off financial support to children if they became involved in the student movement, Dr. Suzuki had never threatened financial retribution for his daughter's political activities. Kimiko, in her fifth year at the university, was putting maximum strains on that tolerance, since her activism was costing him an extra year of financial support. Yet neither Dr. Suzuki nor his wife had registered strong objections to the additional year. As Kimiko put it, "Sometimes they say they wish I'd hurry up and graduate, but basically they don't mind." Kimiko's status as the eldest daughter in a family without sons clearly functioned in support of this pattern. The real measure of her father's attitude of tolerance toward her own experimentation came out in Kimiko's discussion of her experience with arrest. When asked if Dr. Suzuki had reprimanded her or worried about what the neighbors might think, Kimiko weighed her reply carefully and then said, "Well, no . . . my father really doesn't care too much about people's opinions, one way or another. Both he and my mother think that children should be allowed to follow their own course."

It is difficult to convey how extraordinary Kimiko's reply would seem to most Japanese women. For comparative purposes, Neotraditional activists—who, it will be recalled, were almost always participating in groups and causes approved by their families—were asked what their family might do if they were ever arrested. Most thought it too terrible to imagine; many thought their parents would turn them away forever; and many whose father had an important position thought that he would resign to "take responsibility" for his daughter's conduct. A few thought that one or both parents might even commit suicide out of the feeling that the family had been disgraced. This strong burden of responsibility assumed by fathers for unacceptable behavior in their children has long roots in Japan, as was discussed in chapter three. The presence of such a tradition of parental responsibility is surely a strong check on deviant behavior in the young. Dr. Suzuki, in his extraordinarily tolerant attitude, was obviously an unusual man who valued personal freedom for both himself and his children.

In Kimiko's case, her father was the parent to whom she had turned as a role model for her behavior in the political role. As was noted earlier, some other political women had turned to someone else as a model. A crucial factor in the process, however, was the mother's attitude, her willingness to allow her daughter to deviate from the traditional model of female behavior that she herself typically represented. For many mothers, the step was not taken easily, and they continued to experience moments of doubt and fear as they observed their daughters' experimentation. As the next chapter will show, both parents were apt to be more tolerant of a daughter's experimentation at certain stages of her life than at others. During periods in her life cycle when female role demands are most stringent, parents often tried to reassert their authority over their daughter and to hold her to traditional expectations for her behavior, often causing political women to feel resentment and a sense of betrayal. But the support extended to them during key stages of their growth and maturation was crucial in the overall process of becoming politically active.

Concluding Remarks

Much of the discussion in this chapter bears on the process by which both men and women become involved in politics in Japan today. Japanese society presents multiple options to people of both sexes to participate in a variety of political groups or causes. As is explained elsewhere in this volume, those groups that make an active effort to include in their activities young people in the age range for this study tend to be concentrated in the progressive political camp of Japan's polarized political system.[26] Within that camp are to be found many young men and women who are involved in a wide variety of political groups, from the progressive parties and unions to many more informal protest groups, such as citizens' movements, consumer protection groups, the student movement, and the women's movement. Apart from the specific attractions that any one of these types of political activity may hold for young people, all protest activities in the progressive camp have great emotional appeal to the young. As Passin and other writers point out, most Japanese today—even the conservatives—feel that progressives are on the side of moral right in a society long dominated by the conservative camp.[27] Many young people who find themselves in an environment that encourages activism may be

26. See Appendix A.
27. Herbert Passin, "Sources of Protest in Japan," *American Political Science Review* 56 (June 1962): 391–403.

strongly attracted to a political cause. If the level of political interest and social concern in their more immediate family environment was high while they were growing up, then obviously the step is easier to take. In any number of settings in contemporary Japan there will be a number of young people who are psychologically receptive or "predisposed"—at the level of basic needs and drives—to the prospect of joining a political group, and who are thus especially receptive to situational cues.

What this chapter and the two preceding ones have explored, however, is why so few women, relative to men, respond to these various psychological, situational, environmental, and historical cues by becoming politically active, and why certain women do. Explanations for women's lesser rates of participation in politics are well agreed upon in the literature. Normally, for women the combined experience of political socialization and gender-role socialization results in an adult woman who is far less responsive to political cues than are men. Certain women, however, emerge from the same processes with a well-developed notion of a political self and with a greater receptivity to the stimuli provided by the political world around them. This chapter and the two preceding ones have traced the experiences of such women, exploring how and why they came to be different from most women.

As the result of key life experiences and particular patterns of relationships in the family, political women emerged from childhood and adolescence as women who were open to the possibility of experimenting with woman's role and who had come to challenge dominant cultural prescriptions for how women should behave. The "permissiveness" of one or both parents gave them the latitude to engage in role experimentation, often with the active support of the parents, especially the mother. Although the mother was often ambivalent about her daughter's experiment with alternative styles of behavior in and outside of the political role, typically she had conveyed strong support for role change and for her daughter's adventures in politics at key periods of her daughter's growth and maturation. At the same time, however, through a complex dynamic operating in the mother-daughter relation, the mother typically had stepped back from offering herself as a

role model for much of her daughter's behavior and had allowed her to seek alternative models for new styles of behavior. This support was conveyed in the context of an extremely
close affective tie between mother and daughter. A father,
brother, or other person, usually a male, outside the family
then became the model for a political woman's own style of
political behavior. Many of these men had not been active
teachers of the political role. Their own view of appropriate
female behavior was usually more narrowly defined than that
of their wives, and they were reluctant to become active
sponsors of role change. The interesting exceptions were
mainly families in which there were no sons and in which
daughters thus came in for a full share of support and encouragement in and outside the political role. Even when the
normal pattern prevailed, in which fathers or other males had
presented themselves as models for political behavior without encouraging political women to imitate them, their contribution to the overall process by which women become politically active was nonetheless real. These forces at work in
the home environment had resulted in women who were
open to the possibility of acting politically. Confronted with
the right situational, environmental, and historical cues in
late adolescence and adulthood, the women were prepared to
cross the threshold of acceptable female behavior to join a
political group or cause.

6

Handling Role Strain

Political women, like nonactivist women, develop ideologies of woman's role that express how they see work, education, marriage, and other pursuits ideally combined in an adult woman's life. The same ideologies carry with them perspectives on how politics could or should be integrated into a woman's other activities and on what roles should be open to her in a political group. Translating ideology into behavior may be extremely difficult, however, because of role strain—that is, the difficulty that a political woman experiences in trying to meet the expectations of others for her behavior.[1] How political women handle role strain is the subject of this chapter.

1. Goode defines role strain as "the felt difficulty in fulfilling role obligations." William J. Goode, "A Theory of Role Strain," *American Sociological Review* 25 (August 1960): 483.

In addition to the dominant Neotraditional view of woman's role, there are at least two competing views, as was indicated earlier. Each of the latter has sources of support among certain groups and institutions in society as well as among individual women. The New Women's ideology, for example, is supported by the Women's and Minors' Bureau of the Ministry of Labor, numerous women's organizations, such as the League of Women Voters and the Women's Democratic Club, and a number of women's magazines. There is also fairly strong support for the view in the official ideology of the educational system. Support for the Radical Egalitarian ideology is more limited, but there are a number of groups and organizations associated with the New Left or with the Japanese women's movement that back it.

Despite the support that exists for alternative role ideologies, the Neotraditional view, which holds that active political participation is highly inappropriate for women except under the special circumstances described earlier, predominates in Japanese society today. Even if a political woman has come to adopt an alternate ideology of woman's role that sees political activity as fully permissible for women, she must contend with the fact that a great many people in contemporary Japan do not agree with her. Among her circle of significant others—which typically includes parents, brothers and sisters, grandparents and other relatives, significant males in her life, friends, employers and fellow employees, neighbors, teachers and schoolmates—there are likely to be a number of people who regard her political activism as a violation of appropriate role behavior and who send out overt or covert signals of disapproval if and when they learn of her political activism.[2]

2. Biddle and Thomas summarize some of the ways in which violations are made known to the individual: use of positive and negative reinforcements, placing physical or environmental constraints on the individual's behavior, comparing the individual's role performance against a "standard of excellence" (e.g., a person who is in greater compliance with the role demands), conveying or withholding approval, making normative or declaratory statements of role prescriptions, exposing the individual to rituals and ceremonies that present the prescribed behavior in codified form, and punishment. The manner of conveying disapproval ranges from nonverbal behavior (a smile, frown, or knowing look) to physical abuse. Edwin J. Thomas and Bruce J. Biddle, "Basic Concepts for the Variables of Role Phenomena,"

It should be pointed out here that even those political women whose level of political involvement was minimal were not immune to criticism. As chapter one indicated, the threshold beyond which a woman's involvement in politics will be judged questionable or unacceptable is extremely low in Japan, by United States standards. Many citizen modes of participation that are fully acceptable under the terms of the dominant definition of woman's role in the United States are off limits in Japan in most people's definition of woman's proper role and place.

The result, for Japanese women who defy the majority and become politically active, is role strain, and a key problem for them is how to devise strategies to handle it. The political women included in this study had adopted three such strategies. The first involved a variety of coping mechanisms by which women attempted to make their behavior in the political role gender appropriate, and thereby eliminate or minimize role strain. The second involved compartmentalizing roles—that is, screening their political activities from the eyes of potential critics. Finally, women adopting a third strategy confronted their critics. By word or by deed they were engaged in actively challenging the dominant definition of woman's role. As will be discussed later, few women resorted to only one of these strategies to handle role strain. Most, over the course of their activism, had used all three, and at any given time they might be using different strategies to handle role strain in different role relationships. How each strategy worked will now be examined in more detail.

Gender Typing the Political Role

Gender typing is a term that is usually reserved for a description of the larger social process by which the tasks within a given sphere of activity are divided up on the basis of sex. Here, however, the term refers to the same process when it is set in motion by an individual woman to

---

in *Role Theory: Concepts and Research*, ed. Edwin J. Thomas and Bruce J. Biddle (New York, 1966), pp. 52–57.

minimize role strain. Adopting this strategy, women confine their participation in a political group to those activities that stand the best chance of being judged acceptable under the terms of the dominant definition of woman's role, and then justify their activism in ways that their critics may find acceptable.

The actual behavior of women using this strategy is so commonplace and familiar that it seems scarcely to lend itself to analysis. Take, for example, the behavior of a woman who, in a conversation with a skeptical neighbor, is trying to justify her activism. If she is in an antipollution group, she may claim that she is taking part only for the sake of her children's health. If she is campaigning on behalf of a political candidate, she may emphasize how helpful the candidate has been to her father, brother, or husband. In both cases, she is trying to qualify for the special dispensation which even the strongest defenders of the Neotraditional view grant to women who are engaged in what would otherwise be unacceptable behavior, for the sake of their family.

Another version of the same strategy may be used within the political group to avoid criticism not only from outsiders, but from male and female members who hold the Neotraditional view. While verbally justifying her behavior in the ways just described, the woman activist will limit the nature and level of her political participation so that it represents the least possible violation of the expectations of others for her behavior. To the extent possible, she will play a "woman's" political role within the group. She will limit her participation to a wide variety of auxiliary activities, such as handing out pamphlets, doing copy work, and stuffing envelopes. She will perform what Bernard has called woman's "stroking" function, by smoothing over intergroup conflicts, cheering people up when group morale is low, and, in general, creating a pleasant atmosphere in the group.[3] She will perform a number of tasks that are direct carry-overs from the homemaker role, such as pouring tea, straightening up the office or meeting room, or preparing a snack for members who are working late. If she plays a leadership role or takes part in decision making, it will generally be only in those areas

3. Jessie Bernard, *Women and the Public Interest* (Chicago, 1971), pp. 88–102.

of the group's activity falling in the domain of "women's matters."

One of the greatest difficulties in accounting for the political behavior of women who play a "woman's" political role in their political group lies in determining the extent to which their behavior is self-directed, and the extent to which it is directed by structures—that is, the policies, values, and attitudes of the political group.[4] Many political groups in Japan limit the political participation of women members. It was suggested earlier that different types of groups, from large, formal organizations such as the political parties and organized interest groups at one extreme to informal women's groups at the other, impose varying levels of constraints on women's political participation. But the structuralist argument cannot account for the fact that many women "gender type" their participation even in groups that permit or even encourage women to engage in a wide variety of activities, including leadership and decision making. It should also be noted that women in politics in today's Japan are active in an area of behavior in which expectations for their conduct are not yet clearly worked out. A political role for women is so new that a sorting process of the tasks to be performed by females rather than males continues in many organizations. Even in a major organization with prewar antecedents like the Liberal Democratic Party, where a notion of "woman's political role" as a category of activities distinct from those performed by men is fairly well developed, there are still areas where members may not be sure how a given activity is to be sex-typed. In 1972, for example, young women party members and male officials in the Osaka headquarters of the LDP agreed that addressing crowds over a public-address system in a political campaign is a highly appropriate activity for a woman, but the sex typing of this particular activity is

4. Most researchers acknowledge that *both* internal and external structural sets of constraints operate to limit women's participation in politics and in other activities that are dominated by males. See Jeane J. Kirkpatrick, *Political Woman* (New York, 1974), pp. 17–20; Carol A. Whitehurst, *Women in America: The Oppressed Majority* (Santa Monica, Calif., 1977), pp. 90–91; Kirsten Amundsen, *A New Look at the Silenced Majority* (Englewood Cliffs, N.J., 1977), p. 120; Naomi Lynn and Cornelia Butler Flora, "Societal Punishment and Aspects of Female Political Participation," in *A Portrait of Marginality*, ed. Marianne Githens and Jewel L. Prestage (New York, 1977), pp. 139–149.

hardly self-evident and has probably evolved only gradually in the postwar period. In more informal organizations without prewar antecedents, such as citizens' movement groups and many postwar student groups, gender typing of political roles tends to be less developed still. In a radical student sect, for example, there may be a consensus that certain of the political group's tasks are reserved for men, such as carrying a *geba-bō* (stave) in demonstrations.[5] But there are likely to be large areas of activity where members as a whole are not certain of the suitability for women. In the relatively fluid situation that exists in a great many groups, then, the individual woman member's margin of choice is fairly wide. She may expand her participation into a broad range of the group's activities, or she may choose to limit her participation by playing a woman's role in her group. Which route she follows depends in large measure on the degree of role strain she is experiencing and its sources. If significant others within the group (a boyfriend or a husband or certain members she likes or respects) hold her to the dominant definition of woman's role, she may restrict her participation even if the group's leadership, its ideology, and most of the members support the right of women to engage in the full range of the group's activities. Masuda Yōko, the student activist described in chapter five, who swept and cleaned behind the barricades of the University of Tokyo to please her boyfriend while other women members of the sect played leadership roles, is a good example of a political woman who had adopted just such a strategy to minimize role strain.

Role Compartmentalization

Many women opt for a quite different solution to role strain by compartmentalizing roles.[6] In dealing with

5. Since approximately 1967, student political activists generally have worn helmets and carried wooden staves called *geba-bō* (from the German word *Gewalt*) in demonstrations. Kazuko Tsurumi, "Student Movements in 1960 and 1969," *Research Papers of the Institute of International Relations*, Sophia University, Series A-5, (Tokyo, 1972), pp. 28–32.

6. Goode defines role compartmentalization as the ability, on the psychological level, "to ignore the problem of consistency" ("Theory of Role Strain," p. 486).

significant others who are potentially critical of them, these women neither modify the questionable behavior nor try to "excuse it away." Instead, they screen their behavior from potential critics and behave one way inside the political group and another outside it.[7]

One of the most striking examples of role compartmentalization was the way that many political women handled their activism vis-à-vis their families. As chapter five indicated, although many parents were supportive of role experimentation in and outside political roles, the messages they communicated to their daughters were contradictory. Even supportive parents sent out numerous negative signals regarding their daughter's activism, and at certain stages of the daughter's life cycle they were more supportive than at other stages. Anticipating criticism or ambivalent responses from their parents regarding their entry into politics, a number of political women had not told one or both parents that they were planning to join, or had actually joined, a political group. Several women, in fact, had managed to be very active in a political group over a fairly long period without telling their parents anything about it. It often happened, especially if the daughter was living with her family, that she told them eventually, or that they found out on their own sooner or later. But the daughter's initial response was to compartmentalize by saying nothing. Keeping the information from one or both parents often involved elaborate subterfuge and the cooperation of group members (and in some cases, a conspiratorial relationship with one parent to keep the knowledge from the other).

For those young activists involved in radical student groups whose ideology and tactics worry or alienate most Japanese parents, the type of avoidance behavior characterized here as role compartmentalization is found among men as well as women. But because of the special nature of role strain as it affects women, political women of all ages

7. Merton notes that social structural arrangements in any society pave the way for the use of this coping mechanism. In other words, the very fact that a person's role activities are not observed continuously by all those in his or her role set makes it possible for the individual to violate the role expectations of some without undue stress. Robert K. Merton, "Instability and Articulation in the Role-Set," in *Role Theory: Concepts and Research*, ed. Bruce J. Biddle and Edwin J. Thomas (New York, 1966), p. 284.

participating in all types of political groups may resort to role compartmentalization, independent of the ideology and tactics of their group. A good example was a woman of twenty-five who was active in her company's labor union. When the union came out for a Diet candidate in her electoral district, she agreed to put posters up in her neighborhood, but she waited until midnight to do it and persuaded her younger sister to stand guard for her. The candidate was a man whom her family and most people in her upper-middle-class neighborhood supported, but she preferred that the neighbors not know that she was involved in a political campaign. In her own neighborhood, she wanted to be thought of as "feminine" and to avoid behaving in a way that might direct criticism at her parents for having raised her badly. Similarly, a member of the Japan Communist Party resorted to role compartmentalization when she decided to run for public office in a medium-sized city outside Tokyo. She decided not to tell her parents, who lived at some distance from Tokyo, not because of her party allegiance, which they shared, but because of her electoral bid. She knew they would regard her marriage chances as finished because of it and she wanted to avoid the guilt that would result from disappointing them.

It was not only from parents and neighbors that activists screened their political involvement. Husbands were often just as much of a concern. An example was a housewife in an antipollution group. Urged by fellow members to take part in a demonstration in her neighborhood, she agreed to do it, but only "in disguise"—with her hair tied back and wearing a pair of wrap-around sunglasses. If she were recognized, she said, her husband might find out, and he would laugh at her for "trying to look strong" by taking part in a political demonstration. There were even more extreme examples of role compartmentalization. In one case, a thirty-three-year-old housewife and mother who was active in several feminist groups in the suburbs of Tokyo held committee meetings in her home, organized large assemblies, and even allowed herself, her home, and the children to be filmed for a foreign educational film on feminist activities in Japan without telling her husband! Several members of her group followed a similar course with their own husbands. This was a particularly extreme example of compartmentalization, because not only was the fact of membership kept from the husbands, but the women concerned continued to play a role vis-à-vis their husbands to which the group, in their regular meetings, raised strong ideological objections. The same women who argued in meetings that their husbands should learn to clean their own shoes and pour their own coffee performed these same tasks for their husbands in the evenings as if the meeting had not taken place.

It is not argued here that compartmentalization is a unique Japanese solution to role strain. Goode and other writers have seen the same strategy used in the United States. But it can be suggested that the Japanese have a somewhat greater tolerance for the ambiguity that arises when roles are compartmentalized than is true in many other societies, including the United States. Many Western commentators dating from Ruth Benedict have noted in Japanese behavior a high tolerance for ambiguity and a tendency of the Japanese to respond to situational cues in ways that may lead to major contradictions in their behavior as they move from setting to setting.[8] Indeed, some writers have seen that same behavior as the source of the Japanese people's capacity to adapt to rapid social change without experiencing major psychological disruption.[9] If these writers are correct, then role compartmentalization can be seen as a woman's response—for which there is considerable support in the culture—to a situation that involves acute potential stress for her. Anticipated criticism of their political involvement from significant others is so severe and potentially disruptive to their lives that it is easier for political women to "escape" by not confronting others with the reality of their political behavior.

8. Ruth Benedict, The Chrysanthemum and the Sword (Boston, 1946), pp. 195–197. Also see Kazuo Kawai, Japan's American Interlude (Chicago, 1960), pp. 4–6, and George DeVos, "The Relation of Guilt Toward Parents to Achievement and Arranged Marriage among the Japanese," Psychiatry 23 (1960): 299–300, for a discussion of the same phenomenon.

9. Kawai, Japan's American Interlude, pp. 299–300, holds that this ability made it possible for the Japanese to adjust rapidly to military defeat in World War II and to the reforms instituted by the occupation. Tsurumi argues that this same capacity made it possible for them to adjust to the social and psychological tension created by rapid industrialization. See Kazuko Tsurumi, Social Change and the Individual (Princeton, 1970), pp. 33–34, for a discussion

Challenging the Critics

If the demands of woman's role can be met by limiting or justifying political participation or by compartmentalizing it, a third strategy is also available, whereby women challenge the dominant view of woman's role and openly defy their critics. Superficially, this strategy and the strategy described in the first section have much in common, for both involve women's attempts to alleviate role strain by resolving inconsistencies between the way they behave and the way others expect them to behave. But there the similarity ends. Political women described in the first section accept the dominant role ideology and modify their behavior to make it acceptable within those bounds, whereas women who adopt the third strategy reject the definition itself.

Adopting this third strategy places women in the vanguard of efforts to change society's dominant definition of woman's role.[10] Although all political women are to some extent agents of change, those who struggle to keep their activism within acceptable boundaries, or women who screen from others their personal experiment with a new role, are less active agents of change than women who openly defy the restrictive definition itself and who attempt to substitute a new role ideology in its stead.

The process by which women came to challenge society's prescriptions for women's behavior was complex. To the degree that there was support in the family for their role experimentation inside or outside political roles, the task was much easier. Similarly, prior role experimentation itself in areas other than politics gave women the experience and

---

of the "many-layered self" that she sees as a modal Japanese personality type that entails an ability to compartmentalize.

10. The links between an individual's rejection of role obligations and social change are well established. Goode, for example, points out that individuals in a subordinate status who reject role obligations "may, over time, acquire further bargaining power, while those in a superior status may gradually come to feel less committed to the maintenance of the former role pattern" ("Theory of Role Strain," p. 493). Also see Talcott Parsons, "Role Conflict and the Genesis of Deviance," in *Role Theory: Concepts and Research*, ed. Bruce J. Biddle and Edwin J. Thomas (New York, 1966), p. 276.

confidence to argue openly with critics about the appropriateness of their behavior. In addition, political participation itself appeared to provide a powerful impetus for personal change. Membership in a political group gave women a forum in which to test new styles of behavior and to translate an alternative role ideology into behavior. Typically, political groups functioned for women members in much the same way that age-homogeneous groups have been thought to function for young people more generally. They provided women with a sense of solidarity, a "common definition of life-space and destiny," and an opportunity to share role strain and other emotional stress that accompanied their transition to a new identity.[11] The political group also offered them warm affective relationships and a safe haven from the demands of the dominant culture.[12] Surrounded by group members who shared their view of political activism as appropriate behavior for women, political women gradually felt sure enough of their new role ideology to challenge their critics outside the group.

One point needs clarification. Earlier it was noted that most political groups in Japan to some degree gender type political roles within the group and thereby establish structural constraints on women's political participation. One may ask, then, how such groups—particularly the large, formal political organizations that set maximum barriers to women's participation—could serve as a setting for personal change in the way just described. The answer is that for virtually all of the political women interviewed for this study, the political group had offered them *more* opportunities for role experimentation than any other setting to which they had been exposed previously. How political women perceived their political group relative to other settings was presented somewhat differently according to the informant. University students compared the way they were expected to behave at home, in class, or in the dormitory with the way they could act in their political group. Office and factory workers compared the limitations imposed on them in their role as woman

11. S. N. Eisenstadt, *From Generation to Generation* (New York, 1971), p. 46.
12. For these characteristics of small, face-to-face groups, see Sidney Verba, *Small Groups and Political Behavior* (Princeton, 1972), pp. 53–59.

worker with the greater freedom they enjoyed in taking part in activities of the company union. Housewives active in citizens' movements, feminist groups, or other informal political volunteer groups, compared the quality of participation in such groups with that in traditional women's groups, such as those for flower arranging or other Japanese arts, and groups oriented to a mother's responsibilities, such as the PTA.[13]

The experience of a union official at a Mitsubishi company provides an example of how most women saw their political group. Since her election to her half-time union position, the official's workday had been divided between her usual clerical duties and her union responsibilities. Each day, she said, she waited for the moment when she could leave her clerical job and take the elevator upstairs to the union office. It was not only that the content of the two jobs was different, but that the union work offered her more opportunities for self-expression. As she put it, "In the office, relations are vertical. You can't say anything if you're a woman. But in the union I can express myself freely. . . . I can put demands to my boss as a representative of the union." To the outsider observing her in the union office with her four male colleagues, there appeared to be a camaraderie among the male union representatives that did not fully include her. She accepted it as her duty, in the union office as well as in her regular job, to pour tea for the men. She went her separate way cheerfully when the male union officials went out drinking together after hours. If equality of participation is taken to mean that all tasks related to any given role are allocated on the basis of ability rather than sex, this official's behavior in a political group context hardly measured up to an ideal. But on her own scale, relative to how she was required to behave in other social settings, the political group offered her maximum personal latitude.

This having been said, it is also important to note that

13. In the same way, of course, the PTA, for some Japanese women, may be the forum offering maximum opportunities for role experimentation, relative to other settings to which *they* have been exposed. See Keiko Higuchi, "The P.T.A.—A Channel for Political Activism," *Japan Interpreter* 2 (Autumn 1975): 133–140, who argues that the PTA today is a major avenue by which women may acquire the leadership and organizational skills necessary for engaging in political action.

even on an objective scale, most political women to varying degrees *were* engaging in activities which many Japanese people—both inside and outside their circle of significant others—would consider avant-garde or unusual for a
woman. Even in those political parties and unions in which
traditional types of behavior for women were strongly approved, women members, even if they might pour tea for
male members and do a great deal of other "woman's work"
in the organization, generally had an opportunity to take part
in certain activities that many Japanese would consider inappropriate for a woman, such as speaking before large assemblies; addressing crowds from a sound truck; putting up
posters in support of a political candidate; and in the case of
union activists, leading a segment of workers in a May Day
Parade. Of the women active in radical student groups, the
number of those engaged in political activities that many
Japanese would consider "male" activities was even greater:
taking part in demonstrations, violent and nonviolent; appearing on stage at university gatherings to present their
sect's point of view; handing out pamphlets at major train
stations in Tokyo and answering the questions of passers-by;
engaging in a wide range of protest activities in public in de-
fense of an ideological and issue position. The fact that even
the most limited types of political participation involved at
least some behavior that most people would consider inappropriate for women helps explain why all women in the
sample experienced role strain to varying degrees. It also offers a basis for understanding how even the least active political women—whose political roles, to an American, would
seem extremely circumscribed and gender-typed—could experience some degree of change in her view of woman's role
in the political group setting. So far the discussion has explained how exposure to a political group setting over time
can provide the basis for challenging the dominant view of
woman's role by defying critics outside the group. The actual
process of change will be analyzed shortly.

The methods women employed to confront their critics,
and the consequences of their efforts to resolve role strain in
this way, varied widely. The main method was persuasion. In
some cases, political women's desire to convince their friends
to understand and accept their behavior had a missionary

quality. A dramatic example was a meeting held by a radical feminist collective on Mother's Day several years ago, to which the members invited their mothers. The feminists' objective was to explain to their mothers what was wrong with the way women were expected to behave in Japanese society. Only a handful of mothers showed up, and several of those sat stone-faced through the meeting, apparently unconvinced by their daughters' arguments. But the members persisted in their explanations with patience, sincerity, and conviction. Many activists had been much more successful in convincing certain persons, usually parents or other persons especially close to them, not only that their political activism was acceptable, but that it represented a desirable change in the way women were supposed to behave. In essence, they were resocializing persons outside the political group according to the new values they had come to accept inside it. But just as often their arguments fell on deaf ears. Many women, especially university students who had received support for their behavior not only from their political group, but from the larger surrounding subculture provided by the university, described the experience of going home in excitement to tell their parents about their political activities. They had expected a favorable reception and were shocked when they met opposition, criticism, or warnings from one or both parents. Their response to the criticism took several forms. If it was strong enough and if it was from a key figure in their life, some had dropped out of politics in disappointment and regret. Others resorted to compartmentalizing roles vis-à-vis that particular person. Or, they ceased contact altogether. But many women—perhaps sensing the ambivalence in the criticism when it came from their parents—continued their political activities and gradually tried to persuade their critics that it was all right for them as women to do so.

The process by which political women came to adopt the third strategy is important to study, for by defying their critics, women become active agents for change in society's definition of woman's role. By their example, by persuasion, or by active defiance of those who would criticize them, they argue for new views of woman's role under the terms of which political activism becomes acceptable behavior for women. How the process works may be illustrated with a case history.

Politics and Role Strain:
The Case of Satō Sadako

Satō Sadako, at twenty-four a member of the Youth League (Minsei) of the Japan Communist Party and a union activist, was a woman whose role ideology, political ideology, and lifestyle had been transformed over the space of five years in early adulthood. The daughter of impoverished farming parents in northern Japan, Sadako had come to Tokyo seeking work immediately after graduation from senior high school. There were few jobs to be had where she lived, and Tokyo seemed to offer the best prospects. Soon after her arrival she found a job copying letters in a small meat-processing company. The pay was low and the work dull, so after a year she decided to try to find a better job. While she was at loose ends looking for work, she made friends with some members of the All Campus Struggle Congress (Zenkyōtō),[14] a student organization active then, who lived in the working-class neighborhood where her tiny four-mat apartment was located. Soon she was attending the group's meetings and becoming more and more interested in political questions. As she talked with the group's members it had seemed to her increasingly that society was full of contradictions. "Beautiful girls could get all kinds of good positions, but ordinary girls like me who weren't beautiful and had no special skills couldn't get any kind of a decent job."

At last she found a job with a major publishing firm where she was assigned to do clerical work in the textbook division. If the work was still menial, it was more varied than before, and the people in the office were more interesting. The pay was also better. She continued to attend meetings of her political group in the evenings and occasionally took part in demonstrations with other members.

At night in the group's meetings she became increasingly

14. The All Campus Struggle Congress was a student movement group formed in the late 1960s and represented an alliance of various radical sects and also of protestors who were not members of sects. During its peak period in 1969, the group had a substantial student following. A survey of University of Tokyo students in 1969 found that 34 percent supported it. Tsurumi, "Student Movements in 1960 and 1969," pp. 22–23. Also see The Editorial Board, "Tōdai tōsō to gakusei no ishiki" (The Tokyo University struggle and student consciousness), *Sekai* 286 (September 1969): 63–71.

open about discussing her ideas. The group encouraged the members, male and female, to speak up. Gradually, Sadako was becoming something of a leader. At the office Sadako kept her opinions about office matters, her work, her ideas, to herself. She told no one about her political activities and avoided discussing political issues. Vis-à-vis her supervisors, like most of the young women in her office, she volunteered nothing in the way of an opinion unless asked, and did what she was told. If in the evening she agreed with the view of many in her political group that the marriage system oppressed men and women alike, at lunch she sat with other women in the office, appearing to be in pleasant agreement when they discussed their plans for getting a husband. In letters home she never mentioned her political activities. At this point, Sadako appears to have been compartmentalizing roles in her relationships with employers, office mates, and parents.

One day there was a mass meeting at the company of employees from all the various departments. At meetings of this kind, held regularly at the publishing company, the object was for management to explain its goals, policies, and employment practices to those assembled. Although the opinions of the workers were routinely solicited at such meetings, it was fairly well understood by the audience that they were there to listen respectfully. At this particular meeting the employees sat quietly as several new policies were announced. There were to be various new opportunities for male employees of the company, including the chance to study English at company expense. But, as an official mentioned in passing, women, as temporary employees, were not eligible for them. As she listened to the official, Sadako said, it came to her suddenly that women employees would never be treated like the men. They would have less status, less wages, less of a bonus, and as far as the company was concerned, things would always be that way. Sitting there in the audience, Sadako gradually became furious. Before she realized what she was doing, she was on her feet questioning the official. She expressed herself mildly, using the usual polite expressions called for in the situation, but her office mates around her in the audience were dumbfounded. After the meeting, 5 fellow employees came up to her and said that they had been thinking of trying to start a union in the company, and wondered if she would be willing to join them.[15] She agreed. Soon after, the number of their little group swelled to 8, then 10. A year and a half after the incident described above, the membership had grown to 350. It had taken that amount of time to win worker support and recognition by management, but by the time of the interview the union was well on its way, and Sadako was known to most people of the company as one of its main leaders.

At the time she was interviewed, Sadako had worked for a total of five years at the publishing company. She had never been promoted, but she explained that this was simply because of the company's policy toward women employees, not management's response to her union activities. In most ways her life went on as before. The political group had disbanded sometime after the 1968 campus struggles, but along with several former members she had joined a new radical sect with both students and workers in the membership. Most of her friends were in that group or in the union at the company. She continued to live in her four-mat apartment. Except for the time she gave to union activities, the outer form of her life was much the same as in her early years with the publishing company. When Sadako chose to speak up at the company meeting a year and a half earlier, however, she had begun to move in a somewhat new direction. Instead of compartmentalizing her life and limiting her experiment with woman's role to one carefully guarded area of her experience, she had begun to draw together, to integrate, her behavior according to the values to which she had been exposed in her political group, and at the same time had become an active agent for change. She began to talk rather freely in the office and to volunteer her opinions on many matters, political and nonpolitical. The Sadako of the political group became the Sadako of the union and the everyday life at the company.

The costs, by many people's standards, had been high. Al-

15. The majority of all unions in Japan are enterprise unions (composed of the workers in a given company or plant, regardless of their particular trade or skill, or whether they are white-collar or blue-collar) rather than industry-wide unions that are the norm in most advanced industrial societies. This explains why company members, rather than outside organizers, took the initiative in forming the union in this case.

though she had not been fired, Sadako admitted that she was
more or less shunned by many people in her section. "To
them I'm not a woman. They treat me like a man. I quarrel
like a man, talk like a man." When asked if she still poured
tea for the men in her section, she replied simply: "Nobody
asks me now." If there was a satisfaction in being herself in all
her social roles, the costs were greater than many people
would be willing to pay. To be cut off from the normal social
interaction of the office, to be ignored when the other women
went out after work to a coffee shop, to be treated with kid
gloves by the men in her office—these were a few of the costs
of being different.

At one point early in the days of organizing the union,
Sadako had decided to tell her parents about her political
views and activities. Since everyone at the company knew,
she saw no reason not to tell her parents. Because their own
lives had been so hard, she had hoped that they would be
able to understand her personal search for a better life. On
her annual visit home she told them everything. She was
surprised by the anger of their reaction. Her mother told her
that she would never be able to find anyone to marry her. Her
father told her that her efforts to form a union would get her
fired, that she had a good job for a woman, and that she had
risked it to get involved in a useless, futile effort. Both insisted that she get out of the union. Sadako left home in
anger, took the train back to Tokyo, and had not been home
since. She wrote her parents from time to time, and they
answered her letters. But on both sides the tone of the letters
was cool and distant. The subject of the union was never
mentioned.

In the particular way she went about integrating her life
according to the values and behavior she had come to accept
in her political role, Sadako was a bit unusual. If we recall the
young Red Army activist who was described in chapter three,
we see that women who were challenging woman's role as
actively and radically as Sadako was usually withdrew into a
subculture in which they were surrounded by people who
shared their values. In the process, many women had turned
away from conventional work roles, or had taken a job of
some kind connected with their political group or organization. In making almost a total break with a conventional envi-

ronment, these women created a new circle of significant others who supported their activism, and they avoided the disapproval Sadako faced each day at work in trying to maintain a new identity in an unsympathetic environment.

Most political women in the study had not gone so far in defying their critics. New Women, whose role ideology represented a less extreme departure from the norm, were able to take on the criticism directed at them by certain people in their lives without giving up a conventional lifestyle and without trying to confront all their critics. Typically, they tried to resocialize the people closest to them—parents or other close relatives, significant males in their lives, and close friends—while compartmentalizing in most of their other role relationships. But to the extent that they dealt with criticism directed at them from any quarter by attempting to explain why they opposed a restrictive view of woman's role, they too became active agents of social change.

Defying the Critics: Costs

Women who become politically active incur a number of risks to the extent that it becomes known that they are activists. Foremost among the risks were admonishments, social isolation, and rejection from at least some persons important to them. As chapter five indicated, most political women had at least one parent who overtly or covertly supported their role experimentation. In this respect Sadako's experience was unusual. But virtually all political women who defied their critics, even if they retained the love and support of some, risked rejection by others.

In addition, there were certain concrete risks. Holding a conventional job was not always easy for women who had come to challenge a conventional view of woman's role in their political group and who were prepared to confront their critics. Although most women resorted to compartmentalizing in their role relationships with fellow employees or employers, many became angry at sex discrimination in the workplace, which they experienced as an effort to make them conform to role demands they had rejected. But to speak out in a way that was characteristic of their behavior in their political group was to risk losing their job. Even more serious than the economic risks were the concrete costs related to the second of what Freud once described as a human being's two greatest needs, to work and to love. Political women who defied their critics had to weigh the costs of political participation to their marriage prospects, for marriage rather than employment is the normal route to security, prosperity, and status for women in Japan. Realistically, women who openly challenged the conventional definition of woman's role in their relationships with significant males ran a strong risk of rejection. To the average Japanese man and his parents, a political woman—whether a Red Army activist or a party worker in the Liberal Democratic Party—was likely to be seen as overly assertive and unsuitable for a conventional Japanese marriage.

If these were some of the possible costs of defying critics, it should be pointed out that the women who adopted the other two strategies incurred their own kinds of costs. Those who limited their own political participation, who accepted the constraints that many political groups imposed on them, or who struggled to "explain away" their political activism were never completely safe from criticism. Even if they had satisfied most people in their circle that their behavior was acceptable under the terms of the dominant definition of woman's role, many of the informants adopting this strategy seemed fearful of disapproval from some new and unexpected quarter. For example, a Neotraditional woman active in her father's political campaign might feel that everyone, including her present boyfriend, regarded her activities as fully acceptable. But suppose she broke up with her boyfriend, and suppose her political behavior led to a suspicion in the mind of a future candidate for an arranged marriage that she had become difficult to manage? These kinds of worries troubled a number of women who resorted to the first strategy as a way of handling role strain.

Similarly, role compartmentalization carried with it certain costs, foremost of which was the fear of being found out, of being confronted by an angry or critical parent or husband, or being talked about in the office or neighborhood. Even if it is true, as many writers suggest, that Japanese people have a somewhat greater psychological tolerance than people in many other societies for the kind of ambiguity inherent in compartmentalizing roles, the fear of being found out, and the guilt that sometimes accompanied deception, were nonetheless real.

Women who adopted the third strategy were free of risks like these. By stating their views openly, they avoided the ambiguity, deception, and fear that many political women experienced. Many of the most politically active women in the study, who had joined subcultures, by pulling away from significant others who disapproved of them and by building a new circle of friends who shared their values and who offered them strong personal validation, professed to have found—and appeared to have found—a high degree of personal satisfaction. In their subculture they felt free to experiment with a variety of roles and many styles of behavior that would be regarded as unacceptable for women outside it. In Maslow's terms, they were able to engage in self-actualizing behavior. Many had a number of the personal qualities (such as a capacity for empathy and a high level of self-knowledge) that students of "self-actualizing people" have observed in them.[16]

For the large majority of the sample whose role experiment was more modest and who maintained a conventional lifestyle, there was still a great deal of satisfaction in persuading persons close to them of the appropriateness of their behavior. Many married women who had come to a new view of woman's role prior to marriage had resocialized the man they ultimately married. A number of them had met their prospective mates in their political groups.

As this chapter indicated at the outset, few women used a single strategy to handle role strain. Often a woman used one strategy in one role relationship and another strategy in a different role relationship. For example, a political woman might reduce strain in her relationship with a disapproving male friend by "excusing away" her activism or by setting limits on her participation, but she might compartmentalize roles vis-à-vis her parents by not mentioning her political activities to them. Or, alternately, a political woman might confront

16. See Jeanne Knutson, *The Human Basis of the Polity* (Chicago, 1972), pp. 87–91.

FIGURE 1   *Relationship between Level of Female Role Demands and Level of Women's Active Political Participation*

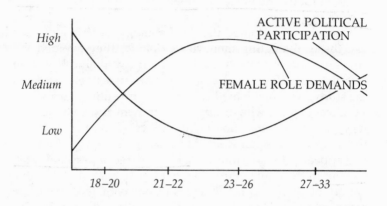

doubtful parents and try to convince them of the appropriateness of her behavior, but she might compartmentalize roles in role relationships with prospective mates. Analysis of the data suggested, however, that there was a close relationship between the level of role strain she experienced and the stage she had reached in the life cycle. The consequences for women's overall level of active political participation over the age range covered in the study are suggested in figure 1. How role strain operates and how women respond to it at various stages of the life cycle will now be examined.

Role Strain and the Life Cycle

Late Adolescence The youngest political women interviewed for the study were in their late teens. It was clear from comparing their experiences and attitudes with those of older activists that role strain was at a lower level for this age cohort than for any other in the age range eighteen to thirty-three. This was true for several reasons. The first related to the larger environment that typically was the setting for their activism. Most were university students, and as such, they were in a setting that appears to give women stronger support for role experimentation than virtually any other major institutional setting in Japan. To some extent, the same is probably true of the university environment in many, if not most, societies. Writers such as Newcomb, Keniston, and many others have long noted the special support the university gives for many types of experimentation, personal and political.[17] But in Japan it is especially true. The educational system, as was noted earlier, is a legacy of the democratizing efforts of the American occupation. Thirty-five years after the end of the war it continues to transmit values that are more nearly egalitarian than do most other institutions. The role demands placed upon women in the educational environment (especially in four-year coeducational institutions) are more consonant with the New Women's ideology or even the Radical Egalitarian ideology, described earlier, than with the dominant definition of woman's role upheld by most mainstream institutions in Japan.[18] Women in this age range can take part in political activities and feel, in doing so, that their behavior is more or less acceptable to most people in the university setting.

A second factor relates to the attitudes of parents during this stage of a daughter's maturation. Much evidence suggests that a great many middle-class and upper-middle-class parents in Japan treat a daughter's late adolescent years as a "grace period" during which they minimize role demands and go along with her experiment with woman's role.[19] As was indicated in chapter five, many such parents

17. See chapter four, n. 5.
18. The influence of higher education in colleges and universities in Japan on women's views of their role has been noted by a number of writers. Herbert Passin, *Society and Education in Japan* (New York, 1965), p. 111, observes its effect on women's expectations in marriage; Robert O. Blood, *Love Match and Arranged Marriage* (New York, 1967), p. 149, offers evidence of its influence on attitudes toward work; and survey results presented in Sumiko Iwao, "A Full Life for Modern Japan Women," in *Text of Seminar on Changing Values in Modern Japan*, ed. Nihonjin Kenkyūkai (Tokyo, 1977), pp. 99–111, offers evidence of its influence on women's attitudes toward woman's role.
19. One way to approach this phenomenon is to say that there are *different* sets of role demands at each developmental stage. See Ruth E. Hartley, "A Developmental View of Female Sex-Role Identification," in *Role Theory: Concepts and Research*, ed. Bruce J. Biddle and Edwin J. Thomas (New York, 1966), pp. 354–360. But at any given developmental stage, the content of the demands is determined in relation to the perceived demands of woman's primary adult role, which serves as an organizing principle for what is deemed acceptable behavior at any stage. As Hartley notes, mothers allowing girls to

encourage role experimentation even while they verbally discourage political activism. For this reason, activists who are in their late adolescence may find the pressure of role demands from their parents to be fairly low, or may even find that the demands are consonant with an alternative ideology of woman's role. A final reason is related to where the women stood in the life cycle relative to the concrete risks associated with activism. The ultimate cost of activism, as was indicated earlier, is to be thought unsuitable as a wife and mother. To adolescents, however, marriageable age seems far away. Asked if their political activities are "unfeminine" or damaging to their marriage chances, many political women in their late teens answered "No" in surprise. Asked about Japanese men's attitudes toward political women, they were likely to point to the men in their own political group who, they said, fully accepted them. Often they added that if they could not find such a man, they simply would not marry.

Young women in this age range could be found using all three strategies to resolve role strain when it arose, but the main point is that the level of role strain was far less during this period than at any other time.

The Early Twenties / As women activists reach their early twenties, there is a gradual increase in the pressures on them from significant others, primarily parents, who increasingly hold them to the dominant definition of woman's role. As they move closer to marriageable age, women also become aware that there may be very little in the way of an alternative to marriage in Japan. Whereas adolescents typically believed that they would be able to find a good job after graduation from college, many women in their early twenties were doubtful about their work prospects as they became increasingly aware of discrimination against women in the job market. Marriage began to loom much larger as their single viable alternative, a perspective driven home in the remarks of parents and peers. As these perceptions took

---

be tomboys fully expect them to shape up later on (p. 357). From that standpoint it makes sense to talk about the *level* of role demands at a given stage, and to talk about adolescence as a "grace period" extended to women before the level of role demands intensifies.

shape, political women became more aware that there was a discrepancy between their own behavior and the behavior expected of adult women in Japan.

At this stage, then, role strain intensified. Although women at all stages of their life may compartmentalize roles as a response to role strain, compartmentalization was an especially common strategy adopted during this period, especially in their relations with parents. By keeping the knowledge of their activism from their parents, political women in effect were attempting to extend the grace period granted to them by one or both parents earlier. Compartmentalization was also a common strategy for dealing with their activism vis-à-vis prospective mates. In their political group these women might be participating fully in a whole range of activities that many outsiders would regard as unfeminine. In the heat of an ideological discussion they might shout at and contradict others, just as the male members did. But outside the group, in interaction with nonactivist male contemporaries, these same women might be found behaving according to the traditional standards of male-female relations. They might drop their eyes demurely as their male companion expressed his opinions about politics, and nod in seeming acquiescence, even if they completely disagreed with him. In quiet moments they might speak seriously about their political convictions or activities, but if they sensed his disapproval, they might hint that they were tiring of their political involvement.

It may be added that similar behavior was sometimes observed in political women who were interacting with male fellow activists outside the political group setting. A number of political women pointed out that many male activists had a double standard of expectations for women who were participating in their political group. If the political woman was a friend or colleague, a male activist held her more or less to the same universalistic standard of behavior to which he held himself. If his relationship with her became more intimate, his attitudes and expectations of her underwent a subtle transformation. He began to hold her to a more traditional set of expectations, not only in their own one-to-one relationship, but in the way he expected her to behave in the political group.

The Marriage Crisis Women active in politics over the period from age twenty-three to about twenty-six typically experience intense role strain. For many, in fact, the strain reaches crisis proportions. There is maximum pressure on them from parents who are worried that the grace period may have lasted too long and that they, by being permissive, may have hurt their daughters' marriage chances. For political women, there is the almost daily experience of hearing friends talk about marriage prospects and marriage plans. There is a strong and growing fear as each year passes, parallel to the one felt by young men in the same age range attempting to establish themselves in careers, that they will be left behind, that they will lose out in the competition for a husband who could be their means to long-term success and prosperity. The prospects of electing the single life become frightening with a growing recognition of the limited nature of the work options available to women. Those working in offices, companies, and various organizations realize that they are expected to marry and leave soon. Those newly graduating from colleges and universities find their employment options extremely limited, which often comes as a surprise to many who have been outstanding students. Those working in blue-collar jobs hear stories of lucky young women who, by marrying up, no longer have to work on the assembly line.

Parents and peers become increasingly explicit in pointing out the costs, in terms of marriage prospects, of what they may see as the informant's "unfeminine" behavior in the political group or movement. Those young women who once spoke optimistically about finding a husband who would share their political convictions and support their plans of continuing in politics after marriage are engaged in an active search for this kind of mate. The search is more difficult than they once suspected because many of their male contemporaries who once shared in their political activities and accepted them as equals in the political setting are now under strong pressure from their *own* parents and nonactivist peers to opt for a traditional lifestyle, which involves not only a conventional work role, but the kind of wife willing to play the traditional woman's role at home.

Women in this age range are especially apt to vacillate in

the strategies they adopt to handle role strain. Many compartmentalize their lives rigidly as they try to attract a mate.
The following exchange with an activist aged twenty-three,
who was preparing to leave the university, demonstrates the
type of ambivalence and confusion they may feel at this stage
of their life:

INTERVIEWER: What kind of man do you want to marry?

INFORMANT: (laughs, very nervous) I don't know. . . .

INTERVIEWER: Many women are concerned about a man's future prospects, his income level, and so on. How do you feel
about that?

INFORMANT: Oh, that doesn't matter.

INTERVIEWER: What about his looks?

INFORMANT: I don't care about that, though of course it would
be nice if he were good-looking. The main thing I care about,
though, is that he be understanding and considerate.

INTERVIEWER: What about his intelligence?

INFORMANT: Oh, I think we should be equal in intelligence
. . . well, I guess it might be better if he were just a little more
intelligent than me. . . .

INTERVIEWER: How about his political attitudes?

INFORMANT: He wouldn't have to have the same views as me,
but I probably couldn't marry a man with completely different
views.

INTERVIEWER: What if you met a man you liked and then it
turned out that he was completely opposed to your having
been involved in the citizens' movement?

INFORMANT: (red, very nervous, in a low voice) I guess I might
marry him anyway if he were attractive enough in other
ways. . . .

INTERVIEWER: Would you tell him you had been active in the
movement?

INFORMANT: I probably wouldn't say openly that I had been
in the movement . . . (weakly) but I would probably insinu-
ate it. . . .

Other young women defied their critics. Confrontations with
parents were common. This was partly because pressure
from parents was mounting, but also because many women
felt angry and betrayed that the grace period that had been

granted to them earlier by one or both parents was being terminated. Though women tried various strategies to handle
role strain, it often appeared to reach intolerable levels. At
this stage, many political women dropped out of politics altogether.

The Late Twenties and Early Thirties / By their late
twenties, most political women had passed through the
period of crisis just described. Although they had responded
to its pressures in many different ways, most patterns of reso-
lution led to a reduction in the level of role strain. As was
indicated above, some women had eliminated the strain altogether by dropping out of politics. But for most of the
women who were still active in politics in their late twenties,
role strain had been reduced by key life choices they had
made during the marriage crisis. It was remarkable to find
that every veteran activist aged twenty-seven to thirty-three
was either single or had married a fellow political activist. In
either case, role strain was greatly reduced, but the implications of this finding are startling. It appears that the fears of
many young activists and their parents are borne out in reality. A conventional marriage (i.e., to a man outside her political group) is not a likely prospect for a political woman in
Japan.

Few political women had survived the marriage crisis
without a confrontation of some kind with their parents.
Some political women had won over their parents. Others
had failed to convince them of the appropriateness of their
behavior. In either case, by their late twenties, they had managed to reduce the level of role strain by surrounding themselves with significant others who shared their values and
who offered them support and personal validation in their
role experiment. Sometimes this involved entry into the subculture provided by a political group; sometimes it meant
marrying a man who shared their view. By their late twenties,
most had evolved a fairly coherent lifestyle in which they
were able to translate an alternative ideology of woman's role
into behavior.[20]

20. This is not meant to imply that marriage to a fellow activist was without problems, or that remaining politically active was easy. Many male activists are ambivalent about what they want from the women they marry,

The discussion so far has focused on veteran activists, women in their late twenties who had been active for some time, dating from their late teens to their mid-twenties. As was indicated, most of these women appeared to have found their personal solutions to role strain. However, when we examine the experiences of new recruits, women who were becoming politically active for the first time in their late twenties, once again role strain was in evidence. The new recruits were married women, some with small children, who had become interested in local civic issues. Their selection of a marriage partner, however, had been made before they became interested in joining a political group, and many found their husband, in-laws, and often their neighbors unsympathetic toward their desire to participate in political activities.

These newcomers to politics handled the role strain by resorting to all three of the strategies discussed earlier, depending on who their critics were. Vis-à-vis their husbands, a number of them compartmentalized roles. Here they were supported by the normal pattern of marriage in Japan (see chapter three), which involves a clear separation of the tasks and responsibilities of the two partners. Japanese husbands tend to be somewhat less inquisitive about what their wife is doing in her own sphere of activity than husbands in many Western societies might be. Those who did not compartmentalize in their role relationship with their husband generally sought to justify their behavior by using the acceptable rationale that their activism was really "for the family's sake"

---

even if their wives are fellow activists. Structural constraints (e.g., the reality of childcare responsibilities) often reduce the level of a woman's activism. Finally, there are social-psychological changes that may alter a woman's political sense of self. As Lynn and Flora note, "Once a woman is defined in terms of child and household duties, it may be difficult to diversify her interaction cycle to permit development—or redevelopment—of a political self." Naomi B. Lynn and Cornelia B. Flora, "Motherhood and Political Participation: The Changing Sense of Self," *Journal of Political and Military Sociology* 1 (Spring 1973), p. 95. In the sample for this study, veteran activists who had married typically remained active in politics, but at a much-reduced level, at least during the early years of child rearing. Also see Cornelia B. Flora and Naomi B. Lynn, "Women and Political Socialization: Considerations of the Impact of Motherhood," in *Women in Politics*, ed. Jane S. Jaquette (New York, 1974), pp. 37–53.

or "for the children's sake." Several women who had adopted this latter strategy expressed regret in the interview that they had done so. Especially if these women had small children, husbands who previously had seldom asked about their daily activities began checking up on them to make sure that their political involvement was not resulting in neglect of their duties. These women wondered aloud if it might not have been better to say nothing. Surprisingly few women handled role strain by confronting a critical husband. Having entered the wife-mother role in a conventional marriage relationship, it was extremely difficult for most women to try to renegotiate the terms of that role, especially during the childbearing years when the level of role demands was highest.

Concluding Remarks

The level of role strain experienced by political women in this study is vivid testimony to why so few women become politically active in Japan, despite the many changes that have occurred since women were granted full political rights after 1945. Except for the youngest activists, women in every age cohort from age eighteen to thirty-three confronted major constraints on their active political participation, and even the youngest activists were not altogether immune to role strain. From the experiences of these political women, it appears that remaining active in politics over the crucial twenties is extremely difficult in Japan unless a political woman is prepared to shape a new lifestyle—a high cost to pay for political activism by many people's standards. Even if many veteran activists were finding satisfaction, and perhaps self-actualization, in adopting alternative lifestyles in or outside a political subculture, few people in any society are prepared to restructure their lifestyle to accommodate a desire to remain active in political groups and causes. Women who had settled on a conventional lifestyle and had married *before* they entered politics encountered their own kinds of problems. As young married women they confronted major opposition and criticism from significant others—husbands, in-laws, neighbors—for attempting to renegotiate the terms of the wife-mother role to accommodate political activism.

The age range set for this study brought together a group of women who were passing through the critical, formative stages of the life cycle when key decisions concerning education, work, and marriage were concentrated. During these stages, role demands are at their highest level. It is true that many women in Japan become involved in voluntary political activities at later stages of the life cycle. Beyond the age of thirty-three, the outer age limit of the study, certain role demands on women begin to subside, especially after the children are in school.[21] But patterns set in the twenties, when so many key life decisions are made, have a major influence on later behavior and on the options and possibilities of the years ahead. Women who in their twenties and early thirties discover that political activism is unacceptable behavior for women, and that it can be engaged in only at high social and psychological costs, are unlikely to enter adulthood with strong, positive feelings about participating in politics. This is a reality important in understanding an overall pattern of political participation in Japan in which the part played by women is as yet quite small.

21. For changes in the life cycle during these years and their implications for women's involvement in outside activities, including political voluntarism, see Linda L. Perry, "Mothers, Wives, and Daughters in Osaka," Ph.D. dissertation, University of Pittsburgh, 1976, pp. 191–218.

7

The Future of Political Women

Political women have been the subject of much recent inquiry. Until the early 1970s, research on women's political behavior focused almost exclusively on women's marginality to political life. Everywhere—in the advanced industrial societies and in the less developed countries as well—studies had shown that women voted at a lesser rate than men, engaged in political discussion less often than men, had less of a sense of political efficacy than men, were less interested in politics than men, and were less likely than men to join political groups, run for office, and attain positions of power. By the late 1960s women's lesser rate of political participation throughout the world had come to be regarded as a fact of modern political life.[1]

1. As Lane noted in the 1950s, "That women should vote less than men has become a fact so familiar now that it has been taken for granted." Robert E. Lane, *Political Life* (New York, 1959), p. 209. See the discussions of

No sooner had gender differences in political behavior come to be taken for granted than the "fact" of women's lesser political participation was itself challenged. By the late 1960s, gaps between the voting rates for men and women were closing in many of the advanced countries.[2] The findings of several recent studies of political socialization conducted in the United States, Britain, and Finland raise questions as to whether some of the male-female differences in children's political orientation and behavior that had turned up in previous research hold today.[3] One explanation of the contradictory findings was that previous studies may have been marred by problems of sampling or measurement; another explanation, compelling in light of an apparent revolution in gender-role attitudes reflected in the results of recent surveys in many countries, was that the differences themselves were disappearing by the early to mid-1970s.[4] Beyond these changes at the level of mass political behavior, a number of writers, noting that women's lesser rates of partic-

women's political behavior in Lester W. Milbrath, *Political Participation* (Chicago, 1965); Gabriel A. Almond and Sidney Verba, *The Civic Culture* (Boston, 1965), p. 325; and Angus Campbell et al., *The American Voter* (New York, 1960), pp. 325. In each case the writers simply document the fact of women's lesser rate of political participation with little discussion.

2. See Marjorie Lansing, "The American Woman: Voter and Activist," in *Women in Politics*, ed. Jane S. Jaquette (New York, 1974), pp. 5–23, who traces this process of change in the United States. For evidence tracing the same overall trend in Europe, see Maurice Duverger, *The Political Role of Women* (Paris, 1955), and Josephine F. Milburn, *Women as Citizens: A Comparative Review* (Beverly Hills, 1976), p. 25.

3. See Anthony M. Orum et al., "Sex, Socialization, and Politics," in *A Portrait of Marginality*, ed. Marianne Githens and Jewel L. Prestage (New York, 1977), pp. 22–33; Veronica Stolte Heiskanen, "Sex Roles, Social Class and Political Consciousness," *Acta Sociologica* 14 (1971): 83–95; Robert E. Dowse and John A. Hughes, "Girls, Boys and Politics," *British Journal of Sociology* 22 (March 1971): 53–67; Richard M. Merelman, *Political Socialization and Educational Climates: A Study of Two School Districts* (New York, 1971). A valuable article by Sapiro notes, however, that findings pointing to an absence of childhood or adolescent sex differences in political attitudes do not necessarily mean that children are not learning gender-typed political roles. Virginia Sapiro, "Is the Child the Mother of the Woman?" *Journal of Politics*, in press.

4. Orum et al., "Sex, Socialization, and Politics," pp. 31–33, discuss both of these alternative explanations, although they do not take a position.

ipation generally had been traced to role conflict, began pointing out that certain political roles, such as activities of support
for political candidates or causes, are probably much easier to
reconcile with female role norms than previous researchers
had assumed, given the long tradition of female volunteerism
on behalf of church or charity in Western countries.[5] By the
mid-1970s, a wave of revisionism had led to the view, supported by much recent research in the United States, that
whatever the situation might have been in the past, dis-
parities between male and female participation had all but
disappeared in all major modes of citizen political activity,
from voting to campaigning on behalf of political candidates.[6]
    As a result of these changes, concern among Western
scholars looking at their own societies focuses increasingly on
women's representation at the elite level, where profound in-
equalities remain. But as the focus of research shifts, it is important to remember that the seeming disappearance of gender differences at lower levels of participation in a few of the
most advanced countries is a very recent phenomenon. Less
than twenty years ago, gaps of 10 to 15 percent between the
voter turnout of men and of women were so common and
persistent in the United States and Western Europe that
many observers regarded them as immutable. Indeed, the
issue of women's representation at the elite level is salient
today in the advanced industrial nations only because now,
as a result of profound changes in women's views of self and
role in those countries in the twentieth century, there is a
large pool of politically interested and aware women who

5. See, for example, Barbara G. Farah and Virginia Sapiro, "New Pride
and Old Prejudice," paper presented at the Annual Meeting of the Southern
Political Science Association, Nashville, 1975, pp. 5–7; Marcia M. Lee, "Towards Understanding Why Few Women Hold Public Office," in *A Portrait of
Marginality*, ed. Marianne Githens and Jewel Prestage (New York, 1977), p.
132; and John W. Soule and Wilma E. McGrath, "A Comparative Study in
Male-Female Political Attitudes at Citizen and Elite Levels," in ibid., pp.
192–193.
    6. Fiedler reached this conclusion after examining data from the 1972 Cen-
ter for Political Studies Election Study, the 1972 CPS Convention Delegate
Study, and the 1972 Virginia Slims poll. Maureen Fiedler, "The Participation
of Women in American Politics," paper presented at the Annual Meeting of
the American Political Science Association, San Francisco, 1975, p. 6. Her
findings and those of other recent studies are reported in Jane S. Jaquette,
"Review Essay: Political Science," *Signs* 2 (Autumn 1976), p. 148.

give much time to politics, yet do not end up in positions of
real power. If the pool did not exist, the question whether
these women make it into the elite would not arise.

Except in a handful of countries, in most of the world today, differences between the political behavior, orientation,
and representation of women and men remain at all levels of
political life, elite and nonelite. The role redefinition process
that has been the central concern of this book is a very
gradual one going on at different rates in all countries. In no
country, including the United States, is that process completed.

When developments in Japan are considered in relation to
world trends, it becomes possible to distinguish four factors
that affect how far the process of role definition has proceeded in any particular country. The first is the timing of the
introduction of suffrage and other political rights for women.
The second is the origin of the impetus for their introduction—specifically, whether the impetus was internal or external to the country. The third is the degree of indigenous
support for the new rights at the time of their introduction.
The fourth is the level of socioeconomic and political development that the country has achieved since.

All of these factors emerge in a review of the steps by
which women's political rights have spread over the world in
the past one hundred years. Women's emergence into political life began in the non-Catholic Western states and in their
most europeanized colonies as a product of far-reaching
changes—economic, social, and ideological—in the eigh-
teenth and nineteenth centuries. During the period when
women were gaining basic political rights in New Zealand
(1893), Australia (1902), the Soviet Union (1917), England and
Germany (1918), the United States (1920), and Canada (1922),
women were excluded from most modes of political participation in the rest of the world (see table 14).[7] Thereafter a second, and eventually a third, wave of countries debated and
finally adopted legal guarantees of women's political rights,
along with many other ideas and institutions of the West. But
as was noted at the outset of the book, the impetus for change
typically came from outside the country in the context of a

7. See Milburn, *Women as Citizens*, pp. 8–9.

TABLE 14 Granting of Suffrage to Women in Selected Countries, by Year, and according to Four Historical Stages, or "Waves"

Fourth Wave* (1972–)	Third Wave (1950–1971)	Second Wave (1923–1949)	First Wave (1893–1922)
Islamic Third World Countries	Newly-independent Third World Countries	Late Developing Societies (Catholic Europe, Eastern Europe, "most developed" countries of the Third World)	Advanced Western Societies (non-Catholic Europe, U.S., USSR, "Europeanized" British colonies)
Saudi Arabia	Pakistan (1950)	Turkey (1934)	New Zealand (1893)
Nigeria (Northern States)	Indonesia (1950)	India (1935)	Australia (1902)
Jordan	Nicaragua (1955)	Philippines (1937)	Denmark (1915)
Yemen	Upper Volta (1960)	Cuba (1940)	Soviet Union (1917)
Kuwait	Malta (1964)	Quebec (1940)	England (1918)
Liechtenstein	Tunisia (1969)	France (1944)	Luxembourg (1919)
	Kenya (1969)	Japan (1945)	Netherlands (1919)
	Syria (1969)	Hungary (1945)	Austria (1919)
	Somalia (1970)	Yugoslavia (1946)	United States (1920)
	Switzerland (1971)	Italy (1947)	Sweden (1921)
		Argentina (1947)	Thailand (1921)
		Belgium (1948)	Canada (except Quebec) (1922)
		Chile (1949)	

*Countries where women were not eligible to vote as of 1971.

SOURCE: For states that granted suffrage prior to 1950, dates are those that appear in U.S. Department of Labor, Women's Bureau, "Women's Suffrage among the Nations," September 1950, or in Josephine F. Milburn, *Women as Citizens: A Comparative Review* (Beverly Hills, 1976). Where the dates given in the two sources conflict, the earlier date is given. For third and fourth waves, data are as reported by the states to the United Nations as of 1970–71. United Nations General Assembly Report No. 8132, *Derechos Políticos de la Mujer* (New York, December 15, 1970), and Report No. 8481, *Droits Politiques de la Femme* (New York, November 30, 1971).

colonial situation, a revolution guided by Western ideology, or in the case of Japan, a military occupation by a foreign power. Indigenous support for women's political rights was lacking, or was found among a Western-educated elite whose views were far out of step with those of the vast majority of the population. As a result, in the great majority of the second- and third-wave states, women's political rights have far shallower roots than in the original suffrage states, where such gains came as the result of centuries of ferment over the issues of human equality and individual rights. Historical factors surrounding the introduction of political rights for women thus set initial parameters within which role redefinition occurs. Thereafter, the pace at which change proceeds is affected by socioeconomic and political variables, as will be discussed shortly.

The historical pattern described above has had a profound influence not only on the overall pace at which role redefinition has progressed in a given country, but on where things stand now. Tension between female role demands and the demands of political roles arises at a "threshold of activism" that varies with the society and that appears to move upward over time as women's political participation at lower levels of activism gains acceptance. Voting, for example, is now acceptable activity for women in a great many countries, including Japan, and is thus below the threshold. Women in such countries can vote, in other words, without experiencing role strain. In the advanced industrial societies, the threshold has shifted upward to a far higher level. As was indicated above, the struggle there for acceptance of women's right to engage in political activity is largely confined to elite types of participation, such as running for and holding elective office or gaining key appointive positions in government or in major political organizations. The disappearance of gender differences in most lower-level, citizen modes of participation in these countries indicates that the dominant definition of woman's role has more or less adjusted to accommodate them. Major variations in women's worldwide gains in the area of politics can be explained in this framework (see figure 2).

In Japan middle-range activities are the battleground on which the struggle over role redefinition is being waged

FIGURE 2   *"Threshold of Activism," according to Historical Stages, or "Waves," in the Granting of Suffrage*

Level of Political Involvement	Fourth-Wave States (some Arab countries and a few other remaining states)	Third-Wave States (Egypt, Mexico, most Third World countries)	Second-Wave States (Catholic Europe, India, Japan)	First-Wave States (Anglo-Europe, Scandinavia, U.S., USSR)
High (holding elective and appointive offices)	unacceptable	unacceptable	unacceptable	marginal
Middle (voluntary political activities)	unacceptable	marginal to unacceptable	marginal	acceptable
Low (voting, other forms of mass political behavior)	unacceptable	marginal	acceptable	acceptable

today. The book has tried to illuminate the nature and dynamics of the role redefinition process that gradually reduces the conflict and at the same time to show how difficult that struggle is. The costs—psychological and social—of engaging in types of political behavior that are not considered fully acceptable for women can be extraordinarily high, as the previous chapter showed. To understand why certain women throughout the world are willing to incur such costs it is important to look back over what has been said so far to discover the major appeals and satisfactions of activism from the vantage point of political women. It is assumed that political involvement holds many attractions that operate equally well for women and men. Political volunteerism satisfies affiliational needs for both sexes. Similarly, both men and women may be strongly attracted to the possibility, in a group situation, of holding positions of leadership and power. Furthermore, the ideological appeals of activism can be great for both sexes. As a number of writers have suggested, causes associated with the political Left carry moral authority and strong ideological attractions in Japan's divided political culture, especially among young people.[8] There was no reason to believe, on the basis of interviews with political women who were involved in such causes, that the ideological appeals of activism were for them any less or any more than for politically active men.

Beyond these and other types of attractions that political volunteerism holds for both sexes there were certain appeals of activism that had special meaning for women. Most of these were directly related to women's roles, status, and options in contemporary Japanese society, or to the dynamics of the role redefinition process as it unfolds in the experience of individual women. If political involvement did not offer some of these role-related attractions and satisfactions, it is doubtful that women would be willing to incur the numerous personal costs of political activism at this stage of Japanese history.

The first set of appeals arises from the content of political roles, relative to the content of most other roles available to women in Japan today. As the book has shown, becoming politically active offered women a chance to engage in many tasks that were normally off limits to them in most settings in Japanese society. Debating political issues, addressing a crowd with a bullhorn, persuading others to join a political cause, making and defending political demands, organizing a group activity, and exercising responsibility as a leader—all were described by various informants as activities that were wholly new to them and that held a measure of excitement and exhilaration, gave them a sense of self-esteem, and were

8. Herbert Passin, "Sources of Protest in Japan," *American Political Science Review* 56 (June 1962): 391–403.

extremely satisfying. From their own vantage point, political roles offered them *more* latitude to engage in new types of behavior than any other roles they played.

The second type of attraction arose from the particular way that voluntary political participation could be fitted into the set of roles typically allocated to women in Japan. The wife-mother role, as many writers have shown and as the informants' lives revealed, sets numerous constraints on how women can use the time that they have available to them for other pursuits. If an adult woman is intent upon finding satisfying activities to combine with the wife-mother role, her range of options is likely to be extremely limited. This is especially true of her employment opportunities, because, as chapter three indicated, work options for the type of highly educated woman who was well represented in the sample are as yet fairly limited in Japan. Although the job market provides opportunities in the manufacturing, sales, and service sectors to less-educated Neotraditional women who are eager for an undemanding job that can be combined easily with traditional role demands, it provides fewer employment opportunities for well-educated women who want a job that is commensurate with their intelligence and training. For that reason, many such women interviewed for this study perceived their work options to be extremely unattractive. Furthermore, even if women can find a job they would accept, work roles, because of problems of finding and paying for regular childcare, because of the inflexibility of hours, and because the type of commitment that is asked of a worker may be too demanding, especially for married women in the age range for this study whose childcare responsibilities typically weigh heavy. In contrast, the role of a political volunteer has flexible demands from the standpoint of scheduling and of the amount of time that has to be committed to it. Membership in a political group does not have to be time-consuming. The level of involvement can be determined by the woman herself. Meetings can be missed if a child is sick. When female-role demands intensify with the birth of another child or as the result of a new set of expectations brought to bear by a husband or in-laws, a political role may be terminated summarily. As Goode points out, it is impossible to drop out of most roles that an individual occupies over a lifetime.[9] Voluntary political roles are exceptions and, for that reason, hold particular attractions.

It is not only for married women that these structural features of active political participation have appeal. The wife-mother role involves extensive anticipatory socialization that sets constraints on women's options prior to entering it. The closer a woman gets to marriageable age, the more intense the level of role demands upon her, as the previous chapter showed. For a woman prior to marriage to make major commitments of her time and energies to activities that cannot be easily terminated when a prospective mate appears is to invite pain, disruption, and personal trauma. It is far easier to drop out of a voluntary political group than it is to drop out of graduate or professional school or to quit a job that holds strong attractions.

A third type of appeal was both psychological and role related. As political psychologists have long noted, one of the attractions of political activism for both men and women is that it offers them a channel for the displacement and release of anger. It is natural, then, that for some women, one of the attractions of activism, consciously or unconsciously, is that it provides a way to release role-related anger. Women in Japan, like women in all societies today, experience many forms of sex discrimination in their daily lives. Few women interviewed for this study failed to recount at least some experiences in which they—despite their talents, abilities, or accomplishments—had been passed over in some way because they were women. Meanwhile, democratic ideology introduced in the postwar period has heightened their awareness of the discrepancy between what the laws say and the reality of everyday life in Japan, making women more conscious of the injustices they may experience. Faced with the sense that there is a gap between what they should be able to expect and what they actually get, women feel disappointment, frustration, and anger. Political participation provides an outlet and target for the release of such feelings. Protest

9. William J. Goode, "A Theory of Role Strain," *American Sociological Review* 25 (August 1960): 486.

activities in particular hold these attractions, but all types of political activity, because they involve the dimension of struggle against opposing forces, whether on behalf of a point of view or a candidate, offer an outlet for strong feelings.

A fourth attraction is derived from the intrapsychic dimensions of the process of role redefinition, as they have been described in this study. Most women's entry into politics had been preceded by role experimentation. Such experimentation, it was pointed out, was generally supported indirectly by the hopes and aspirations of their mothers, even when those same mothers were outwardly voicing disapproval over their daughters' behavior. To the extent that this factor was in evidence, political women undoubtedly derived strong psychological gratification from living out the aspirations of mothers who were obtaining vicarious satisfaction from their adventures in a new area of activity.

A fifth set of appeals of political volunteerism related to particular types of affiliational needs that were met for women through group participation. As was noted earlier, group membership answers affiliational needs for both men and women. In Japan, however, because of demands associated with the male and female gender roles, women may have a special receptivity to the types of ties represented by group membership. Urban, unemployed housewives in particular are likely to have rather limited social networks compared with those of their husbands, as chapter three indicated. Because of work demands on their husbands and because much male leisure activity in Japan does not include wives, the urban housewife may experience considerable isolation, especially if her own family of origin lives elsewhere. A civic or political group made up of age peers thus offers considerable attraction.

For young women prior to marriage, group membership meets other types of affiliational needs. As a result of the change in values that has occurred since 1945, a great many young people today are attracted to new styles of relations with the opposite sex in which there is more camaraderie and openness than have characterized male-female relations in Japan in the past. Yet it is still relatively difficult in Japan to find informal settings that bring together men and women in a situation where they can get to know each other, where

they can work together to realize shared goals. Voluntary political groups met women's need to experiment with a new
and more open style of relating to men and, in some cases,
had led them to prospective mates who were willing to accept
their experiment with woman's role.

A sixth attraction was the appeal of service to others. Many
types of voluntary political activities call on the participant to
do something for others, whether for a candidate, for victims
of pollution, or for members of a minority group in Japan.
Even within political groups themselves, there are opportunities to serve and nurture other group members. This feature of volunteerism, which is highly consonant with the
norms associated with many other social roles women play,
had strong emotional attractions for a number of political
women. Even when they objected, as many did, to pressures
to do "women's work" for the group by serving food or per-
forming other related chores, the ideal of service itself, in an
emotional sense, had strong attractions for them. This appeal
of political volunteerism—in fact, of volunteer activities in
general—draws women to such activities in Western countries as well.[10] It can be argued, however, that the strong emphasis on nurturing, service to others, and self-sacrifice in the
dominant ideology of woman's role makes this appeal especially salient in Japan.

Finally, as was discussed throughout this study, political
activism represented an important opportunity for women to
experiment with woman's role and to translate an alternative
role ideology into behavior in a setting that provided strong
support for personal change. As was indicated earlier, not
only did some degree of role change precede most women's
entry into politics, but political participation in a group context supported still further change in women's notions of self
and role. Many factors contributed to this process: the opportunity to engage in activities new to women; the sense of
self-esteem that accompanied the performance of challenging
new roles; the experience of crossing the boundaries of ap-

10. See Doris B. Gold, "Women and Voluntarism," in *Woman in Sexist
Society*, ed. Vivian Gornick and Barbara K. Moran (New York, 1971), pp.
533–554; Ingunn Norderval Means, "Women in Local Politics: The Norwegian Experience," *Canadian Journal of Political Science* (September 1972), pp.
365–388; and Farah and Sapiro, "New Pride and Old Prejudice," pp. 3–7.

propriate role behavior, which tended to increase political women's sense of self-confidence and spirit of adventure; and, perhaps most important, the validation from others engaged in a similar experiment.

All these factors help explain why political women are drawn to political groups and what special satisfactions they may be deriving from political participation. Despite the numerous costs and risks associated with women's entry into politics, the appeals of political volunteerism are very great for many women. In the end, the role redefinition process is under way throughout the world because increasing numbers of women find the attractions and satisfactions of activism greater than the risks and costs associated with it.

One remaining question deserves consideration in this book. What will be women's place in political life in Japan in the years ahead? Throughout the book, role redefinition has been viewed as a worldwide process going on at various rates and involving similar stages. Following the logic of that view, it is possible to predict that political volunteerism and other citizen modes of participation in the not-so-distant future will gain full acceptance in Japan as activities appropriate for women. At the same time, other aspects of the analysis throw doubts on such an optimistic prediction. The conditions under which women gained political rights in Japan, as in most of the non-Western world, were vastly different from those that obtained in the original suffrage states, as this chapter showed. Can women's political rights, planted late in unfriendly soil by foreigners who did not fully understand local conditions, flourish in Japan and, by implication, elsewhere outside the original suffrage states?

The prediction of this book is that they can and will, in the presence of the types of key socioeconomic and political factors that so far have operated in Japan since the granting of women's suffrage. A close look at postwar trends in Japan reveals much evidence that the number of women who engage in political volunteerism will increase, and that the pace at which role redefinition is proceeding will accelerate. Behind this change and behind the process of role redefinition itself are the forces that support change in the dominant ideology of woman's role, which, in turn, will affect attitudes

—on the part of individual women and of society at large—toward women's political participation. As chapter three showed, urbanization, the spread of the nuclear family, and economic prosperity all have major influence on the options and possibilities open to women. There is no sign of abatement in the first two processes in Japan, and as for the third factor, most predictions are that prosperity in Japan will continue and that the middle-class lifestyle associated with it will spread. All of the advanced industrial societies, it is true, are adjusting in the 1980s to lower levels of growth; still, among those countries, Japan's relative economic position is fairly secure. Education for women is another key force supporting role change, and on that front, too, there are no major signs of a reversal of current trends. As chapter three indicated, trends over the postwar period point to ever-increasing numbers of women entering higher education, including the types of universities where they are at present least represented. Demographic factors are an equally powerful spur to role change for women, for they set the broad parameters that define women's options. Today in Japan, family size is small, and most married women complete their childcare responsibility by their late thirties. Because average life expectancy for women now is over seventy-seven, women increasingly face a long stretch of their lives during which the wife-mother role cannot fully occupy their time. These underlying demographic changes press women toward a variety of activities to round out their lives, from part-time and full-time employment, to hobbies and other leisure activities, to participation in politics. All these forces operate to modify the dominant view of woman's role and thus to support role redefinition in the area of politics. Socioeconomic factors operating in Japan at present, and probably for some time to come, provide a powerful impetus for change in women's views of self and role and push Japan down the path already followed by the original suffrage states.

Political factors support the same direction of change. Recent writers, pointing to trends in Japan as well as in the United States and Western Europe, suggest that there is a growing popular commitment in all three settings to the belief that political change is a natural and desirable goal in a modern society. [11] This development has a strong influence on the growth of participant orientations among citizens, and leads to greater diversification in the number and types of political roles available to men and women. [12] That such roles hold attractions for Japanese women today is indicated in the results of a recent national survey in which one out of every five women questioned stated an interest in participating in civic activities—a very high number given the relatively small proportion of people in any society who become politically active. [13]

Socioeconomic and political factors, then, strongly support the contention that increasing numbers of women in Japan will seek out active political roles in the future. For those women, the process of entry into political life will have been made easier by political women today who, as agents of change, are smoothing the way for them. As the dominant definition of woman's role expands to accommodate middle-range political activities of the type represented by volunteerism, the front line of the struggle over role redefinition will move forward into the area of elite-level participation. What will happen at that stage in Japan is difficult to predict. As recent studies conducted in the United States have shown, resistance to women's entry at the highest levels of political life can be great, even in societies where virtually all other modes of political participation for women have gained acceptance. What we do know is that as a result of changes that are occurring today in Japan, there will be a large pool of women who have the *potential* of vying for top elective and appointive positions in government and in parties and po-

11. Michael Crozier, Samuel Huntington, and Joji Watanuki, *The Crisis of Democracy* (New York, 1975).

12. Ibid. Also see Taketsugu Tsurutani, *Political Change in Japan* (New York, 1977); Robert E. Ward, *Japan's Political System* (Englewood Cliffs, N.J., 1978), pp. 69–70; and Heinz Eulau, Samuel Eldersveld, and Morris Janowitz, *Political Behavior* (Glencoe, Ill., 1956).

13. Ministry of Foreign Affairs, *Status of Women in Modern Japan* (Tokyo, 1975), p. 28. Twenty-one percent stated their interest in participating in such activities, and 7 percent expressed a positive willingness to do so. For comparative purposes, it may be noted that only approximately 4 to 8 percent of all Americans are political volunteers. (Marjorie Lansing, "The American Woman: Voter and Activist," in *Women in Politics*, ed. Jane S. Jaquette (New York, 1974), p. 16.) Even if the level of Japanese women's participation falls far short of the desires they express in surveys, the figure is still high.

litical organizations. Through participating in political activities in the middle range, they are acquiring the political skills and experience that are prerequisites for leadership roles. Whether they will take the steps toward equal representation at the highest levels, and if so, whether society will accommodate their struggles, are questions for the future. But they are questions that cannot be answered today for any country in the world. In no state has equal representation in positions of real power been achieved for women.

APPENDIX A

The Study: Supplementary Notes

This section is intended to tell interested persons more about the research design of the study and how it was operationalized in the field. It is especially hoped that this section may be of use to people who are conducting fieldwork abroad for the first time, and who wonder how to begin the awesome task of making a research design fit the complex reality they find around them.

The design for this particular project had been developed well in advance of my arrival in Japan in January 1971. The fall of 1971, however, found me still thrusting around for a way to locate women who not only met the objective requirements I had set for the sample (i.e., were activists aged eighteen to thirty-three), but who would be willing to cooperate in the research. At the time I began my search for the informants I had been living in Tokyo for some nine months, and the terrain was becoming familiar. Over these months I had worked with sociologist Tsurumi Kazuko of the Institute of International Relations at Sophia University, where I was a Visiting Foreign Research Scholar. I was greatly aided in refining the research design in various discussions with Professor Tsurumi. However, when it came down to the question of how to go about meeting suitable political women, Professor Tsurumi pointed out that in this, no one could really help me. Although people might introduce me to young women activists, there was no guarantee that they would talk to me about their personal lives. The key, she said, would be gaining their confidence.

My first efforts were heavy-handed and embarrassing to recall. The most visible young women activists in Tokyo are students, members of various sects of the Japanese student movement, who along with their male colleagues distribute political leaflets at major subway stations in the city. Finally one day, feeling ready, I went up to one of these young women, introduced myself, and asked if she would be willing to tell me something about herself and her group. She was taken completely off-guard, mumbled a hasty "No, I can't," and rushed off to join other members of her radical faction. By that time, they were all regarding me with dark, suspicious faces. I left hastily.

Then one day I had the good fortune to hear through a Japanese friend about a demonstration that was to take place out of the city at the site of a U.S. military base near Mount Fuji. The demonstration was to be sponsored by a number of peace groups, the women's sections of the Socialist and Communist parties, and other groups. Most important, there was to be a bus leaving from Shinjuku station in Tokyo that would take some fifty women members of these and other political groups to the site of the demonstration. A *busload* of political women!

Through a young man I knew who was active in the student movement at Tokyo University I began a long and circuitous series of introductions that led me at last to a leader of Amnesty International, a peace group that was organizing the demonstration at Mount Fuji. This gracious woman, a longtime political woman then in her late fifties, took me in without qualms, pleased to have a foreigner participate in what was otherwise to be an all-Japanese demonstration. I told her about my plans to interview young women who were active in political groups, and she became enthusiastic about introducing me to the many she knew. Plans were made to include me on the bus to the demonstration.

On a crisp day in early October of 1971 I turned up at the appointed place for what proved to be a day and evening crammed with experiences I shall long remember. Every seat on the bus was taken. A few people crouched in the aisles. Although there were several men in the group, most were women, and many of them younger women in their twenties and early thirties. I began to talk to some of them sitting near me. Then once the bus was in motion, formal introductions began. It is the custom in Japan when groups take bus trips for any particular purpose, whether it be a company outing or a political demonstration, to have a microphone system set up so that each person can make a few remarks. When groups attend demonstrations together, these introductory remarks often include a statement of the individual's purpose in attending the demonstration and some remarks about how he or she became concerned about that particular cause. Statements of various women on the bus introduced me to a number of issues and causes in Japan that I had known little about. On the bus were members of a number of groups that were later to be represented in my sample. The demonstration's attraction for women who were active in a wide array of political groups was a result of its focus on antimilitarism, a cause that in Japan unites the disparate groups in the progressive camp perhaps more than any other.

When my own turn at the microphone came, I related, in a somewhat shaky voice, my own purpose for coming to Japan and my interest in the political goals of young Japanese women and their struggle to attain them. I was overwhelmed at the response. Throughout the day, on the bus and later at the demonstration site, women young and old came up to me, expressed their interest in my work, and offered to help me meet young women to interview. Phone numbers were scrawled on odd bits of paper by the light of the bonfire that was raging at the demonstration site to provide warmth. Several hundred people had come to attend the demonstration on various buses. A number of distinguished leaders in the progressive camp were present, including perhaps the best-known female member of the Diet in the Socialist Party, Tanaka Sumiko. In the program that followed an afternoon of informal chatter and feasting on *oden* (vegetables, meats, and fish cooked in broth), a number of these notables spoke. The program was a long one, and toward the end, my sponsor pushed me forward to introduce myself and to repeat what I had said earlier on the bus about my work. I protested, having never addressed a large gathering, much less one with a number of notables present, in Japanese. But it was too late. She was already on the large platform that had been set up for the day, introducing me herself in glowing terms. I followed her and once more described my research. Fortunately the blaze from the fire between me and the audience made it impossible to see anyone beyond it and I was able to get through my account. Afterwards, as the area was cleared and a *bon* dance began, still more young women came up to me and offered to help. By the time the demonstration ended and the bus had safely returned to Shinjuku station late in the evening, I had made a number of valuable contacts with people willing to aid me in the days ahead. Even more important, the experience had given me an opportunity in an informal setting to learn how to present myself and my work in a way that would elicit support from young women active in political causes. From then on I had no difficulty locating informants and securing their cooperation.

As the selection of informants proceeded thereafter, several guidelines were devised to assure that things went smoothly and to avoid overrepresentation of any given group or point of view among the sample. First, I met with informants only after they had been introduced to me by a third party, generally an older person they trusted. The experience with the student radical in the subway station had convinced me that even among progressives and young people in Japan, it is difficult to win their cooperation and trust unless one is introduced by someone they respect. Second, not more than five informants were introduced by any one person. Usually only one or two were introduced by a given individual. After an initial introduction, I telephoned the prospective informant and secured her agreement to be interviewed.

The introductions that preceded the interviews were often quite circuitous. For example, to meet young women active in the Liberal Democratic Party I first was introduced by an American professor to a policy spokesperson for the LDP at the Tokyo party headquarters. This person then introduced me to a woman working with him at the headquarters, who then introduced me by phone to the head of the LDP headquarters in Osaka. The latter then introduced me to a subordinate of his at the Osaka headquarters, who at last introduced me to three young women active in the student section (*gakuseibu*) of the LDP Osaka office. I found little difference between the conservative and progressive camps in Japan when it came to the need for introductions. Properly introduced, many things became possible for a foreign researcher working in Japan. But without an introduction linking one to the particular world known to any given individual in Japan, the prospects of success are fairly limited.

If there were many advantages to the system just described, there were certain consequences that should be made explicit. One of these was that political women in leadership positions in their group tend to be somewhat overrepresented in the sample. Approximately one-fourth held leadership positions of some kind. This was because those making the introductions were generally eager to have me meet young women who were especially committed and articulate. Although this bias did make for a sample of political women in the best sense of the term, it did skew the sample in the direction of women who strongly identified with a political role rather then toward women who were less sure about their place in the political world. A second consequence of the selection method was that it required that the informants be introduced by someone they respected, whose opinion of them they generally valued. Although this factor had the great advantage of almost insuring the complete cooperation of the informant, it necessarily introduced the possibility that the informant would try to give the "right" answer out of concern than what she said would get back to the person introducing her. I dealt with this problem as best I could by making sure whenever possible that introductions were made over the phone rather than in person, in an attempt to minimize my links to the introducing party. Also, in all but a few cases, the interviews were conducted far away from the setting where the informant had contact with the person who had introduced her. Finally, in the preliminaries of the interviews, the informant was assurred that her name would not be used and that her privacy would be carefully guarded. She was told that she was free to say whatever she wished, and could choose to answer or not answer particular questions. These assurances were repeated through the use of various interviewing techniques. These precautions made it reasonably possible to collect data that accurately reflected the particular balance of feeling and opinion of a given informant. Nevertheless, the problem of possible bias because of the method of selection is one that must be recognized and dealt with constantly in research of this nature.

The research design did not call for the selection of a sample that was representative of (1) all women in Japan or (2) all political women in Japan. Rather, the aim was to choose women who, in the types of groups they had joined and in the nature of their activities, were broadly representative of Japanese political women in their age range.

A list of political groups, parties, and organizations in which young women participate as volunteers was made with the help of a great many "knowledgeables." Scholars, journalists, and a number of well-known political women were especially helpful. In identifying groups from which I hoped to select informants, I kept in mind several organizational characteristics. Since I wanted to control for structural limitations on women's participation in political groups (i.e., limitations posed by the values, policies, and attitudes of the group and its members regarding women's role in the group), I distinguished three broad categories of political groups, according to the degree to which structural constraints were present. The three categories, along with descriptive characteristics that were weighed in distinguishing them from one another, are as follows:

I. *Political Parties and Organizations* (political parties and large, organized interest groups)
Organizational structure: formal
Sex composition of membership: male and female
Leadership: paid professional
Structural constraints on women's participation: high

II. *Political Groups and Movements* (small, informal interest groups, including protest movements)
Organizational structure: informal
Sex composition of membership: male and female
Leadership: voluntary and unpaid
Structural constraints on women's participation: medium

III. *Women's Groups* (political groups, including feminist groups, with only women in the membership)
Organizational structure: informal to formal
Sex composition of membership: all female
Leadership: voluntary and unpaid
Structural constraints on women's participation: none

Operating behind this categorization was the general assumption, which was later verified through observation of the internal activities of a number of political groups, that structural limitations on women's participation were more likely to be present in large, formal organizations where leadership carried numerous rewards, in terms of money or power or both. The smaller and less formal the organization, the lower the "power stakes"; therefore, there was likely to be less opposition to women's full participation in all the group's activities, including those involving leadership. The fewest barriers of all were to be found in groups that were limited to women, since the possibility for sex-based discrimination was precluded. In assessing the degree to which structural barriers to women's participation were present within each of the three broad categories, other variables were relevant, including the group's political ideology (with more opportunities for women in groups with a Marxist ideology) and the age composition of the membership (with more opportunities in groups made up of age peers). However, since the focus of the book was on women's "route" to activism rather than on their experiences within the political groups they had joined, I did not undertake further refinement of the broad categories I had established. A complete list of the political groups represented in the sample is found in Appendix B.

Two biases in the selection of groups must be noted. The first of these is geographical. The interviewing was conducted in Tokyo and its environs and in the Kyoto-Osaka area. Groups meeting outside these areas were not included. The decision to confine most of the interviewing to major cities was based chiefly on financial and time limitations. However, patterns of women's political participation in Japan also suggested the appropriateness of this strategy. As observers of Japanese political behavior have noted, young women's participation in political groups today is highest in urban areas. In smaller cities and in the Japanese countryside there are numerous political activities that include women. However, for reasons dealt with in the book, the women who take part in them tend to be well above the age range for this study.

A second bias is found in the ideological persuasion of the sample overall. The close observer of Japanese political life may feel that the parties, groups, and organizations listed in Appendix B are weighed too heavily in favor of left-wing activities in a country where the conservatives have long been in power. Women active in the Liberal Democratic Party, Japan's conservative party, are included, of course, and many groups on the list, such as most interest groups, have goals that are specific rather than ideological. Nevertheless, a fairly high percentage of the women were taking part in protest politics rather than "conservative" politics in Japan. In the abstract this represents an apparent bias in the sample collection. But in fact it reflects a reality of Japanese political life. In today's Japan, the conservative establishment, including the LDP, represents the status quo. In a country that many writers have described as polarized over basic values into a "progressive" (*kakushin*) camp of intellectuals, labor unions, students, and the opposition parties, and a "conservative" (*hoshu*) camp of businessmen, farmers, shopkeepers, and the LDP, it is the progressives who are trying to change that status quo. It is they who are more politically active, particularly in informally organized interest groups and political movements. If this formulation does not always apply to the political participation of the older generation in Japan, it almost certainly applies to persons in the age range represented in the sample. If one looks at those aged eighteen to thirty-three in the conservative camp, one is hard-pressed to turn up large numbers of women *or* men who are political activists.

In the case of young women activists this is especially true. Conflict between the conservatives and the progressives in Japan involves basic value differences over such questions as how individuals should relate to authority, what should be the nature of the political process, and how individuals should conduct their lives. The conservative view of a properly functioning society sees it comprising hardworking men who forward Japan's ends, economic and otherwise, in the world today, and of hardworking women who, through their service to the family, make man's work possible. In the context of such a view, it is only natural that most members of the conservative camp feel that a woman in the age range for this study should be resolving the basic concerns of her future: preparing for marriage, finding a suitable mate, mastering the art of caring for a home, giving birth to children, and then devoting herself to them and to the family as a unit. It is almost impossible for most conservatives, male or female, to imagine how a young woman would have time from these "primary" responsibilities to be active in politics. An extensive search for young women participating in political groups in the conservative camp produced only a handful of women, all of whom were somehow exceptions to the thinking described above: a politician's wife, several women so young that they had not yet started getting ready for marriage, and several women who described themselves in forthright terms as somehow unsuited for marriage. If there is a bias in the sample toward women in progressive politics, it is born of the bias in the conservative camp against an active political role for young women.

The Interviews: Administration

The interviews were conducted in Japanese, and ranged in length from two to eight hours. The average interview lasted three hours. The total interviewing time, then, for the one hundred informants was about four hundred hours.

Approximately four-fifths of the informants were interviewed in a single, extended session. The other fifth were interviewed in additional meetings as well. Apart from these formal contacts, a number of informants whom I had gotten to know well included me in various political and nonpolitical activities in which they were engaged.

The interviews were held in a variety of places depending on the circumstances, but two-thirds of them were held in coffee shops that dot the Japanese urban landscape. There, for the price of a cup of coffee, one can sit undisturbed for as long as one wants. This choice of interview site was dictated by practical considerations. Tokyo, where two-thirds of the interviews took place, is a vast and far-flung city, and the informants were extremely busy people. The researcher was not able to pay them for their time (even had they been willing to accept payment, which is doubtful—many even insisted, to the point where there was no choice left, on paying for their own coffee). To meet them, the most practical solution was to go to them, to meet them in coffee shops in an area of the city convenient to them. In a few cases, especially in Kyoto where coffee shops were less numerous outside the central area of town, informants were interviewed in their homes or in some other designated place. This was also true in several cases where informants had small children and needed to be at home. The ordinary routine, however, was to arrange a meeting in the informant's favorite coffee shop and then to set off with a complex set of directions on how to find the right place.

In all but four of the interviews the writer was aided by one of four Japanese assistants, all of them young women in the same age range as the informants. These assistants helped immeasurably in maintaining the flow of communication by clarifying points that either the interviewer or the informants had difficulty understanding. They were instructed to remain at the sidelines of the interview setting and to make their presence felt only when there were impediments to understanding. In all the interviews, and after them as well, extensive and detailed notes were taken. Twenty of the one hundred interviews were taped.

Political Groups Represented in Study, by Category and Type, with Number of Respondents Participating in Each

Name of Group	General Description	Location[1]	Sex of Membership	Type of Organization[2]	Respondents
A. *Political Parties and Organizations*					
Jimintō (Liberal Democratic Party)	Party in power	T,O	m,f	lg.,form.	8
Shakaitō (Japan Socialist Party)	Opposition party	K	m,f	lg.,form.	3
Minshatō (Democratic Socialist Party)	Opposition party	T	m,f	lg.,form.	2
Kōmeitō (Clean Government Party)	Opposition party	O	m,f	lg.,form.	4
Kyōsantō (Japan Communist Party)	Opposition party	T,K	m,f	lg.,form.	5
Mitsubishi Rōdō Kumiai (Mitsubishi Union)	Company union, industry	T	m,f	lg.,form.	3
Ōbunsha Rōdō Kumiai (Ōbunsha Union)	Company union, publishing	T	m,f	lg.,form.	2

Name of Group	General Description	Loca-tion[1]	Sex of Member-ship	Type of Organi-zation[2]	Respon-dents
Kyōto Shiyakusho Rōdō Kumiai (Kyoto City Office Workers' Union)	Union, city employees	K	m,f	lg.,form.	2
Tsūshin Rōdō Kumiai (Communi-cation Workers' Union)	Labor union, communications	K	m,f	lg.,form.	2
Zensenbai (United Workers in Government Monopoly Company)	Union, national government employees in tobacco and salt industries	T	m,f	lg.,form.	1
Sheru Rōdō Kumiai (Shell Oil Company Union)	Company union, industry	T	m,f	lg.,form.	1
Asahi Garasu Rōdō Kumiai (Asahi Glass Company Union)	Company union, industry	T	m,f	lg.,form.	1
Nihon Kikaki Seisaku Rōdō Kumiai (Japan Gas Register Company Union)	Company union, utilities	T	m,f	lg.,form.	1
Kyōdai Byōin Shokuin Rōdō Kumiai (Kyoto University Hospital Workers' Union)	Hospital union	K	m,f	lg.,form.	1
Nihon Shuppansha Hanbai Rōdō Kumiai (Japan Publications Sales Workers' Union)	Labor union, publishing	T	m,f	lg.,form.	1

B. *Political Groups and Movements*

Beheiren (Citizens' League for Peace in Vietnam)	Peace group	T,O,K	m,f	lg.,infor.	7
Koe Naki Koe ("Voiceless voices")	Peace group	T	m,f	sm.,infor.	3
Heieki Kyohi no Chikai ("Anti-draft Pledge" Group)	Peace group (anti-draft)	T	m,f	sm.,infor.	2
Pax	Peace group	T	m,f	lg.,infor.	1
Kyūen Sentā (Aid Center)	Citizens' movement: legal aid to political radicals	T,K	m,f	sm.,infor.	7
Nyūkan Taisei (Organization for Korean Immigrants)	Citizens' movement: aid to Koreans in Japan	T	m,f	sm.,infor.	2
Buraku o Kangaeru Kai ("Group for Thinking about the *Burakumin* [Outcasts]")	Citizens' movement: aid to *Burakumin*	T,O,K	m,f	sm.,infor.	3
Hyakumin Kai ("Group of One Hundred")	Peace group	T	m,f	sm.,infor.	2
Okinawa Deigo Kai ("Okinawa Flower Group")	Citizens' movement: aid to Okinawans	O	m,f	sm.,infor.	1
Kokusai Shōkyō Rengō (National Anti-Communist League)	Right-wing protest group	T	m,f	sm.,infor.	1
Campus protest group (no name)	Campus group supporting radical teacher dismissed from university	T	m,f	sm.,infor.	1

Name of Group	General Description	Location[1]	Sex of Membership	Type of Organization[2]	Respondents
Campus protest group (no name)	Campus group supporting Korean dissidents	T	m,f	sm.,infor.	1
Minsei (Democratic Youth League)	Student movement group affiliated with Japan Communist Party	T,O,K	m,f	sm.,infor.	9
Hansen (Anti-war Faction)	Student movement group	T	m,f	sm.,infor.	2
Zenkyōtō (All Campus Struggle Congress)	Student movement group	T	m,f	sm.,infor.	4
Bundo ("The Bund")	Student movement group	T	m,f	sm.,infor.	2
Chūkaku (Middle Core Faction)	Student movement group	T	m,f	sm.,infor.	5
Kakumaru (Revolutionary Marxist Faction)	Student movement group	T	m,f	sm.,infor.	1
Shaseidō (Socialist Youth League)	Student movement group	T	m,f	sm.,infor.	2
Daiyon Intā ("Fourth International")	Student movement group	K	m,f	sm.,infor.	1
Furonto ("The Front")	Student movement group	K	m,f	sm.,infor.	1
Sekigun (Red Army)	Student movement group	T	m,f	sm.,infor.	2
Non-sect radicals	Student movement group opposed to sects	T,K	m,f	sm.,infor.	5
Unspecified sect (militant)	Student movement sect	Y	m,f	sm.,infor.	1

C. Women's Groups

Name	Description				
Fujin Minshu Kurabu (Women's Democratic Club)	Organization to improve women's status	T,Y,O	f	sm.,infor.	7
Idobata ("Gossiping around the Well")	Consciousness-raising group: suburban housewives		f	sm.,infor.	5
Ajia Fujin Kaigi (Asia Women's Conference)	Organization to improve women's status	T	f	sm.,infor.	1
Nihon Josei Kaihō Junbi Kai (Group Preparing for Liberation of Japanese Women)	Women's group: artists, students, and white-collar workers	T	f	sm.,infor.	2
Tatakau Onna ("Fighting women")	Women's rights group	T	f	sm.,infor.	5
Tatakau Onna Collective	Women's collective	T	f	sm.,infor.	3
S.E.X. collective	Women's collective	T	f	sm.,infor.	1
Yama no Kami ("Gods of the Mountains")	Citizens' movement: environmental protection	T	f	sm.,infor.	2
Shufuren (Housewives' Assoc.)	Consumer interest group	T	f	lg.,form.	3
Hoikujo Undō (Movement for Daycare Centers)	Citizens' movement: group for daycare centers	T,K	f	sm.,infor.	5
Josei Sabetsu o Danko Yurusanu Kai ("Group Firmly Opposing Discrimination against Women")	Women's rights' group: teachers and professionals	T	f	sm.,infor.	2

Name of Group General Description	General Description	Location[1]	Sex of Membership	Type of Organization[2]	Respondents
Women's group (no name)	Consciousness-raising group: Tokyo University students	T	f	sm.,infor.	3
Women's group (no name)	Consciousness-raising group: Waseda University students	T	f	sm.,infor.	1
Women's group (no name)	Consciousness-raising group: artists, writers, housewives	K	f	sm.,infor.	3
Women's group (no name)	Consciousness-raising group: daycare center nurses	T	f	sm.,infor.	2

[1] Refers to the city where the group was located:
T = Tokyo
O = Osaka
K = Kyoto
Y = Yokohama

[2] Refers to the organizational type of the group to which the informant belonged.
sm. (small) = under 100 regular members
lg. (large) = more than 100 regular members
form. (formal) = organizations or groups with an established headquarters and a full-time, paid professional staff
infor. (informal) = organizations or groups without the above.

The above classification applies to that group of which the informant was an active member. In numerous cases the total membership of an organization, such as Minsei, is far more than 100. But the particular branch, or unit, of the organization in which the informant was participating had a membership of less than 100. In this case, the group is classified as "small."

Interview Topic List

I. General Background Information
  a. Name.
  b. Respondent's present age.
  c. Where born and grew up, with attention to size of geographical unit (village; city or town under 50,000; city 50,000 to 1,000,000; city over 1,000,000).
  d. Composition of family respondent grew up in, with attention to birth order of children.
  e. Respondent's complete educational history: when, where, what type of school?
  f. Respondent's complete work history: when, where, what type of job?
  g. Marital status of respondent.
  h. Children: how many, what ages, sex?
  i. Current living arrangement: type of residence? whom is she living with?
  j. Current status: student, worker, housewife, etc.?

II. Background Information: Mother
a. Marital history: how parents met, ages at marriage, what type of marriage (arranged marriage [*miai kekkon*] or "love match" [*renai kekkon*]).
b. Work history: when, what type, childcare arrangements if worked after marriage?
c. Age.
d. Educational history (if the respondent's mother had more or less education than was usual, reasons were explored).

III. Background Information: Father
a. Work history: when, what type, status?
b. Age.
c. Educational history.

IV. Background Information: Siblings
a. Marital information on all siblings.
b. Age(s).
c. Present status of each.
d. Education of siblings relative to education of the respondent: in particular how did her level, quality of education compare with that of male siblings?

V. Background Information: Husband or Other Significant Male
a. History of relationship: when met, how met, current status of relationship?
b. Nature of present living arrangement: private apartment, public housing, private house, other?
c. Current work status.
d. Educational history.
e. Age.

VI. Political Attitudes and Experience of Mother
a. Party preference of mother.
b. Does the respondent's mother usually vote?
c. Is the respondent's mother interested in politics?
d. Does the respondent's mother discuss politics? how often? with whom? does she enjoy discussing? do parents agree on most political issues?
e. Is the respondent's mother a member of a political group? what kind? ever been an officer? how became interested?
f. Other political activities of mother.

VII. Political Attitudes and Experience of Father
    a. Party preference of father.
    b. Does respondent's father usually vote?
    c. Is respondent's father interested in politics?
    d. Does respondent's father discuss politics? how often? with whom? does he enjoy discussing?
    e. Is respondent's father a member of a political group? what kind? ever been an officer? how became interested?
    f. Other political activities of father.

VIII. Political Attitudes and Experience of Significant Others
Questions similar to those in VI and VII were asked about any person (e.g., husband, other significant male, sibling, grandparent) who was clearly a key figure in the informant's political development.

IX. Background to Political Activism and Role Change: Childhood and Adolescence of Respondent
    a. Which parent (or other person) did the respondent go to first (i.e., prefer to go to) with the following types of problems when growing up?
      1. Money problems.
      2. To talk about sex, boyfriends.
      3. To talk about school work.
      4. To talk about future plans: marriage.
      5. To talk about future plans: work.
      6. To talk about future plans: education.
    b. When the respondent was 18 years old or so and thinking about her life, what course in adult life she might have chosen would have pleased her father the most? Follow-up questions, depending on answer to above:
      1. Did his ideal plan for the respondent include marriage?
      2. Did his ideal plan for the respondent include working?
      3. How did he feel about a woman's working after marriage?
      4. How did he feel about a woman's working after having children?
      5. What did he see ideally as the best education for the respondent after high school: what level?

what type of school or program? coed or woman's college?

6. If the respondent were academically able to compete to enter a national university, how would her father have felt about her taking an entrance exam to enter such a university?

c. Same question series repeated for mother.

In questions b and c, an effort was made to get the respondent to distinguish between parental expectations in her formative years (i.e., at 18 or so) and her parent's present attitudes, to help determine whether parental attitude changes might have taken place. In the case of young respondents (18 to 22 or so) this kind of differentiation generally could not be made.

d. What was respondent's own ideal plan at age 18 or so?

e. Question series in b repeated for any significant other in family (grandparent, sibling).

f. If the respondent were to live with a man (outside marriage), how would her father feel about it?

g. Same question repeated for mother.

h. How does the respondent's father feel about arranged marriage? did he ever try to arrange an *omiai* (formal introduction, which is preparatory to arranged marriage) for her?

i. Same question for mother.

X. Political History of the Respondent

a. When did the respondent first become interested in politics: age, circumstances, nature of issue, event?

b. Was the respondent interested in politics or social problems in high school? circumstances? what type? did she become involved in any way?

c. Did the respondent join any political- or social-problem-oriented group in high school or earlier? circumstances? what type? leadership position?

d. Did father discuss politics with the respondent when she was growing up?

e. Same question repeated for mother.

f. Did father discuss politics with the respondent's male siblings when she was growing up?

g. Same question repeated for mother.

h. What was her father's reaction when the respondent first became interested in politics and talked about it at home?

i. Same question repeated for mother.

j. History of political group memberships through the present: when joined, what circumstances, influences leading to joining, leadership positions, how long a member, why left.

At this stage, based on the political background data gathered so far, one particular political group (in cases where the respondent had current multiple memberships) was picked as the primary focus of the questions in the next section, generally the group in which the respondent was playing the most active role. If the respondent had a long history of political group memberships, the question series was asked separately for the most significant *current* membership and for the respondent's *first* significant political group affiliation.

XI. Becoming a Political Activist

a. When did respondent first become interested in her present group?

b. What influences led to joining: role of significant others (classmates, teachers, office mates, employer, boyfriend), books, events, specific incidents?

c. Which factor of those discussed under (b) influenced the respondent the most?

d. When the respondent first joined her present group, did she tell her father? (If so, what was his reaction? if not, why not?)

e. Same question repeated for mother.

f. Same question repeated for significant other(s) outside the political group.

g. Does the respondent now talk with her father about the political group?

h. Same question repeated for mother.

i. Same question repeated for significant other(s) outside the political group.

j. A reference was made to a widely reported news event in Japan at the time concerning five young radical (male) activists who had taken a hostage and barricaded themselves in a mountain lodge. During the period when the lodge was surrounded by the police, who were urging the activists to surrender, several of the activists' parents came to the lodge, addressed them through megaphones, and pleaded with them to give themselves up. The father of one activist committed suicide, presumably over the disgrace caused him by his son's actions. With appropriate references to the above news story, the respondent was asked how her own father would have responded if she had been an activist inside the lodge. She was presented with four possible hypothetical responses of a parent in such a case, and asked which would have been her own father's probable response.

1. Some fathers might have said "She's not my daughter" and washed their hands of the whole matter.
2. Some fathers might have disapproved of her actions, but might have pleaded with their daughter to give herself up.
3. Some fathers might have felt that their daughter had her own life to lead and that she should do whatever she felt was right.
4. Some fathers might have committed suicide.

    k. Same question repeated for the mother.

XII. Nature of Present Political Involvement
    a. Nature of current group.
        1. Size.
        2. Organizational structure.
        3. Sex composition.
        4. Goals.
        5. Strategies.
    b. Sex-role allocation within the respondent's political group (if coed): tasks allocated to women, tasks allocated to men, tasks allocated to both sexes on an equal basis.
    c. Respondent's roles within group: what tasks does she generally do? ever been a leader?
    d. Attitudes of group members toward women occupying leadership positions in the group: attitudes of male members, attitudes of female members.

e. Has the respondent ever taken part in a political demonstration? (If so, what role did she play? if physical combat was involved, did she engage in it?)
f. Has the respondent ever been injured, arrested in political activities? (If so, a series of follow-up questions were asked, including questions about the attitudes of the parents in this case.)
g. Has the respondent ever run for political office? (In the few cases where this has occurred an extensive series of follow-up questions were asked.)
h. In her group, can the respondent think of times when it was a handicap to be a woman? An advantage?
i. The respondent was asked a question that may be paraphrased as follows: "Some respondents have told me that men in their group treat the women members more or less equally, and consider them friends, but that when it comes to having girl-friends or getting married, these same men prefer traditional women, who're not involved in politics, as girlfriends or wives. What about the men in your group?"
j. Respondent's party preference.
k. Does the respondent generally vote?
l. How does the respondent's father feel about her present political activity?
m. Question repeated for mother.
n. How do significant males in the respondent's life (husband, boyfriend, brother) feel about her political activity: warmly support, mildly support, indifferent, disapprove?
o. Respondent is told that some people think that for a woman to be involved in politics is unfeminine, and is asked what she thinks.
p. Respondent is told that some people think that women can afford to be more politically radical than men, because they have fewer constraints (job, family responsibilities, parental expectations, etc.), and is asked to respond.
q. Respondent is told that many Japanese people

laugh when I tell them that I am in Japan to study women's political consciousness, and asked why she thinks they laugh.

XIII. Respondent's Attitudes and Behavior Regarding Gender Roles

a. In the respondent's political group, are there certain tasks that she thinks are best done by male members?

b. In the respondent's political group, are there certain tasks that she thinks are best done by female members?

c. Has the respondent ever used "men's language" (i.e., words and expressions generally used only by men in Japan)? If not, why not? How does she feel about women using such expressions? If so, how does she feel when she uses such language? How do significant others feel about her using it?

d. How does the respondent feel about being asked to make tea: for members of her political group, for employees in her office, in other contexts?

e. How would the respondent feel if she were asked to be a leader of her political group? would she do it? Does she think it is harder for a woman to be a leader than for a man? if so, why?

f. Does the respondent smoke, drink? Does she feel these activities are appropriate for women?

g. How does the informant feel about marriage? If single, does she want to get married? If married, how did she feel about it at time of marriage and now?

h. How does the informant feel about arranged marriage (*miai kekkon*)? Has the respondent ever had a *miai*, or been under pressure from her parents to have one?

i. What kind of man does the respondent want to marry (asked of unmarried women): more, less, or equally intelligent relative to the respondent?

j. If the respondent met a man she wanted to marry, would she tell him about her political activities?

k. If the respondent met a man she wanted to marry who objected to her political activities, what would she do?

l. If the respondent were married and if her husband objected to her working, what would she do?

m. If the respondent marries, how would she prefer to address her husband: *anata* (traditional deferential term of respect to husbands, literally "you"), first name with polite suffix, first name without polite suffix, or other? (Married respondents were asked how they addressed their husband.)

n. If the respondent marries, how would she prefer to be addressed by her husband: first name without polite suffix, first name with polite suffix, diminutive form of first name (e.g., Kimi-chan)? (Married respondents were asked how they were addressed by their husband.)

o. If the respondent currently had a dating or intimate relationship with a man (other than a husband), she was asked how they addressed each other.

p. Does the respondent feel that she is treated equally (i.e., not discriminated against because of sex) in the following contexts: home, school (if a student), office (if a worker), or any other setting significant for the particular respondent?

XIV. Future Plans

a. Marriage plans: does the respondent plan to marry? any specific marriage plans? (Asked of single women.)

b. If the respondent marries, will she continue working?

c. If the respondent marries, would she plan to continue in her present political group (or other group)?

d. Does the respondent plan to have children: how many, ideally? How does the respondent feel about daycare?

e. Educational plans: what type, when to be undertaken?

f. Work plans: what type? What position(s) would the respondent like to achieve, if possible?

g. Political plans: continue with present group, plan to join new groups, seek a leadership position, run for office (questions geared to nature of current participation, traditional or protest)?

   h. (Asked of full-time housewives with children.) What life does the respondent envision for herself once her children are in school or thereafter? (At what point in her children's maturation would she consider herself free to act on these plans?)

   i. Has the respondent discussed her future plans with her father? if so, what reaction?

   j. Same question asked for mother.

   k. Same question asked for husband or other significant male.

Note: At the conclusion of the interview, the respondents were invited to add anything they wished, and also to ask questions of the interviewer, if they so desired.

Selected Bibliography

English Language Materials on Japan

Ackroyd, Joyce. "Women in Feudal Japan." *Transactions of the Asiatic Society of Japan*. Third Series, vol. 7 (Tokyo, 1959). Pp. 31–68.

Akamatsu, Tadashi Hanami. "New Problems Facing the Protective Labor Law." *Japan Labor Bulletin*. Part I (May 1970): 7–10; Part II (June 1970): 5–8.

———. "The Retirement Age System in Japan." *Japan Labor Bulletin* 6 (October 1967).

Anderson, Ronald S. *Japan: Three Epochs of Modern Education*. Bulletin No. 11. Washington, D.C.: Department of Health, Education and Welfare, 1959.

Andrew, Nancy. "The *Seitōsha*: An Early Japanese Women's Organization, 1911–1916." *Papers on Japan*. East Asian Research Center, Harvard University. Vol. 6, pp. 45–69. Cambridge, 1972.

Ariga, Kizaemon. "Contemporary Japanese Family in Transition." *Transactions of the Third World Congress of Sociology* 4. Amsterdam: International Sociological Association, 1956. Pp. 215–221.

———. "The Family in Japan." *Marriage and Family Living* 16 (1954): 362–368.

Austin, Lewis, ed. *Japan: The Paradox of Progress*. New Haven, Conn.: Yale University Press, 1976.

Beard, Mary. *The Force of Women in Japanese History*. Washington, D.C.: Public Affairs Press, 1953.

Beardsley, Richard K.; Hall, John W.; and Ward, Robert E. *Village Japan*. Chicago: University of Chicago Press, 1959.

Beckmann, George M. *The Making of the Meiji Constitution*. Lawrence, Kans.: University of Kansas Press, 1957.

Benedict, Ruth. *The Chrysanthemun and the Sword*. Boston: Houghton Mifflin, 1946.

Bennett, John W.; Passin, Herbert; and McKnight, Robert K. *The Japanese Overseas Scholar in America and Japan*. Minneapolis, Minn.: University of Minnesota Press, 1958.

Blacker, Carmen. *The Japanese Enlightenment: A Study of the Writings of Fukuzawa Yukichi*. Cambridge: Cambridge University Press, 1964.

Blaker, Michael K., ed. *Japan at the Polls*. Washington, D.C.: American Enterprise Institute, 1976.

Blood, Robert O. *Love Match and Arranged Marriage: A Tokyo-Detroit Comparison*. New York: Free Press, 1967.

Borton, Hugh. *Japan's Modern Century*. New York: Ronald Press, 1955.

Brinkley, F. A. *A History of the Japanese People from the Earliest Times to the End of the Meiji Era*. New York: Encyclopaedia Britannica, 1915.

Caudill, William. "Anthropology and Psychoanalysis: Some Theoretical Issues." In *Anthropology and Human Behavior*, edited by Thomas Gladwin and William C. Sturtevant, pp. 174–214. Washington, D.C.: Anthropological Society of Washington, 1962.

————. "Around the Clock Patient Care in Japanese Psychiatric Hospitals: The Role of the *Tsukisoi*." *American Sociological Review* 26 (April 1961): 204–214.

————. "Patterns of Emotion in Modern Japan." *Japanese Culture: Its Development and Characteristics*, edited by Robert J. Smith and Richard K. Beardsley, pp. 115–231. Chicago: Aldine, 1962.

————. "Sibling Rank and Style of Life Among Japanese Psychiatric Patients." Reprinted from the Joint Meeting of the Japanese Society of Psychiatry and Neurology and the American Psychiatric Association, May 13–17, 1963. (Printed as a supplement to *Psychiatria et Neurologia Japanicas*.)

————. "Some Problems in Transnational Communication (Japan–United States)." *Application of Psychiatric Insights to Cross-Cultural Communication*. New York: Group for the Advancement of Psychiatry, 1961.

————. "Thoughts on the Comparison of Emotional Life in Japan and the United States." *Seishinigaku* 6 (February 1964): 29–33.

————. "Tiny Dramas: Vocal Communication between Mother and Infant in Japanese and American Families." Paper presented at the

Conference on Culture and Mental Health, Honolulu, East-West Center, March 1969.

Caudill, William, and Weinstein, Helen. "Maternal Care and Infant Behavior in Japan and America." *Psychiatry* 32 (February 1969): 12–43.

Curtis, Gerald L. *Election Campaigning Japanese Style.* New York: Columbia University Press, 1971.

DeVos, George. "The Relation of Guilt toward Parents to Achievement and Arranged Marriage among the Japanese." *Psychiatry* 23 (August 1960): 287–301.

DeVos, George, and Wagatsuma, Hiroshi. "Status and Role Behavior in Changing Japan: Psychocultural Continuities." In *Sex Roles in Changing Society,* edited by Georgene H. Seward and Robert C. Williamson. New York: Random House, 1970.

DeVos, George, and Wagatsuma, Hiroshi. "Value Attitudes towards Role Behavior of Women in Two Japanese Villages." *American Anthropologist* 63 (December 1961): 1204–1230.

Doi, Takeo. "*Amae*—A Key Concept for Understanding Japanese Personality Structure." *Psychologia* 5 (1962): 1–7.

Dore, Ronald P. *City Life in Japan.* Berkeley and Los Angeles: University of California Press, 1958.

———. *Education in Tokugawa Japan.* Berkeley and Los Angeles: University of California Press, 1965.

Dore, Ronald P., ed. *Aspects of Social Change in Modern Japan.* Princeton, N.J.: Princeton University Press, 1967.

East-West Center. *Women's Movement in Postwar Japan.* Selected articles from *Shiryō: Sengo Nijū-nen Shi* (Source Book on Twenty Postwar Years in Japan). Translated by Wake A. Fujioka. Honolulu: East-West Center, 1968.

Embree, John. *Suye Mura: A Japanese Village.* Chicago: University of Chicago Press, 1939.

Flanagan, Scott C. "The Japanese Party System in Transition." *Comparative Politics* 3 (January 1971): 231–254.

Flanagan, Scott C., and Richardson, Bradley M. "Political Disaffection and Political Stability: A Comparison of Japanese and Western Findings." In *Comparative Social Research,* vol. 3, edited by Richard F. Tomasson. Greenwich, Conn.: JAI Press, 1980.

Fujimoto, Taizo. *The Story of a Geisha Girl.* London: T. W. Laurie, 1916?

Fujita, Taki. *Japanese Women in the Post-War Years.* Twelfth Conference, Institute of Pacific Relations, Kyoto, 1954.

———. "Women and Politics in Japan." *Annals of the American Academy of Political and Social Science* 375 (January 1968): 91–95.

Furuya, Tsunatake. "Meiji Women: Landmarks They Have Left." *Japan Quarterly* 14 (July–September 1967): 318–325.

Griffin, Edward G. "The Universal Suffrage Issue in Japanese Politics, 1918–1925." *Journal of Asian Studies* 31 (February 1972): 275–290.

Hall, John W., and Beardsley, Richard K. *Twelve Doors to Japan*. New York: McGraw-Hill, 1965.

Havens, Thomas R. H. "Women and War in Japan, 1937–45." *American Historical Review* 80 (October 1975): 913–934.

Higuchi, Keiko. "The PTA—A Channel for Political Activism." *Japan Interpreter* 10 (Autumn 1975): 133–140.

Hoshino, Ai. "The Education of Women." In *Western Influences in Modern Japan: A Series of Papers on Cultural Relations*, edited by Nitobe Inazō. Chicago, 1931.

Ike, Nobutaka. "Economic Growth and Intergenerational Change in Japan." *American Political Science Review* 67 (December 1973): 1194–1203.

Iwao, Sumiko. "A Full Life for Modern Japanese Women." In *Text of Seminar on Changing Values in Modern Japan*, edited by Nihonjin Kenkyūkai. Tokyo: Nihonjin Kenkyūkai, 1977.

Jansen, Marius, ed. *Changing Japanese Attitudes towards Modernization*. Princeton, N.J.: Princeton University Press, 1965.

Japan, Government of. *Seminar in (sic) Public Administration Officers on Women's Problems*. Tokyo, 1973 and 1975.

————. Ministry of Education. *Educational Standards in Japan 1970*. Tokyo, March, 1971.

————. Ministry of Foreign Affairs. *Status of Women in Modern Japan*. Tokyo: The Ministry, 1975.

————. Ministry of Labor. Women's and Minors' Bureau. *The Status of Women in Japan*. Tokyo, 1968, 1973, 1977.

Japan External Trade Organization. "Female Employment in Japan." *Now in Japan* 19 (December 1975): 1–25.

Japan Institute of Labor. *Japan Labor Bulletin*. Tokyo: The Institute, July 1, 1973.

Kaji, Etsuko. "The Invisible Proletariat: Working Women in Japan." *Anpo* 18 (Autumn 1973): 48–58.

Kawai, Kazuo. *Japan's American Interlude*. Chicago: University of Chicago Press, 1960.

Kawai, Michi, and Ochimi, Kubushiro. *Japanese Women Speak*. Boston: The Central Committee on the United Study of Foreign Missions, 1934.

Kiefer, Christie W. "The Psychological Interdependence of Family, School, and Bureaucracy in Japan." *American Anthropologist* 72 (February 1970): 66–75.

Kosaka, Masaaki. "The Status and Role of the Individual in Japanese Society." In *The Japanese Mind: Essentials of Japanese Philosophy and Culture*, edited by Charles A. Moore. Honolulu: University of Hawaii Press, 1967.

Koyama, Takashi. "Changing Family Structure in Japan." In *Japanese Culture: Its Development and Characteristics*, edited by Robert J. Smith and Richard K. Beardsley. Chicago: Aldine, 1962.

————. *The Changing Social Position of Women in Japan*. Paris: UNESCO, 1961.

Krauss, Ellis S. *Japanese Radicals Revisited: Student Protest in Postwar Japan*. Berkeley and Los Angeles: University of California Press, 1974.

Kubota, Akira, and Ward, Robert E. "Family Influence and Political Socialization in Japan: Some Preliminary Findings in Comparative Perspective." *Comparative Political Studies* 3 (July 1970): 140–175.

Küchler, L. W. "Marriage in Japan." *Transactions of the Asiatic Society of Japan* 13 (July 1885): 114–137.

Kuroda, Yasumasa. "Agencies of Political Socialization and Political Change: Political Orientation of Japanese Law Students." *Human Organization* 24 (Winter 1965): 328–331.

————. *Reed Town, Japan: A Study in Community Power Structure and Political Change*. Honolulu: University of Hawaii Press, 1974.

Lebra, Joyce; Paulson, Joy; and Powers, Elizabeth, eds. *Women in Changing Japan*. Boulder, Colo.: Westview Press, 1976.

Lifton, Robert Jay. "Individual Patterns in Historical Change: Imagery of Japanese Youth." *Journal of Social Issues* 20 (October 1964): 96–111.

————. "Japanese Youth: The Search for the New and the Pure." *American Scholar* 30 (Summer 1961): 332–344.

————. "Woman as Knower: Some Psychohistorical Perspectives." In *The Woman in America*, edited by Robert Jay Lifton. Boston: Beacon Press, 1967.

————. "Youth and History: Individual Change in Postwar Japan." In *The Challenge of Youth*, edited by Erik H. Erikson, pp. 260–290. New York: Anchor Books, 1963.

Maki, John M., ed. *Court and Constitution in Japan*. Seattle: University of Washington Press, 1964.

Maruyama, Masao. *Thought and Behavior in Modern Japanese Politics*. London: Oxford University Press, 1963.

Massey, Joseph A. "The Occupation and the Sheriff of Nottingham: The Legacy of Election Reform." In *The Occupation of Japan: Impact of Legal Reform*, edited by L. H. Redford. Norfolk, Va.: The MacArthur Memorial, 1978.

————. *Youth and Politics in Japan*. Lexington, Mass.: Lexington Books, 1976.

Mishima, Sumie. *The Broader Way: A Woman's Life in the New Japan*. New York: John Day, 1953.

Miyamoto, Ken. "Itō Noe and the Bluestockings." *Japan Interpreter* 10 (Autumn 1975): 190–204.

Moore, Barrington. "Asian Fascism." In *Social Origins of Dictatorship and Democracy*, pp. 228–313. Boston: Beacon Press, 1966.

Morris, Ivan. *The World of the Shining Prince: Court Life in Ancient Japan*. New York: Knopf, 1964.

Morris, J. *Kotaka: A Samurai's Daughter*. London: Wyman, 1885.

Murasaki Shikibu. *The Tale of Genji*. Translated by Arthur Waley. London: Allen and Unwin, 1925.

Murray, Patricia. "Ichikawa Fusae and the Lonely Red Carpet." *Japan Interpreter* 10 (Autumn 1975): 171–189.

Nagai, Michio. *Higher Education in Japan: Its Take-off and Crash*. Translated by Jerry Dusenbury. Tokyo: University of Tokyo Press, 1971.

Nagano, Yoshiko. "Women Fight for Control: Abortion Struggle in Japan." *Anpo* 17 (Summer 1973): 14–20.

Nakane, Chie. *Japanese Society*. Berkeley and Los Angeles: University of California Press, 1970.

Nishio, Harry K. "The Changing Japanese Perspectives and Attitudes Towards Leisure." *Humanitas: Journal of the Institute of Man* 8 (November 1972): 367–388.

Passin, Herbert. *Society and Education in Japan*. New York: Teachers College, Columbia University, 1965.

———. "Sources of Protest in Japan." *American Political Science Review* 56 (June 1962): 391–403.

Perry, Linda. "Mothers, Wives, and Daughters in Osaka: Autonomy, Alliance and Professionalism." Ph.D. dissertation, University of Pittsburgh, 1976.

Pharr, Susan J. "Japan: Historical and Contemporary Perspectives." In *Women: Role and Status in Eight Countries*, edited by Janet Z. Giele and Audrey C. Smock, pp. 219–255. New York: Wiley, 1977.

———. "The Japanese Woman: Evolving Views of Life and Role." In *Japan: The Paradox of Progress*, edited by Lewis Austin, pp. 301–377. New Haven, Conn.: Yale University Press, 1976.

———. "A Radical U.S. Experiment: Women's Rights Laws and the Occupation of Japan." In *The Occupation of Japan: Impact of Legal Reform*, edited by L. H. Redford. Norfolk, Va: The MacArthur Memorial, 1978.

Plath, David W. *The After Hours: Modern Japan and the Search for Enjoyment*. Berkeley and Los Angeles: University of California Press, 1964.

Raper, Arthur F.; Tsuchiyama, Tamie; Passin, Herbert; and Sills, David L. *The Japanese Village in Transition*. General Headquarters, Supreme Commander for the Allied Powers, Report No. 136, Tokyo, 1950.

Reich, Pauline C. "Japan's Literary Feminists: The *Seitō* Group." Translated by Pauline C. Reich and Fukuda Atsuko. *Signs* 2 (Autumn 1976): 280–291.

Reischauer, Edwin O., and Fairbank, John K. *East Asia: The Great Tradition*. Boston: Houghton Mifflin, 1958.

Richardson, Bradley M. *The Political Culture of Japan*. Berkeley and Los Angeles: University of California Press, 1974.

————. "Urbanization and Political Participation: The Case of Japan." *American Political Science Review* 67 (June 1973): 433–452.   *Leh JA LA6*

Salamon, Sonya. "'Male Chauvinism' as a Manifestation of Love in Marriage." In *Adult Episodes in Japan*, edited by David W. Plath. Leiden: Brill, 1975.

————. "The Varied Groups of Japanese and German Housewives." *Japan Interpreter* 10 (Autumn 1975): 151–170.

Scalapino, Robert A. *Democracy and the Party Movement in Prewar Japan*. Berkeley and Los Angeles: University of California Press, 1962.

Shibusawa, Keizo. *Japanese Life and Culture in the Meiji Era*. Translated by Charles Terry. Tokyo: Obunsha, 1958.

Shimbori, Michiya. "The Sociology of a Student Movement—A Japanese Case Study." *Daedalus* 97 (Winter 1968): 204–228.

Stoetzel, Jean. *Without the Chrysanthemum and the Sword: A Study of Attitudes of Youth in Post-war Japan*. New York: Columbia University Press, 1955.

Sumiya, Mikio. "The Function and Social Structure of Education." *Journal of Social and Political Ideas in Japan* 5 (December 1967): 117–138.

Supreme Commander for the Allied Powers (SCAP), General Headquarters, Government Section. *Political Reorientation of Japan, September 1945 to September 1948*. 2 vols. Washington, D.C.: U.S. Government Printing Office, 1949.

Taira, Koji. *Economic Development and the Labor Market in Japan*. New York: Columbia University Press, 1970.

Takabatake, Michitoshi. "Citizens' Movements: Organizing the Spontaneous." *Japan Interpreter* 9 (Winter 1975): 315–323.

Tomoda, Yasumasa. "Educational and Occupational Aspirations of Female Senior High School Students." *Bulletin of the Hiroshima Agricultural College* 4 (December 1972): 247–262.

Totten, George O. *The Social Democratic Movement in Prewar Japan*. New Haven, Conn.: Yale University Press, 1966.

Tsurumi, Kazuko. *Social Change and the Individual: Japan Before and After Defeat in World War II*. Princeton, N.J.: Princeton University Press, 1970.

————. "The Japanese Student Movement: Group Portraits." *Japan Quarterly* 16 (January–March 1969): 25–44.

————. "The Japanese Student Movement: Its Milieu." *Japan Quarterly* 15 (October–December 1968): 430–455.

————. "Student Movements in 1960 and 1969: Continuity and

Change." *Research Papers of the Institute of International Relations.* Sophia University, Series A-5. Tokyo, 1971.

Tsurutani, Taketsugu. *Political Change in Japan.* New York: McKay, 1977.

U.S. Department of Labor and Japan Ministry of Labor. *The Role and Status of Women Workers in the United States and Japan.* (A Joint U.S.–Japan Study). Washington, D.C.: U.S. Government Printing Office, 1976.

Vavich, Dee Ann. "The Japanese Woman's Movement: Ichikawa Fusae, A Pioneer in Woman's Suffrage." *Monumenta Nipponica* 22 (1967): 402–436.

Vogel, Ezra. "Beyond Salary: Mamachi Revisited." *Japan Interpreter* 6 (Summer 1970): 105–113.

———. "The Democratization of Family Relations in Japanese Urban Society." *Asian Survey* 1 (June 1961): 18–24.

———. "The Go-Between in a Developing Society: The Case of the Japanese Marriage Arranger." *Human Organization* 20 (Fall 1961): 112–120.

———. *Japan's New Middle Class: The Salary Man and His Family in a Tokyo Suburb.* Berkeley and Los Angeles: University of California Press, 1963.

Vogel, Ezra, and Vogel, Suzanne H. "Family Security, Personal Immaturity and Emotional Health in a Japanese Sample." *Marriage and Family Living* 23 (May 1961): 161–166.

Ward, Robert E. *Japan's Political System.* Englewood Cliffs, N.J.: Prentice-Hall, 1978.

———. "The Origins of the Present Japanese Constitution." *American Political Science Review* 50 (December 1956): 980–1010.

Ward, Robert E., and Rustow, Dankwart A., eds. *Political Modernization in Japan and Turkey.* Princeton, N.J.: Princeton University Press, 1964.

Watanuki, Jōji. "Patterns of Politics in Present-Day Japan." In *Party Systems and Voter Alignments: Cross-National Perspectives,* edited by Seymour M. Lipset and Stein Rokkan, pp. 447–466. New York: Free Press, 1967.

———. "Social Structure and Political Participation in Japan." Laboratory for Political Research, Report no. 32. Iowa City, Iowa: University of Iowa, 1970.

"White Paper on Sexism: Japan" Task Force. *Japanese Women Speak Out.* Tokyo: PARC, 1975.

General English Language Materials

Allport, Gordon, "A Test for Ascendance-Submission." *Journal of Abnormal and Social Psychology* 23 (1928–29): 118–136.

Almond, Gabriel A. *The Appeals of Communism.* Princeton, N.J.: Princeton University Press, 1954.

Almond, Gabriel A., and Verba, Sidney. *The Civic Culture.* Boston: Little, Brown, 1965.

Amundsen, Kirsten. *A New Look at the Silenced Majority: Women and American Democracy.* Englewood Cliffs, N.J.: Prentice-Hall, 1977.

Angrist, Shirley S. "The Study of Sex Roles." *Journal of Social Issues* 25 (January 1969): 215–232.

Arnold, David O., ed. *Subcultures.* Berkeley, Calif.: Glendessary Press, 1970.

Ash, Mildred. "Freud on Feminine Identity and Female Sexuality." *Psychiatry* 34 (August 1971): 322–327.

Bales, R. F. *Interaction Process Analysis: A Method for the Study of Small Groups.* Cambridge, Mass.: Addison-Wesley, 1950.

Bardwick, Judith M., ed. *On the Psychology of Women: A Survey of Empirical Studies.* Springfield, Ill.: Charles C. Thomas, 1971.

————, ed. *Readings on the Psychology of Women.* New York: Harper & Row, 1972.

Bardwick, Judith M., and Douvan, Elizabeth. "Ambivalence: The Socialization of Women" In *Woman in Sexist Society,* edited by Vivian Gornick and Barbara K. Moran, pp. 225–241. New York: Mentor, 1971.

Bendix, Reinhard. "Compliant Behavior and Individual Personality." In *A Source Book for the Study of Personality and Politics,* edited by Fred I. Greenstein and Michael Lerner, pp. 47–59. Chicago: Markham, 1971.

Bernard, Jessie. *Women and the Public Interest: An Essay on Policy and Protest.* Chicago: Aldine-Atherton, 1971.

Biller, Henry B. *Father, Child and Sex Role: Paternal Determinants of Personality Development.* Lexington, Mass.: Heath Lexington, 1971.

Blau, Francine D. "Comment on Mueller's 'Economic Determinants of Volunteer Work by Women.'" *Signs* 2 (Autumn 1976): 251–254.

Boserup, Ester. *Woman's Role in Economic Development.* New York: St. Martin's, 1970.

Brim, Orville G., Jr. "Socialization Through the Life Cycle." In *Socialization after Childhood,* edited by Orville G. Brim, Jr., and Stanton Wheeler, pp. 1–49. New York: Wiley, 1966.

Brown, D. G. "Masculinity-Femininity Development in Children." *Journal of Consulting Psychology* 21 (June 1957): 197–202.

————. "Sex-role Development in a Changing Culture." *Psychology Bulletin* 55 (1958): 232–242.

Bullock, Charles, and Hays, Patricia. "Recruitment of Women for Congress." *Western Political Quarterly* 25 (September 1972): 416–423.

Campbell, Angus; Converse, Philip E.; Miller, Warren E.; and Stokes, Donald E. *The American Voter.* New York: Wiley, 1960.

Campbell, Angus; Gurin, Gerald; and Miller, Warren E. *The Voter Decides*. Evanston, Ill.: Row Peterson, 1954.

Commission of the European Communities. *European Men and Women: A Comparison of Their Attitudes to Some of the Problems Facing Society*. Brussels: The Commission, 1975.

Constantini, Edmond, and Craik, Kenneth H. "Women as Politicians: The Social Background, Personality, and Political Careers of Female Party Leaders." *Journal of Social Issues* 28 (1972): 217–236.

Dahlstrom, Edmond. *The Changing Roles of Men and Women*. Translated by Gunilla and Steven Anderman. Boston: Beacon Press, 1962.

Dahrendorf, Ralf. "Homo Sociologicus." In *Essays in the Theory of Society*, pp. 19–81. Stanford, Calif.: Stanford University Press, 1968.

Davies, James C. *Human Nature in Politics*. New York: Wiley, 1963.

Dawson, Richard E., and Prewitt, Kenneth. *Political Socialization*. Boston: Little, Brown, 1969.

Dennis, Jack, and McCrone, Donald J. "Preadult Development of Political Party Identification in Western Democracies." In *Comparative Political Socialization*, edited by Jack Dennis and M. Kent Jennings, pp. 115–135. Beverly Hills, Calif.: Sage Publications, 1970.

Denzin, Norman K. "The Significant Others of a College Population." In *Symbolic Interaction*, edited by Jerome G. Manis and Bernard N. Meltzer, pp. 185–197. Boston: Allyn and Bacon, 1972.

Douvan, Elizabeth, and Adelson, Joseph. *The Adolescent Experience*. New York: Wiley, 1966.

Dowse, Robert E., and Hughes, John A., "Girls, Boys and Politics." *British Journal of Sociology* 22 (March 1971): 53–67.

Duverger, Maurice. *The Political Role of Women*. Paris: UNESCO, 1955.

Easton, David, and Dennis, Jack. *Children in the Political System*. New York: McGraw-Hill, 1969.

Easton, David, and Hess, Robert. "The Child's Political World." *Midwest Journal of Political Science* 6 (August 1962): 229–246.

Eisenstadt, S. N. *From Generation to Generation*. New York: Free Press, 1964.

Elshtain, Jean Bethke. "Women and Politics: A Theoretical Inquiry." Ph.D. dissertation, University of Massachusetts, 1973.

Epstein, Cynthia F. *Woman's Place: Options and Limits in Professional Careers*. Berkeley and Los Angeles: University of California Press, 1970.

Epstein, Gilda F., and Bronzaft, Arline L. "Female Freshmen View Their Roles as Women." *Journal of Marriage and the Family* 34 (November 1972): 671–672.

Epstein, Leon D. *Politics in Wisconsin*. Madison: University of Wisconsin Press, 1958.

Erikson, Erik H. *Gandhi's Truth*. New York: Norton, 1969.

———. "Identity and the Life Cycle." *Psychological Issues* 1, no. 1 (1959): 18–171.

———. *Identity: Youth and Crisis*. New York: Norton, 1968.

Eulau, Heinz; Eldersveld, Samuel; and Janowitz, Morris. *Political Behavior*. Glencoe, Ill.: Free Press, 1956.

Fairbanks, John K; Reischauer, Edwin O.; and Craig, Albert. *East Asia: The Modern Transformation*. Boston: Houghton Mifflin, 1965.

Farah, Barbara G., and Sapiro, Virginia. "New Pride and Old Prejudice: Political Ambition and Role Orientations Among Female Partisan Elites." Paper presented at the Annual Meeting of the Southern Political Science Association, Nashville, November 1975.

Festinger, Leon. *A Theory of Cognitive Dissonance*. Chicago: Row Peterson, 1957.

Feuer, Lewis S. *The Conflict of Generations: The Character and Significance of Student Movements*. New York: Basic Books, 1969.

Fiedler, Maureen. "The Participation of Women in American Politics." Paper presented at the Annual Meeting of the American Political Science Association, San Francisco, 1975.

Flacks, Richard. "The Revolt of the Advantaged: Explorations of the Roots of Student Protest." In *Learning about Politics*, edited by Roberta S. Sigel. New York: Random House, 1970.

Flora, Cornelia B., and Lynn, Naomi B. "Women and Political Socialization: Considerations of the Impact of Motherhood." In *Women in Politics*, ed. Jane S. Jaquette, pp. 37–51. New York: Wiley, 1974.

Freeman, Jo. *The Politics of Women's Liberation*. New York: McKay, 1975.

Gehlen, Frieda L. "Women Members of Congress." In *A Portrait of Marginality*, edited by Marianne Githens and Jewel L. Prestage, pp. 304–319. New York: McKay, 1977.

Giele, Janet Z. "Introduction: Comparative Perspectives on Women." In *Women: Role and Status in Eight Countries*, edited by Janet Z. Giele and Audrey C. Smock. New York: John Wiley, 1977.

Gillespie, James M., and Allport, Gordon W. *Youth's Outlook on the Future*. Doubleday Papers in Psychology, No. 15. New York: Doubleday, 1955.

Ginzberg, Eli. *Life Styles of Educated Women*. New York: Columbia University Press, 1966.

Githens, Marianne. "Spectators, Agitators, or Law Makers: Women in State Legislatures." In *A Portrait of Marginality:* edited by Marianne Githens and Jewel L. Prestage, pp. 196–209. New York: McKay, 1977.

Githens, Marianne, and Prestage, Jewel L. *A Portrait of Marginality:*

The Political Behavior of the American Woman. New York: McKay, 1977.

Goffmann, Erving. *Encounters.* Indianapolis and New York: Bobbs-Merrill, 1961.

Gold, Doris B. "Women and Voluntarism." In *Woman in Sexist Society,* edited by Vivian Gornick and Barbara K. Moran, pp. 553–554. New York: Mentor, 1971.

Goode, William J. "Norm Commitment and Conformity to Role-Status Obligations." *American Journal of Sociology* 66 (November 1960): 246–258.

——. "A Theory of Role Strain." *American Sociological Review* 25 (August 1960): 483–496.

——. *World Revolution and Family Patterns.* New York: Free Press, 1970.

Gosnell, Harold F. *Democracy, the Threshold of Freedom.* New York: Ronald Press, 1948.

Greenstein, Fred I. *Children and Politics.* New Haven, Conn.: Yale University Press, 1965.

——. "Sex Related Political Differences in Childhood." *Journal of Politics* 23 (May 1961): 353–371.

Greenstein, Fred, and Lerner, Michael. *A Source Book for the Study of Personality and Politics.* Chicago: Markham, 1971.

Gruberg, Martin. *Women in American Politics.* Oshkosh, Wis.: Academia Press, 1968.

Haavio-Mannila, Elina. "Sex Roles in Politics." In *Towards A Sociology of Women,* edited by Constantina Safilios-Rothschild, pp. 154–172. Lexington, Mass.: Xerox College Publishing, 1972.

Hacker, Helen Mayer. "Women as a Minority Group." *Social Forces* 30 (October 1951): 60–69.

Hanna, William, ed. *University Students in Politics.* New York: Basic Books, 1971.

Hartley, Ruth E. "A Developmental View of Female Sex-Role Identification." In *Role Theory: Concepts and Research,* edited by Bruce J. Biddle and Edwin J. Thomas, pp. 354–361. New York: Wiley, 1966.

Heiskanen, Veronica Stolte, "Sex Roles, Social Class and Political Consciousness." *Acta Sociologica* 14 (1971): 83–95.

Hess, Robert D., and Torney, Judith V. *The Development of Political Attitudes in Children.* Garden City, N.Y.: Anchor Books, 1968.

Horner, Matina S. "Femininity and Successful Achievement: A Basic Inconsistency." In *Feminine Personality and Conflict,* edited by J. Bardwick et al. Belmont, Calif.: Brooks/Cole, 1970.

——. "Towards An Understanding of Achievement-Related Conflicts in Women." *Journal of Social Issues* 28 (1972): 157–175.

Huntington, Samuel. *Political Order in Changing Societies.* New Haven, Conn.: Yale University Press, 1964.

Hyman, Herbert H. *Political Socialization.* Glencoe, Ill.: Free Press, 1959.

Iglitzin, Lynne B. "The Making of the Apolitical Woman: Femininity and Sex-Stereotyping in Girls." In *Women in Politics,* edited by Jane Jaquette, pp. 25–36. New York: Wiley, 1974.

Inglehart, Ronald, "The Silent Revolution in Europe: Intergenerational Change in Post-Industrial Societies." *American Political Science Review* 65 (December 1971): 991–1017.

Inkeles, Alex. "Social Change and Social Character: The Role of Parental Mediation." *Journal of Social Issues* 11, no. 2 (1955): 12–23.

Jancar, Barbara. "Women and Elite Recruitment into the Central Committee of Bulgaria, Czechoslovakia, Hungary, and Poland." Paper presented at Midwestern Political Science Association Meeting, Chicago, 1977.

Janeway, Elizabeth. *Man's World, Woman's Place.* New York: Delta Books, 1971.

Jaquette, Jane S. "Review Essay: Political Science." *Signs* 2 (Autumn 1976): 147–164.

Jennings, M. Kent. "Preadult Orientations to Multiple Systems of Government." *Midwest Journal of Political Science* 11 (August 1967): 291–317.

Jennings, M. Kent, and Thomas, Norman. "Men and Women in Party Elites: Social Roles and Political Resources." *Midwest Journal of Political Science* 12 (November 1968): 469–492.

Jennings, M. Kent, and Langton, Kenneth P. "Mothers versus Fathers: The Formation of Political Orientations among Young Americans." *Journal of Politics* 31 (May 1969): 329–357.

Jennings, M. Kent, and Niemi, Richard G. "The Transmission of Political Values from Parent to Child." *American Political Science Review* 62 (March 1968): 169–184.

Johnson, Kay Ann. "The Politics of Women's Rights and Family Reform in China." Ph.D. dissertation, University of Wisconsin, Madison, 1976.

Johnson, Miriam M. "Sex Role Learning in the Nuclear Family." *Child Development* 34 (June 1963): 317–333.

Kagan, Jerome, and Moss, Howard A. "The Stability of Passive and Dependent Behavior from Childhood through Adulthood." *Child Development* 31 (September 1960): 577–591.

Kammeyer, Kenneth. "Birth Order and the Feminine Sex Role Among College Women." *American Sociological Review* 31 (August 1966): 508–515.

Kanter, Rosabeth. "Women and Hierarchies." Paper presented at the Annual Meeting of the American Sociological Association, San Francisco, 1975.

———. *Women and Organization.* Englewood Cliffs, N.J.: Prentice-Hall, 1976.

Keniston, Kenneth. *Young Radicals: Notes on Committed Youth.* New York: Harcourt, Brace & World, 1968.

Key, V. O., Jr. *Public Opinion and Democracy.* New York: Knopf, 1961.

Kirkpatrick, Jeane J. *The New Presidential Elite.* New York: Basic Books, 1976.

———. *Political Woman.* New York: Basic Books, 1974.

Kluckhohn, Clyde. "Values and Value Orientations in the Theory of Action." In *Toward a General Theory of Action,* edited by Talcott Parsons and Edward Shils, pp. 388–433. Cambridge, Mass.: Harvard University Press, 1951.

Kluckhohn, Florence Rockwood. "Some Reflections on the Nature of Cultural Integration and Change." In *Sociological Theory, Values, and Sociocultural Change,* edited by Edward A. Tiryakian, pp. 217–247. New York: Harper Torchbooks, 1963.

Knutson, Jeanne, ed. *Handbook of Political Psychology.* San Francisco: Jossey-Bass, 1973.

———. *The Human Basis of the Polity: A Psychological Study of Political Man.* Chicago: Aldine-Atherton, 1972.

Kohlberg, Lawrence. "A Cognitive-Developmental Analysis of Children's Sex-Role Concepts and Attitudes." In *The Development of Sex Differences,* edited by Eleanor Maccoby, pp. 82–173. Stanford, Calif.: Stanford University Press, 1966.

Komarovsky, Mirra. "Cultural Contradictions and Sex Roles." *American Journal of Sociology* 52 (November 1946): 184–189.

———. "Functional Analysis of Sex Roles." *American Sociological Review* 15 (August 1950): 508–516.

Lane, Robert E. "Fathers and Sons: Foundations of Political Belief." *American Sociological Review* 24 (August 1959): 502–511.

———. "The Need to be Liked and the Anxious College Liberal." *Annals of the American Academy* 361 (September 1965): 711–780.

———. *Political Life: Why and How People Get Involved in Politics.* New York: Free Press, 1959.

———. *Political Thinking and Consciousness: The Private Life of the Political Mind.* Chicago: Markham, 1969.

Langton, Kenneth P. *Political Socialization.* New York: Oxford University Press, 1969.

Lansing, Marjorie. "The American Woman: Voter and Activist." In *Women in Politics,* edited by Jane S. Jaquette, pp. 5–24. New York: Wiley, 1974.

Lapidus, Gail. "Modernization Theory and Sex Roles in Critical Perspective: The Case of the Soviet Union." In *Women in Politics,* edited by Jane S. Jaquette, pp. 243–256. New York: Wiley, 1974.

Lasswell, Harold D. *Psychopathology and Politics.* New York: Viking, 1960.

Lee, Marcia M. "Towards Understanding Why Few Women Hold

Public Office." In *A Portrait of Marginality*, edited by Marianne Githens and Jewel L. Prestage, pp. 118–138. New York: McKay, 1977.

Levinson, Daniel J. "Role, Personality and Social Structure in the Organizational Setting." In *A Source Book for the Study of Personality and Politics*, edited by Fred I. Greenstein and Michael Lerner, pp. 61–74. Chicago: Markham, 1971.

Levy, Marion J. *Modernization and the Structure of Societies*. Princeton, N.J.: Princeton University Press, 1966.

Liebert, Robert. *Radical and Militant Youth: A Psychoanalytic Inquiry*. New York: Praeger, 1971.

Linton, Ralph. "Role and Status." In *Readings in Social Psychology*, edited by T. H. Newcomb and E. L. Hartley. New York: Holt, 1957.

Lipset, Seymour Martin. *Political Man: The Social Bases of Politics*. Garden City, N.Y.: Doubleday, 1960.

Lynn, David B. "A Note on Sex Differences in the Development of Masculine and Feminine Identification." *Psychological Review* 66 (March 1959): 126–135.

Lynn, Naomi B., and Flora, Cornelia Butler. "Motherhood and Political Participation: The Changing Sense of Self." *Journal of Political and Military Sociology* 1 (Spring 1973): 91–103.

———. "Societal Punishment and Aspects of Female Political Participation." In *A Portrait of Marginality*, edited by Marianne Githens and Jewel L. Prestage, pp. 118–138. New York: McKay, 1977.

Maccoby, Eleanor, ed. *The Development of Sex Differences*. Stanford, Calif.: Stanford University Press, 1966.

Maccoby, Eleanor, and Jacklin, Carol. *The Psychology of Sex Differences*. Stanford, Calif.: Stanford University Press, 1974.

Maccoby, Eleanor; Mathews, Richard; and Morton, Anton. "Youth and Political Change." *Public Opinion Quarterly* 18 (Spring 1954): 23–39.

Manderson, Lenore. "The Shaping of the Kaum Ibu (Women's Section) of the United Malays National Organization." *Signs* 3 (Autumn 1977): 210–228.

Mannheim, Karl. "The Problem of Generations." In *Essays on the Sociology of Knowledge*, edited by Paul Kecshemeti, pp. 276–320. London: Routledge and Kegan Paul, 1952.

Means, Ingunn Norderval. "Women in Local Politics: The Norwegian Experience." *Canadian Journal of Political Science* (September 1972), pp. 365–388.

Merelman, Richard M. *Political Socialization and Educational Climates: A Study of Two School Districts*. New York: Holt, Rinehart & Winston, 1971.

Merton, Robert K. "Instability and Articulation in the Role-Set." In

Role Theory: Concepts and Research, edited by Bruce J. Biddle and Edwin J. Thomas, pp. 282–287. New York: Wiley, 1966.

————. *On Theoretical Sociology.* New York: Free Press, 1967.

————. "The Role-Set: Problems in Sociological Theory." *British Journal of Sociology* 8 (June 1957): 106–120.

Merton, Robert K., and Barber, Elinor, "Sociological Ambivalence." In *Sociological Theory, Values, and Sociocultural Change,* edited by Edward A. Tiryakian, pp. 91–120. New York: Harper and Row, 1963.

Middleton, Russell, and Putney, Snell. "Political Expression of Adolescent Rebellion." *American Journal of Sociology* 68 (March 1963): 527–535.

Milbrath, Lester W. *Political Participation: How and Why Do People Get Involved in Politics.* Chicago: Rand McNally, 1965.

Milburn, Josephine F. *Women as Citizens: A Comparative Review.* Beverly Hills, Calif: Sage Publications, 1976.

Moses, Joel. "Women in Political Roles." Paper presented at Conference on Women in Russia, Stanford University, Palo Alto, 1975.

Mulvey, Mary Crowley, "Psychological and Social Factors in Prediction of Career Patterns of Women." *Genetic Psychology Monographs* 68 (1963): 309–386.

Newcomb, Theodore M. *Personality and Social Change.* New York: Dryden Press, 1943. Second printing, 1957.

Newcomb, Theodore M., and Feldman, K. *The Impact of Colleges upon Their Students.* New York: Jacob, Losey, 1969.

Nogee, Philip, and Levin, Murray. "Some Determinants of Political Attitudes among College Voters." *Public Opinion Quarterly* 22 (Winter 1958): 449–463.

Orcutt, James D. "The Impact of Student Activism on Attitudes towards the Female Sex Role." *Social Forces* 54 (December 1975): 382–391.

Orum, Anthony M.; Cohen, Roberta A.; Grasmuck, Sherri; and Orum, Amy W. "Sex, Socialization, and Politics." In *A Portrait of Marginality,* edited by Marianne Githens and Jewel L. Prestage, pp. 17–37. New York: McKay, 1977.

Parsons, Talcott. "Age and Sex in the Social Structure of the United States." *American Sociological Review* 7 (October 1942): 604–616.

————. *Essays in Sociological Theory Pure and Applied.* Glencoe, Ill.: Free Press, 1949.

————. "Role Conflict and the Genesis of Deviance." In *Role Theory: Concepts and Research,* edited by Bruce J. Biddle and Edwin J. Thomas, pp. 275–276. New York: Wiley, 1966.

Parsons, Talcott, and Shils, Edward A., eds. *Toward a Theory of General Action.* Cambridge, Mass.: Harvard University Press, 1951.

Porter, Mary Cornelia, and Ann B. Matasar. "The Role and Status of Women in the Daley Organization." In *Women in Politics*, edited by Jane S. Jaquette, pp. 85–108. New York: Wiley, 1974.

Prewitt, Kenneth. "Political Efficacy." *International Encyclopedia of the Social Sciences*, vol. 12, pp. 225–228.

Rose, Arnold M. "The Adequacy of Women's Expectations for Adult Roles." *Social Forces* 30 (October 1951): 69–77.

Rossi, Alice S. "Naming Children in Middle-Class Families." *American Sociological Review* 30 (August 1965): 499–513.

Sapiro, Virginia. "Is the Child the Mother of the Woman? Socialization to Political Gender Roles among Women." *Journal of Politics*, in press.

Sapiro, Virginia, and Farah, Virginia. "Women as Political Elites: A Literature Review and Agenda." Paper presented at the Annual Meeting of the Midwest Political Science Association, Chicago, April 1976.

Sears, R. R. "Dependency Motivation." In *Symposium on Motivation*, edited by Marshall R. Jones. Lincoln: University of Nebraska Press, 1965.

Sheridan, Mary. "Young Women Leaders in China." *Signs* 2 (Autumn 1976): 59–88.

Siegel, A. E.; Stolz, L. M.; Hitchcock, E. A.; Adamson, J. A. "Dependence and Independence in the Children of Working Mothers." *Child Development* 4 (December 1959): 533–546.

Smith, M. Brewster; Bruner, Jerome S.; and White, Robert W. *Opinions and Personality*. New York: Wiley, 1956.

Smock, Audrey C. "Bangladesh: A Struggle with Tradition and Poverty." In *Women: Role and Status in Eight Countries*, edited by Janet Z. Giele and Audrey C. Smock. New York: Wiley, 1977.

Smock, Audrey C., and Youssef, Nadia Haggag. "Egypt: From Seclusion to Limited Participation." In *Women: Role and Status in Eight Countries*, edited by Janet Z. Giele and Audrey C. Smock. New York: Wiley, 1977.

Soule, John W., and McGrath, Wilma E. "A Comparative Study of Male-Female Political Attitudes at Citizen and Elite Levels." In *A Portrait of Marginality*, edited by Marianne Githens and Jewel L. Prestage, pp. 178–195. New York: McKay, 1977.

Stoper, Emily. "Wife and Politician: Role Strain Among Women in Public Office." In *A Portrait of Marginality*, edited by Marianne Githens and Jewel L. Prestage, pp. 320–337. New York: McKay, 1977.

Stucker, John J. "Women as Voters: Their Maturation as Political Persons in American Society." In *A Portrait of Marginality*, edited by Marianne Githens and Jewel L. Prestage, pp. 264–283. New York: McKay, 1977.

Sullivan, Harry Stack. *The Interpersonal Theory of Psychiatry.* New York: Norton, 1953.

Szalai, Alexander. *The Situation of Women in the United Nations.* Research Report No. 18, United Nations Institute for Training and Research, 1973.

Thomas, Edwin J., and Biddle, Bruce J. "Basic Concepts for the Variables of Role Phenomena." In *Role Theory: Concepts and Research,* edited by Edwin J. Thomas and Bruce J. Biddle, pp. 51–63. New York: Wiley, 1966.

Tiller, Per Olav. "Parental Role Division and the Child's Personality Development." In *The Changing Roles of Men and Women,* edited by Edmund Dahlstrom, pp. 79–104. Boston: Beacon Press, 1962.

Tingsten, Herbert. *Political Behavior: Studies in Election Statistics.* London: P. S. King, 1937.

Tolchin, Susan, and Tolchin, Martin. *Clout: Womanpower and Politics.* New York: G. P. Putnam, 1973.

Verba, Sidney. *Small Groups and Political Behavior: A Study of Leadership.* Princeton, N.J.: Princeton University Press, 1972.

Verba, Sidney, and Nie, Norman H. *Participation in America: Political Democracy and Social Equality.* New York: Harper & Row, 1972.

Werner, Emmy E. "Women in Congress: 1917–1964." *Western Political Quarterly* 19 (March 1966): 16–30.

Werner, Emmy E., and Bachtold, Louise M. "Personality Characteristics of Women in American Politics." In *Women in Politics,* edited by Jane S. Jaquette, pp. 75–84. New York: Wiley, 1974.

Whitehurst, Carol A. *Women in America: The Oppressed Majority.* Santa Monica, Calif.: Goodyear Publishing, 1977.

Wilson, James Q. *The Amateur Democrat.* Chicago: University of Chicago Press, 1962.

Woodward, Julian L., and Roper, Elmo. "Political Activity of American Citizens." In *Political Behavior,* edited by Heinz Eulau et al., pp. 133–137. Glencoe, Ill.: The Free Press, 1956.

Japanese Language Materials

Arichi Tōru. *Fujin no chii to gendai shakai* (The position of women and contemporary society). Tokyo: Nōritsu Bunkasha, 1971.

Ariga Kizaemon. *Nihon koninshiron* (A study of the history of marriage in Japan). Tokyo: Nikkō Shoin, 1948.

Doi Takeo. *Amae no kōzō* (The structure of *amae*). Tokyo: Kōbundō, 1971.

Editorial Board, "Tōdai tōsō to gakusei no ishiki" (The Tokyo University struggle and student consciousness). *Sekai* 286 (September 1969): 63–71.

Endō Motoo. *Nihon josei no seikatsu to bunka* (The life and culture of Japanese women). Tokyo: Shikai Shobō, 1941.

Fukaya Masashi. *Ryōsai kenbo shugi no kyōiku* (Education to be a virtuous wife and wise mother). Tokyo: Reimei Shobō, 1966.

Harada Tomohiko. *Nihon josei shi* (History of Japanese women). Tokyo: Kasui Shobō Shinsha, 1965.

Higa Masako. *Onna no tatakai* (Women's struggle). Tokyo: Nippon Jitsugyō Shuppansha, 1971.

Hiratsuka Raichō. *Genshi, josei wa taiyō de atta* (In the beginning, woman was the sun). 3 vols. Tokyo: Ōtsuki Shoten, 1971.

———. *Watakushi no aruita michi* (The road I walked). Tokyo: Shin Hyōronsha, 1955.

Hosoi Wakizō. *Jokō aishi* (A tragic history of girl operatives). Tokyo: Iwanami Shoten, 1954.

Ichikawa Fusae. *Ichikawa Fusae jiden: senzenhen* (Autobiography of Ichikawa Fusae: the prewar years). Tokyo: Shinjuku Shobō, 1974.

———. *Watakushi no seiji shōron* (My case for politics). Tokyo: Akimoto Shobō, 1972.

Ide Fumiko. *Seitō* (The Bluestockings). Tokyo: Kōbundō, 1962.

Institute of Newspaper Research of the University of Tokyo. *Tōdai funsō no kiroku* (Record of struggle at Tokyo University). Tokyo: Nihon Hyōronsha, 1969.

Isomura Ei-ichi; Kawashima Takeyoshi; and Koyama Takashi, eds. *Gendai kazoku kōza* (Lectures on the contemporary family). 6 vols. Tokyo, 1955–1956.

Japan. Economic Planning Agency. *Kokumin seikatsu hakusho* (Report on national life). Tokyo, 1971.

———. Ministry of Education. *Gakkō kihon chōsa* (Basic school survey). Tokyo, 1961 and 1971.

———. *Zenkoku gakkō sōran* (National school report). Tokyo, 1961 and 1971.

———. Ministry of Labor, Women's and Minors' Bureau. *Fujin no genjō* (The condition of women). Tokyo, 1971–1976.

———. *Fujin rōdō no jitsujō* (The status quo of women workers), Reports No. 128–133. Tokyo, 1972–1976.

———. *Me de miru fujin no ayumi* (A look at women's progress). Tokyo, April 1971.

———. Office of Prime Minister. *Fujin ni kansuru ishiki chōsa* (Survey of consciousness relating to women). Tokyo: The Office, 1973.

"Kageki-ha mo onna jōi??" (Women on top—even in radical factions??) *Nihon Keizai Shimbun*, November 11, 1972, p. 22.

Kawashima Takeyoshi. *Kekkon* (Marriage). Tokyo: Iwanami Shoten, 1954.

———. *Nihon shakai no kazoku-teki kōsei* (The familistic structure of Japanese society). Tokyo: Nihon Hyōron Shinsha, 1950.

232   SELECTED BIBLIOGRAPHY

Kitakōji Satoshi, et al. *Gakusei undō no genjō to tenbō* (The present condition and future prospects for the student movement). *Shisō no Kagaku*, 62 (May 1967).

Koyama Takashi. *Gendai kazoku no oyako kankei* (The parent-child relation in the contemporary family). Tokyo: Baifūkan, 1973.

Koyama Takashi, et al. *Gendai kazoku no yakuwari kōzō* (The role structure of the contemporary family). Tokyo: Baifūkan, 1967.

Kunitachi-shi Kōminkan Shimin Daigaku Seminā. *Shufu to onna* (Housewives and women). Proceedings of the Citizens' College Seminar of Kunitachi City Hall. Tokyo, 1973.

Matsushita Kei-ichi. *Gendai fujin mondai nyūmon* (An approach to problems of women today). Tokyo: Nihon Hyōronsha, 1970.

Morosawa Yōko. *Onna no rekishi* (History of women). 2 vols. Tokyo: Miraisha, 1970.

Murakami Nobuhiko. *Meiji josei shi* (The history of Meiji women). 3 vols. Tokyo: Rironsha, 1970–1972.

Sankei Shimbun. *Iken to ishiki no hyakkajiten: Sankei Shimbun 1000-nin chōsa kara* (Encyclopedia of opinion and thought: from Sankei Shimbun's survey of 1000 persons). Tokyo: Sankei Shimbun, 1972.

"Sekigun geisha" (Red Army geisha). *Josei Jishin* 1 (May 1972): 29–31.

Shakai Mondai Kenkyū Kai (The social problems study group), ed. *Zengakuren kakuha-gakusei undō jiten* (The Factions of the National Federation of Student Self-Government Associations—The Dictionary of the Student Movement). Tokyo: Futabasha, 1969.

Takahashi Akira. "Nihon gakusei undō no shisō to kōdō" (Thought and behavior in the Japanese student movement). *Chūō Kōron* 5 (May 1968), 6 (June 1968), 8 (August 1968), 9 (September 1968).

Takemure Itsue. *Zenshū: josei no rekishi 1, 2* (Collected works: History of women. Parts I and II). Vols. 4 and 5. Tokyo: Rironsha, 1966.

Tamanoi Sumi. *Omiai desu yo* (Time for omiai). Tokyo: Nihon Hyōron Shinsha, 1968.

Tamura Kenji and Tamura Makie. *Anata wa dare to kekkon shiteru ka* (Whom will you marry?). Tokyo: Sekkasha, 1961.

Tanaka Mitsu. *Inochi no onna tachi e* (That women might live). Tokyo: Tabata Shoten, 1972.

Tanaka Sōgorō. *Nihon shakai undō shi* (A history of Japanese social movements). 3 vols. Tokyo: Sekai Shoin, 1947–1948.

Tanaka Sumiko and Hidaka Rokurō. *Fujin seisaku: Fujin undō* (Women's policy: The women's movement). Vol. 1 of *Gendai fujin mondai kōza*. 6 vols. Tokyo: Aki Shobō, 1969.

Uno Riemon, ed. *Shokkō mondai shiryō* (Data on the problems of factory operatives). Osaka: Kōgyō Kyōiku-kai, 1912.

Wakamori Tarō and Yamamoto Fujie. *Nihon no josei shi* (A history of women in Japan). Vol. 4. Tokyo, 1965.

Yamamura Yoshiaki. *Nihonjin to haha* (The Japanese and their mothers). Tokyo: Tōyōkan Shuppansha, 1971.

Yoshimi Kaneko. *Fujin sansei ken* (Women's political rights). Vol. 1 of *Gendai nihon josei shi* (Contemporary history of Japanese women). Tokyo: Kajima Kenkyūjo Shuppansha, 1971.

Index

Designer: Barbara Llewellyn
Compositor: Interactive Composition Corporation
Printer: Vail-Ballou
Binder: Vail-Ballou
Text: VIP Palatino
Display: VIP Palatino
Cloth: Holliston Roxite B 51548
Paper: 50 lb. Writers Offset B32

993